'A must-read from a key figure in Ireland's LGBTQ+ youth movement that combines the rigour of careful academic treatment with the insight of extensive experience in the field.'
Conor O'Mahony, University College Cork

'Barron is a force of nature who has been a pivotal, tireless, good-humoured voice at the forefront of deep and dramatic social change in Ireland for over three decades. Never one to be underestimated, he's managed to pull off another unlikely coup here: making what could have been a rather dry treatise on civil society and forging change into something personal, vital and entertaining!'
Rory O'Neill, AKA drag performer Panti Bliss

'Michael Barron's book is a powerful reminder that change is built from the margins, by those most excluded yet most resilient. As an activist working in a context where queer visibility is still punished, I found deep affirmation in this honest, strategic and hopeful account of youth-led transformation. It's not just Ireland's story – it's a blueprint for us all.'
Xheni Karaj, Executive Director of the Alliance against LGBT Discrimination

'Barron's book delivers a powerful message of hope: that love wins despite institutional barriers, ignorance and hate. At its heart is youth leadership and organising – urgently needed in an era of disinformation and global turmoil.'
Tomas V. Raskevičius, Leader of the Freedom Party, Lithuania

'Now more than ever, we must approach our shared struggles with an intersectional lens and remain vigilant in the face of oppressive forces that seek to divide those furthest from power. Michael Barron's powerful and timely book is a vital reminder of the necessity of radical solidarity – without it, we risk working against emancipation for all.'
Senator Lynn Ruane, Seanad Éireann

'Michael Barron generates a unique social memory of how transformative social change was achieved in Ireland, particularly among self-organised communities of LGBTQ+ youth. Making a compelling case for the link between activism and academia and a radical multi-layered approach to research, this insightful analysis reveals the critical role of LGBTQ+ civil society organisations in policy making.'
Ursula Barry, University College Dublin (Emerita)

'This book captures how class-conscious queer youth activism built real power. It reflects the solidarity we built together – with Michael Barron's strategic clarity and relentless commitment helping shape its course.'
Gillian Brian, Executive Director of Swan Youth Services, Dublin

HOW IRELAND'S LGBTQ+ YOUTH MOVEMENT WAS BUILT

Civil Society in the Pursuit of Social Justice

Michael Barron

First published in Great Britain in 2025 by

Policy Press, an imprint of
Bristol University Press
University of Bristol
1–9 Old Park Hill
Bristol
BS2 8BB
UK
t: +44 (0)117 374 6645
e: bup-info@bristol.ac.uk

Details of international sales and distribution partners are available at policy.bristoluniversitypress.co.uk

© Bristol University Press 2025

British Library Cataloguing in Publication Data
A catalogue record for this book is available from the British Library

ISBN 978-1-4473-6869-4 hardcover
ISBN 978-1-4473-6870-0 paperback
ISBN 978-1-4473-6871-7 ePub
ISBN 978-1-4473-6872-4 ePdf

The right of Michael Barron to be identified as author of this work has been asserted by him in accordance with the Copyright, Designs and Patents Act 1988.

All rights reserved: no part of this publication may be reproduced, stored in a retrieval system, or transmitted in any form or by any means, electronic, mechanical, photocopying, recording, or otherwise without the prior permission of Bristol University Press.

Every reasonable effort has been made to obtain permission to reproduce copyrighted material. If, however, anyone knows of an oversight, please contact the publisher.

The statements and opinions contained within this publication are solely those of the author and not of the University of Bristol or Bristol University Press. The University of Bristol and Bristol University Press disclaim responsibility for any injury to persons or property resulting from any material published in this publication.

Bristol University Press and Policy Press work to counter discrimination on grounds of gender, race, disability, age and sexuality.

Cover design: Lyn Davies
Front cover image: Alamy/Stephen Barnes

To Jaime
And to the memory of my friends, lifelines and warriors
Kieran Dunne and Eoin Collins

Contents

List of figures and tables		viii
Acknowledgements		x
1	Introduction	1
2	Context: LGBTQ+ youth in the crosshairs	28
3	Building a civil society platform	59
4	Community youth work: the BeLonG To model	79
5	A new narrative: queer optimism	104
6	Alliances and political power	123
7	Self-organised community model for policy change	141
8	Defending our civil society platforms	153
9	Conclusion	165
References		170
Index		181

List of figures and tables

Figures

1.1	Organising framework	21
1.2	Sinéad O'Connor, RTÉ *Late Late Show*, 1990	26
1.3	Parade float (Kevin and Anthony, Dublin Pride, 2006)	26
1.4	Image of an early BeLonG To at Dublin Pride	27
2.1	*Gay Community News* youth issue 2007 'Look who's talking!' cover	55
2.2	*Gay Community News* youth issue 2006 'Generation next' cover	56
2.3	International Day Against Homophobia & Transphobia	57
2.4	BeLonG To 'Key principles for working with LGBT asylum seekers and refugees' (2011)	58
3.1	'Oh be nice!!', Jamie O'Brien	78
4.1	Process of policy development of Action Plan on Bullying	88
4.2	LGBTQ+ civil society strategic advocacy to improve mental health	91
4.3	LGBTQ+ civil society strategic advocacy in education system	95
4.4	Michael Barron as Dublin Pride Grand Marshall 2010, and husband Jaime Nanci	99
4.5	Donegal LGBTQ+ Pride parade rainbow flag	100
4.6	Michael Barron and Glen Edward McGuinness at Dublin Pride 2009	101
4.7	The first BeLonG To LGBTQ+ Prom poster	102
4.8	Gay Prom poster	103
5.1	Timeline of LGBTQ+ youth campaigns	109
5.2	'He's gay and we're cool with that' poster 2007 from the Equality Authority and BeLonG To, later used by Lil Nas X to address his coming out on social media	120
5.3	BeLonG To young people James Kavanagh, Esther Twieg and Senator David Norris promote Ireland's first Gay Prom	121
5.4	'Stand Up!' poster for LGBT Awareness Week (2012)	122
6.1	Michael Barron and husband Jaime Nanci kissing at Marriage Equality Referendum count centre	136
6.2	Activists Lisa Kenny and Karen McLoughlin in the BeLonG To campervan for Yes	137
6.3	Michael Barron with former President of Ireland Mary McAleese and Dr Martin McAleese	137
6.4	Michael Barron with Minister Richard Bruton, ending baptism barrier announcement	138
6.5	BeLonG To Yes children's rights organisations coalition T-shirt	139
6.6	International LGBTQ+ activist panel discussion at the LGBT Youth forum in Croke Park	140
7.1	Framework for civil society-driven public policy development	143

7.2	Cyclical framework for civil society role in public policy development	150
8.1	Dublin far-right riots 2023, on Dublin's main street – O'Connell Street	164
9.1	Love, Organise, Resist! Artist and cultural activist Holly Pereira stands in front of her design created with queer elder and lifer Rita Wild and ResiStickers Ireland, which was used in an anti-hate campaign following the Dublin riots	169

Tables

| 1.1 | Participant profile | 15 |
| 1.2 | Theories and concepts | 18 |

Acknowledgements

Writing this book has been a profound privilege, a culmination of decades of activism and exploration as a queer man with a passion for justice. It became a deeply personal journey, shaped by memories of my late friend Kieran, who introduced me to a vibrant, joyful world, and Eoin, the first queer activist I met, who taught me generosity and quick thinking. Initially built on my doctorate thesis, this book evolved into something entirely different, a creative process that reconnected me with the countless young people I've met in my work – many now adults, yet still bound by shared experiences – and lifelong activists, mentors and elders who continue to inspire me. Writing during a time of global crises, from the climate emergency to the erosion of rights for women and trans people, reminded me of what matters most: the strength of communities that care for one another. With the support of my husband Jaime and the generosity of friends across all walks of life, I rediscovered the enduring warmth and hope that fuels this work.

I want to acknowledge and thank the following who were incredibly wise and generous in helping me to produce this book. They are a community who worked so closely with me as we retraced old steps to tell this story.

Jaime Nanci-Barron, Amel Yacef, Rita Wild, Aisling Staunton, Kris Clarke, Oonagh McArdle, Fiona Finn, Paula Gerathy, Fiona Carey (for designing all the tables), Brian Melaugh, Patricia Prendiville, Maurice Devlin, Hilary Tierney, Carys Thomas, Domenico Gambino, Anna Quigley, Lynn Ruane, Caoimhín Gaffney, Jamie O'Brien, Andrew Byrne, Sinead Keane, Aoife Kelleher, Hugh Rodgers.

I want to thank all the people who were so generous with their time and shared their analysis with me and who allowed me to interview them for this book.

I especially need to thank all the incredible young people and colleagues and friends at BeLonG To who inspired this work, Lisa O'Hagan, Aoife Kennedy, my colleagues and friends at EQUATE and all the communities I have had the privilege to work with.

Thank you.

1

Introduction

This is a story of how Ireland's LGBTQ+ youth-focused civil society pursued social justice and in doing so changed children and youth legislation and policy to an extraordinary degree. It's a story that has remained untold – how Ireland's LGBTQ+ young people moved from a position of being unnamed, or as one queer academic observed, 'unmentionable', in any government policy to being included across a wide spectrum of public policy, and to the introduction of the government's National LGBTI+ Youth Strategy in 2018. It is a story that moves between erasure and violence, violence and visibility, visibility and defiance, and defiance and the possibility of liberation.

Rather than focusing on the 'big ticket items' of this period, I delve deeper, to examine how a movement is built and sustained. This journey has been neither triumphantly linear nor tragically static, and in taking a long-term view of it, I aim to move beyond campaign stories (some of which I have written myself in the past) to paint a fuller picture.

I consciously enter into telling this story as myself. As a queer person, whose personal life and experience embody the issues I speak about – from erasure towards liberation – which I carry in my bones, in my heart and in how I move in this world. As a social justice advocate and activist, I am driven by a deep-seated need to take action against injustice and towards liberation, and I desire to encourage and uplift other activists on their journeys. As an academic, I want and need to make sense of it all – of our lives and the world we live in.

I set out to make a contribution in two main ways. Through narrative and storytelling, to shed new light on the experience of a movement for social justice over a number of decades. I do this through incorporating the reflections on the period of 21 key interviewees involved in differing ways in this movement, through my own reflections and memory work and through analysis of media and documentation such as government policy and organisational strategies.

Drawing on existing public policy frameworks, in this work I produce a specific model for public policy change driven by the communities who seek social justice due to their marginalisation. The model I produce centres the role of minority community organisations in the creation and implementation of government policies, including laws and constitutional changes. It's a model based on the experience of being part of a movement which brought marginalised needs from the community hall to the constitution.

'Memory work' (Bryant and Bryant, 2019) is a driving factor in this book – a desire to capture social memory before it is lost, to give a context to these social changes and tips for future organising. To do this, I believe that we need to share and understand the personal context, motivations and emotions involved in our advocacy. This is a departure for me. I have spent much of my life advocating for LGBTQ+ rights while keeping my own life hidden from view. This is due in part to a learnt sense of professionalism. This taken-for-granted standard of politeness did not – and in many ways still does not – allow myself or other queer people to truly be ourselves when we speak about some of the most personal issues in our communities and our own lives. In the pursuit of liberation, which included changing the rules of the advocacy game, I accepted one rule – that to be an effective queer rights advocate, I needed to keep my personal experience, my traumas and my liberations out of sight. It was always so vital that we made others feel comfortable. To be successful, including getting those initial seats at the decision-making tables, we had to work harder, we had to come up with solutions. We made it safe for others to move towards equality, and we kept quiet about our own lives.

I have seen this mirrored in advocates and friends from other minority communities – we have always had a common ground in understanding that in the mainstream world of public policy development, we had to be careful about how much of ourselves we could share. For the LGBTQ+ community and for communities of people seeking international protection (asylum) and for members of the Traveller and Roma communities, for example, we have had a shared experience and stigma of presumed 'illegality', which has stymied our ability to let our guards down. Homosexuality was only decriminalised in Ireland in 1993, and even today there is a strong and growing movement, as in the UK, to outlaw puberty blockers for young trans people. For people seeking international protection/asylum, there is an assumption of illegality ('illegal immigrants'), and for members of the Traveller and Roma communities there is a hugely bigoted association with criminality. I remember these assumptions being brilliantly addressed by the Cork Traveller Visibility Group at the start of a training session when they indicated that they were there to talk about the socio-economic and political barriers faced by Travellers, and they didn't want to hear about 'the time your bike was stolen from you by a Traveller when you were six!'

I do not disavow carefulness in presenting personal and community details as a strategy which is used by many great advocates today. We do what we have to do, and I feel so much respect for those who go to bat for our community, often in crisis situations and against phenomenal opposition. I believe our advocates need to be celebrated, not taken down. I acknowledge that I can now reflect on my time in advocacy without this intense pressure and with a clarity which some distance affords me. Writing this book has allowed me the space and opportunity to engage in social memory work (French, 1995) and to place myself inside the LGBTQ+ community and movements for social justice so that I can bring my life and my emotions to this work. I have also taken time and space to heal that part of myself that has been damaged by the 'passing' or dimming and minimising of myself that I felt was needed. In this time, I have come to see how oppressive this has been, the impact that doing this for two decades has had on my spirit and the ongoing repair work that it needs. I share my memories, emotions and analysis as a queer person and activist alongside those of the people I interviewed and combine them with historical context and sociological theory with the intention of offering you real, useful and usable insights.

This book builds on my doctoral thesis, which I spent six years writing, carefully analysing many hours of interviews and hundreds of policy documents and media articles. It allowed me to spend time theorising the social justice movements I was part of and to develop a specific model for analysing government policy making. These years of research provide the backbone to this book, which in turn empowers me to speak with greater freedom, confidence and intention now.

In reflecting upon the journey of LGBTQ+ young people in Ireland from 1993 to 2015, a period marked by significant strides in public policy and social acceptance, I am reminded of the fragility of these advances. As I write this Introduction, the world witnesses a disconcerting resurgence of conservative and far-right ideologies, manifesting in an alarming rollback of human rights of women, people of colour, indigenous people, disabled people and those of sexual and gender minorities. This global trend, marked by legislative attacks and societal backlashes against LGBTQ+ communities, starkly contrasts with the progress we championed in Ireland. The positive changes which happened in Ireland for the LGBTQ+ community, in a relatively short period, must be understood within a long history of national and international fear and scapegoating of minorities and not as 'equality achieved'. As I move into new roles to pursue liberation for the LGBTQ+ community and all communities pushed to the margins, I do so in an era that is becoming increasingly defined by extremist pushback. I believe it is time that we reflect on the narratives which drive this pushback, ones we have experienced and won out against before. Each generation of social justice activists needs to plough their own furrow and breathe life into new, creative and extraordinary strategies. We also have an intergenerational responsibility to share learning. This sharing includes how strategies of community organising, campaigning, direct action and solidarity worked in the past and to help explore how they can be built on today.

While I chronicle an era of far-reaching advancement of LGBTQ+ rights in Ireland, I am acutely aware of the international environment where these rights are increasingly contested. This duality of progress and peril influenced this work greatly, driving home the message that the road to equality is not guaranteed. Our story is one of resilience and relentless pursuit of justice, but it is also a cautionary tale of the ongoing struggle to safeguard our hard-won gains against the backdrop of a world where rights are precariously poised at the edge. In August 2022, Victor Madrigal-Borloz, a United Nations expert on the protection of LGBTQ+ people, reported from the United States that '[d]espite five decades of progress, equality is not within reach, and often not even within sight, for all persons impacted by violence and discrimination based on sexual orientation and gender identity in the United States'. In 2023, 546 anti-LGBTQ+ Bills were proposed in state legislatures across the United States. Meanwhile, in Europe, Hungary passed a 'don't say gay' law in 2021, banning the discussion of LGBTQ+ issues in schools and on children's TV. The focus of much of the global pushback against LGBTQ+ equality is based on removing access to LGBTQ+ information from young people. In Ireland in 2023 and 2024, hundreds of letters were sent to schools and election leaflets sent to homes claiming that the government had 'put in place a very sexualised curriculum in our school system … [which] promotes gender identity ideology … contrary to established science not to mention all known religious systems' (leaflet distributed by an anonymous source, May 2024). In the November 2024 General Election in the Republic of Ireland, far-right political parties campaigned on 'halting gender ideology', while in Northern Ireland political parties on the government executive voted to extend the United Kingdom's ban on puberty blockers for trans teenagers to Northern Ireland (The Journal, 11 December 2024).

Recent events highlight how the progress made by LGBTQ+ civil society in Ireland between 1993 and 2015 is now facing new challenges from far-right activism. Protests against LGBTQ+ books in libraries and events like Drag Story Hour reflect tactics imported from extremist movements in the US and UK. Disinformation campaigns and harmful 'grooming' rhetoric are reviving fears and stigmas that earlier LGBTQ+ advocates worked hard to dismantle. This book examines how civil society, policy making and public discourse have shaped LGBTQ+ rights, reminding us that every generation must protect and build upon the freedoms hard won by those who came before.

Yet, I remain optimistic. Our journey in advocacy and policy development for LGBTQ+ young people has often been a bumpy one, where we have not always been in a period of progress. We must remain hopeful as we move into the next stages, reinforcing gains, holding back the tide of reactionary bias and ultimately continuing our journey towards liberation.

My motivations

I was born in 1975 and grew up in County Kilkenny, in a rural part of the south-east of Ireland. As a gay young person in the late 1980s and early

Introduction

1990s, it did not seem possible for me to discuss my sexuality with anyone, and I received strong gender-normative and homophobic messages from peers, family and media. These arose particularly in relation to sport and acceptable masculine gender performance.

I was fortunate when at the age of 13 my soon to be best friend Kieran Dunne and his family moved from London to rural Kilkenny too. As two 'newbies' in the same class in the Good Counsel College in the town of New Ross, we became fast friends, bonding over music and fashion and a shared anarchic humour that catapulted us from the status of weird new boys (Kieran's English accent, my emerging gayness) to troublemakers. Kieran and his siblings Sean, Ivan and Michelle offered me a window into the bigger world of London, and new dance music (Salt-N-Pepa, Soul II Soul, Eric B. & Rakim, Neneh Cherry). Their family was wild, open and worldly. This was a much-needed salve from the normality of a rural machismo that filled me with fear and dread and which until then I couldn't find a way out of. One of Ivan's friend's visited from London, and there were rumours that he was gay, but it was ok with everyone. Together with our friend Tom, also a music lover and mischief maker, we formed a tribe, and it all added up to an early taste of freedom.

Then in 1990, when I was 15, I consumed three iconic pop cultural moments which exploded this sense of freedom in me and attached it to being gay. First, Madonna performed her legendary Marie Antoinette production of her hit song 'Vogue' on the MTV Music Awards with her beautiful and clearly, even to a 15 year old in Kilkenny, gay dancers. We didn't have MTV in my family home, but I video recorded it at Kieran's house and watched it on repeat, transfixed by her and by these stunning Black and Latino fem men. That same year, Sinéad O'Connor, whom I had been obsessed with since her album *The Lion and the Cobra* (1987), became a global superstar with an interpretation of the Prince song 'Nothing compares to you'. By this stage, I was aware of my attraction to men, and pieces of the jigsaw started to fall into place. Sinéad sang about overthrowing the old Catholic patriarchal theocracy, and the depth in her voice both warmed and electrified me. I loved her. Then O'Connor appeared on the Irish late night TV chat show *The Late Late Show* with legendary host (and national father figure) Gay Byrne, wearing a Dublin AIDS Alliance T-shirt with members of the gay community to raise awareness of AIDS and its impact on the queer community.

Two years later, I left Kilkenny with Kieran and Tom to attend university in Dublin. After spending a year on the sexually diverse rave scene in London with Sean and Ivan, I came out as gay while on a summer trip with Tom in New York City. It was a wonderfully liberating time, where I met my first holiday boyfriend, who was from Puerto Rico and introduced us to the hectic queer closing days of what was described as 'The Club Kid era' in New York (Boardman, 2024). Thrown in at the deep end, I swam. For the second time, I found my tribe. We became part of a group of young queers, mostly of colour and mostly of people who had left home (or were forced to leave home) to find community too. Among that motley crew, I experienced queer community and queer joy for the first time.

I reluctantly came back to Ireland to finish university in 1997 but was delighted to find a queer scene that was booming, edgy and hilarious. There was the bar The George (Fartukh, 2023), the club H.A.M (Tiernan, 2024) and what became known as 'Gay Christmas' – the Alternative Miss Ireland (AMI), an 'annual beauty pageant that is open to men, women and animals' run by a non-profit collective dedicated to raising money for Irish HIV/AIDS organisations (Tiernan, 2021). AMI irreverently clashed with St Patrick's Day and really committed to its aim of presenting an alternative Ireland – I was sold!

My life took an unexpected turn in the summer after college when I became involved in community youth work. I was living in the North Inner City of Dublin, where I noticed much racist graffiti, which led me to volunteer with the Irish Refugee Council to teach English to migrant children. I loved this volunteer work – spending time with young people at schools and sometimes with their parents at their homes. I became particularly close with a family from Angola and committed to supporting their son through school in Dublin, which was incredibly difficult for him due to the language barrier, culture shock and trauma of fleeing his home country because of violence. Volunteering with this family, I began to learn how the system was stacked against people coming to the country for international protection.

In 1998, I undertook a Youth Studies certificate course with Maynooth University and the City of Dublin Youth Services Board. As part of this course, I carried out a piece of research entitled 'Lesbian, gay and bisexual experiences of school'. This research was carried out through focus groups and a survey with OutYouth – the gay, lesbian and bisexual youth group supported by Gay Switchboard Dublin. This was my introduction to youth work with the LGBTQ+ community and also to a number of LGBTQ+ activists. That study revealed that LGB young people were experiencing a striking level of homophobia and biphobia in school.

At this time, I was employed by Focus Ireland, a charity that supports homeless people, to work at their day centre for teenagers who were experiencing homelessness, 'The Loft'. Young people at the centre experienced a multitude of marginalisations and were most often from specific working-class areas which have been neglected by the state or were members of the Traveller community. They had often had early exposure to extreme poverty, violence, drug use and racism as well as intergenerational trauma. I was the only 'out' gay person on the team, and my progressive manager Jean Rafter often asked me to key work (work closely with and advocate for young people internally and externally, for example in court or with education bodies) young people who were gay and/or perhaps involved in sex work. During this time, I came to understand that a good number of young people coming to the centre were somewhere on the LGBTQ+ spectrum, and as a team we began to discuss at meetings how we might provide more specific support to homeless queer youth. Dr Carol-Anne O'Brien, whom I would later work with at BeLonG To, had written 'No safe bed: lesbian, gay and bisexual youth in residential services', about working with homeless queer youth and which provided inspiration at this time. I believe it is significant that my initial direct work with queer youth was with young people living on the extreme margins of society who were, often violently, excluded from the supports that all young people should have access to.

In 2001, I moved organisations to take on a new role with the Gay Men's Health Project. As an outreach worker, I had three specific briefs – to work with homeless gay men, to work with people seeking asylum and to work with younger gay people. As part of this role, I worked with an extraordinary group of community members and youth workers, convened by OutYouth and led by Fran McVeigh, to establish a specific state-supported LGBT youth service, which was to become BeLonG To in 2003. In addition to the intersectional analysis I brought from my years working with young people of colour, young migrants, young Travellers and young homeless people, Fran brought a powerful class analysis. As a very experienced youth work manager from Belfast who had spent most of her life advocating with working-class communities, Fran was tireless in ensuring that BeLonG To would reach working-class queer young people and would bring this analysis to the centre of the work. This focus on class analysis had a deep impact on the approach we took and was further deepened by Anna Quigley, a long-time chairperson of BeLonG To and Dublin Inner City community activist, as well as Dr David Carroll (Youth Work Manager, National Development Manager and Executive Director), Gillian Brien (Youth Work Manager) and Ger Roe (Drugs Programme Manager), who continuously combined queer and class analysis so that it became embedded in the work.

I was the organisation's first worker and remained with it, including as Executive Director, until 2015. During this period, I advocated with others for much of the policy change discussed in this book. I approach the work of advocacy from a social justice position. This position, borne out through experience of working with marginalised young people and communities, determines that inequalities and oppressions are embedded in systems and 'sewn into the fabric of society through institutions that support both cultural norms and personal beliefs' (Thompson, 2003).

I began advocating for policy change in the areas of education and mental health from 2004 as a result of working with LGBTQ+ young people who were experiencing difficulties in school and at home and who were displaying the effects of mental ill health, including self-harming and attempting suicide. As a youth worker, I had been attempting to refer young people to mental health supports and had been advocating on their behalf with limited success.

In a BeLonG To submission to the National Suicide Review Group in 2005, we made the argument that '[i]nternational studies have linked homophobic harassment, which is clearly endemic in Irish schools, with suicidal behaviour among LGBT youth' (BeLonG To, 2005, p 3). This argument was accepted, and LGBT people became a named priority group in 'Reachout: national action plan for action on suicide prevention' (Health Service Executive [HSE], 2005). In an Irish context, this was the first time LGBTQ+ young people, indeed LGBTQ+ people in general, had been featured in a policy document relating to mental health. This is not an unproblematic framing of LGBTQ+ youth, but it was an authentic one and does mark a milestone in the inclusion of their concerns across public policy more broadly. It represented a 'ground-up' approach to influencing government policy and also began a cycle with BeLonG To, a grass-roots organisation in its origin, of planning, action, observation and reflection in order to influence policy.

At the heart of my motivation for writing this book is all that I learned and carried with me from my time with BeLonG To. My time in this role was a profound catalyst. Those early years opened my eyes to the stark reality of LGBTQ+ young people's exclusion from public policy and decision making. Witnessing their journey to becoming significantly included towards the end of my time there was both a privilege and a powerful motivator. This book has provided me the opportunity to delve deeply and critically into the transformative processes that facilitated such change.

Early on in my work with BeLonG To, I became keenly aware of the profound risk and violence LGBTQ+ youth faced. When opening BeLonG To as a youth service, initially, my focus was squarely on the LGBTQ+ youth I interacted with directly in my role as a frontline youth and community worker. That work alone was a significant commitment, but my relationships with these young people revealed oppressive systems they courageously navigated every day: education, healthcare, social work, homeless services, international protection and criminal justice, in addition to often precarious or violent family environments. As one former member of BeLonG To said:

> There was so much going on in my life – violence in school and at home, growing up in an environment where it was normal to have a social worker involved and where peers were in jail. For me, no one was taking my queer identity seriously, or the damage that the

experience of homophobia, on top of all the rest, was having on my health and ability to see a future.

It became clear that in order for the young people I knew and came to deeply care about to have a fair and just interaction with the world, these systems required radical transformation. This analysis broadened my advocacy work to include systemic change, enlarging the circle of those I considered in our fight. I grew to understand that my work extended beyond the hundreds of young people I met personally to include the thousands of LGBTQ+ youth I would never meet. This broader understanding fuelled a commitment to fighting for a world where the rights and dignity of LGBTQ+ youth are fully recognised and respected, challenging a deeply embedded status quo. Early on in this work, with the support of many elders and mentors, I began to develop an understanding that advocacy for policy changes, community building and strategic narrative shifts were essential to address the complex challenges in the lives of LGBTQ+ young people.

As a scholar deeply engaged in social justice processes, the omission of the critical role played by LGBTQ+ youth civil society in Ireland during the transformative years of 1993–2015 struck a chord with me. This period marked substantial social and policy shifts, yet, without a thorough exploration of these years and the pivotal role of LGBTQ+ youth in civil society, our grasp on this significant transformation is incomplete. I feel the need to reinforce our social memory of this period so that it runs deeper and expands to empower more of our community to partake in it. As one interviewee for this book said of this period: 'If marriage equality was the issue of this time, LGBTQ+ youth in schools was the locus.' In this book, I focus attention on this central point (school and youth) and how work there, which faced fierce resistance, came to uplift the rest of the LGBTQ+ movement. It was also the LGBTQ+ youth civil society movement that really brought an intersectional approach, class and race analysis, to the battle for rights which was both urgently needed and which was successful in building solidarity. Much writing about the LGBTQ+ community, globally and in Ireland, has had an inherent middle-class White settled bias. In Ireland, it has overlooked the huge shift in the demographics (where 20 per cent of the population were born outside of Ireland, for example) and the huge contribution of working-class queer people and the vitality of class analysis by failing to move beyond LGBTQ+ identity to address material inequalities and lived realities. Intersectionality – class, gender, sexuality, race, disability – should guide research, and advocacy efforts to avoid reinforcing privileged narratives and underscoring intersectionality was a conscious position taken by LGBTQ+ youth civil society as it reflected both the adults and, more so, the young people involved. This intersectionality created an urgency in the work and a motivation for me to write this book.

My identity as a queer person, a scholar and a social justice advocate brings an informed sense of this urgency to this work. The current threats from governments to civil society freedoms, particularly civil society groups representing minority communities, coupled with the ascendancy of far-right ideologies, underscore the fragility of our gains. Despite the progress made by minority communities and women, the reversal of such progress globally is alarming. This book stems from a conviction in the central role of independent civil society, of communities on the margins speaking and acting for themselves, in championing social justice and the imperative to safeguard these spaces within democracies. The restriction of LGBTQ+ rights has long been a 'canary in the coalmine' for the restriction of rights in general and the oppression of all minority groups. Further, within LGBTQ+ rights, the rights of young people have consistently been among the most precarious. In contesting dominant erasures and narratives of memory, I aim to show the strategic complexity and resilience of these social justice fighters against a wall of resistance.

Self-organised civil society

In 1993, LGBTQ+ young people were invisible in Irish public policy. Today, their presence is acknowledged across a wide range of national mainstream children and youth policy and is highlighted by the creation of a dedicated National LGBTQ+ Youth Strategy. The Council of Europe's (CoE) 2018 publication, 'Safe at school: education sector responses to violence based on sexual orientation, gender identity/expression or sex characteristics in Europe', highlighted that Ireland was just one of six of the council's 46 member states that had implemented a 'full comprehensive response' to such violence (CoE, 2018, p 31). In this book, I explore the profound shift from invisibility to visibility, analysing the driving forces and mechanisms behind these changes.

When I refer to 'civil society', I draw on a number of descriptions such as civil society is 'an intermediate realm situated between state and household, populated by organised groups or associations which are separate from the state, enjoy some autonomy in relations with the state and are formed voluntarily by members of society to protect or extend their interests, values or identities' (Manor et al, 1999, pp 3–4). Crotty describes civil society as

> [t]hose non-governmental groups and institutions within a society that focus and direct into politically accessible channels the interests of their constituents. Their key features are their independence from political control; the political space allowed these institutions to evolve and prosper; and the capacity of such agencies to direct member needs into political channels. (Crotty, 1998, p 9)

Combining these definitions with others, I am referring to the collective of community groups, labour unions, minority rights groups, anti-poverty groups, non-governmental and charitable organisations. Civil society is also referred to as 'the third sector' (alongside government and commerce). It is a space where people can express their fundamental human rights and have these acted upon by their organisations, who work to have their members' rights realised. Civil society can be characterised by its attempt to realise public benefit and promote social justice and common good.

I address the troubling reduction in civil society advocacy, drawing on original primary research and analysis of media and policy documents to emphasise the crucial role of LGBTQ+ youth civil society organisations. These groups have been key in shaping policy debates and collaborating with government agencies to formulate and implement effective policies. This book marks the first time the significant impact of public moral discourse on LGBTQ+ youth issues in Ireland has been highlighted, showing how strategic foresight and narratives developed by LGBTQ+ organisations have transformed public opinion and policy over two decades.

The synergy between community development, narrative innovation and political engagement spearheaded by LGBTQ+ youth civil society has led to significant legislative advancements and a shift towards greater recognition of LGBTQ+ rights. This tripartite model of action, operating under often challenging conditions, has set a new standard in public policy discourse, proving that consistent, visionary efforts can lead to substantial societal and political change.

This work dives deep into the barriers facing LGBTQ+ young people's recognition, including the entrenched influence of Christian churches in critical areas like education and health and pervasive historical homophobia and transphobia. In this often extreme environment, I explore how LGBTQ+ civil society's response was persistent and strategic and focused on turning the ideals of social justice and equality into practical community, cultural and policy changes. I examine how these efforts required careful social analysis to identify policy issues, imaginative solutions and cooperative actions with the government to drive policy reform.

By underscoring the essential role of self-organised civil society in achieving sustained change across community organisations, policy change and political collaboration, this book challenges conventional policy analysis which often separates these elements and critiques queer history narratives focused solely on ephemeral campaigns and milestones.

Providing insights into organised social change spanning a number of decades, the book aims to offer support for ongoing and future work for justice. Here I draw on my own experience, in combination with the 21 people I interviewed and a great deal of previous analysis in the area. What emerges is a 'haunting', as Gordan describes it – the persistence of unresolved injustices and conflicts which intertwine our personal experiences, social structures and historical context (Gordan, 1997, p 338).

In highlighting the indispensable role of a robust civil society at a time when its autonomy is under global pressure, I make the case that creative partnerships between government and civil society hold huge potential to foster progressive social change. Rather than increasing limitations on civil society, which many governments are, there is an urgent need in an era marked by the rise of far-right movements to breathe new life and independence into civil society so that communities and human rights advocates are emboldened to pursue radical and lasting social justice.

My aim here is to dig into the heart of how, in real life, public policy making towards communities pushed to the margins can be made through an open engagement by government – both civil service and elected politicians – with communities themselves. It is based on an analysis of policy change towards LGBTQ+ young people across decades, which centres the role played by LGBTQ+ civil society in bringing about legislative and policy change. It is a story, in many ways my story, of working with LGBTQ+ young people to articulate their needs and rights, and building trust and understanding with policy makers, which allowed the voices of this hugely marginalised community to drive policy change in an often hostile environment.

There is an abundance of research into public policy development, including agenda setting, trends, formation, governance and public administration systems. However, very little focused work has been produced which explores the longitudinal processes of public policy formation about the LGBTQ+ community. Where LGBTQ+ issues are discussed in Irish public policy texts, very little attention has been paid to young people or to the processes that lead to their concerns becoming public policy issues that demand legislative and policy change. Where LGBTQ+ youth are discussed in an Irish policy context, the focus has been on the analysis of policy text with no input from the LGBTQ+ community and no consideration of the broader LGBTQ+ movement for liberation. This work addresses this gap, this *erasure*, with consideration to historical, cultural and social specificities of gender and sexual minority identities in Ireland in the late 20th century and the first two decades of the 21st.

Methods used to create the book

The nature of my work as a social justice advocate and my intention for this book to be useful to other advocates means that I consciously apply an 'advocacy and participatory worldview'. By this, I mean that I carried out the research in a way that is 'intertwined with politics and a political agenda' to address issues such as 'empowerment, inequality, oppression, domination, suppression, and alienation' (Creswell, 2009, p 9) and that I want to 'advance an agenda for change' (Kemmis and Wilkinson, 1998, p 24).

I set out in this research to explain how insights from the Irish policy community, LGBTQ+ young people themselves and my own experience contribute to our understanding of civil society organisations' role in the changing status of LGBTQ+ young people in Irish public policy. I also wanted to explain *how* policy changed, *why* it changed and *what learning* can be shared.

Because of this, I applied three methods to my research work:

- qualitative interviewing of 21 people;
- documentary analysis of public policies, organisational documents and media reports;
- autoethnographic and memory work – to surface my own memories and learning.

Qualitative interviewing

As Rubin and Rubin put it, '[q]ualitative interviewing projects are especially good at describing social and political processes, that is, *how and why* things change' (Rubin and Rubin, 2012, p 3).

With each of the people I interviewed, I approached the work of knowledge generation as a co-creation process in which both interviewee and interviewer are active. I approached data collection as a series of 'conversations in which a researcher gently guides a conversational partner in an extended discussion' and in acknowledgement that 'in qualitative interviews, each conversation is unique, as researchers match their questions to what each interviewee knows and is willing to share' (Rubin and Rubin, 2012, p 4). Conversational partnerships also demand reciprocity and emotional engagement: '[R]ather than just asking and listening, sometimes researchers may need to answer some of the same questions about themselves that they have posed to the conversational partner' (Rubin and Rubin, 2012, p 84). As Jacquie Aston puts it: 'I believe that a certain amount of disclosure is essential. It facilitates a sense of trust and mutuality and it increases the comfort level of the narrator' (Aston, 2001, p 147). This approach is in line with my own position as an actor in the work being discussed and an honest acknowledgement that the key actors and I had varying existing relationships. These relationships did not mean that we came from a singular perspective – in fact we often came from very different perspectives – but I approached the conversations from a position of honouring our shared commitment.

Interviewees were invited to participate on the basis that they had been involved in work to improve the lives of LGBTQ+ young people in varying ways over the period of the study. This process of purposive sampling was made possible due to my own work.

I chose to interview four groups of people. Three of them are part of what is widely described in public policy theory as 'the policy community' (Kingdon, 1984; Jenkinson-Smith and Sabatier, 1993; Pross, 1995; Pal, 2014). Kingdon describes policy communities as being 'composed of specialists in a given policy area ... scattered both through and outside of government' (p 7).

These groups were:

- members of civil society groups;
- members of the civil and public service;
- politicians – in this case, former government ministers for education and children and youth;
- members of the community in question itself – in this case, queer people who were members of LGBTQ+ youth services and campaigns during this period.

Civil society participants came from LGBTQ+ organisations who advocated directly for policy change; mainstream youth organisations, whose involvement came about through specific advocacy initiatives, as well as through the general principle of equality for all young people; and actors from the media – who were active both in reporting on and in developing media about LGBTQ+ young people.

Civil and public service participants were each invited to take part based on their involvement in the development and implementation of LGBTQ+ youth inclusive policies. Each participant had been involved at a senior level in this work across four government bodies – the Department of Education and Skills, HSE, the Department of Children and Youth Affairs (DCYA) and the Equality Authority.

The political participants were all former government ministers during times of significant change for LGBTQ+ young people: two had been Minister for Children and Youth Affairs, and one had been Minister for Education and Skills.

In addition to these three groups, I interviewed a fourth group – people who had been youth participants in LGBTQ+ youth services and advocacy campaigns during the period. Each of these now queer adults had invested a huge amount of time, energy and bravery while they were young people working for greater equality and provide unique insights which are generally overlooked when we explore how public policy change happens.

My goal was to gather a rich tapestry of insights by compiling this varied matrix of experiences, exploring the depths of how policies impact LGBTQ+ youth and the broader implications of these policies on society. Through this lens, my research seeks to contribute to the academic discourse and to challenge it to aim for effecting tangible change in the lives of

LGBTQ+ young people, underpinned by a philosophy of co-creation and mutual respect in the quest for knowledge.

Documentary analysis

One key element of my research involved an extensive review of documentary evidence. I analysed 83 articles from the *Irish Times* archives covering 2003 to 2015 and 124 documents from LGBTQ+ civil society groups from the same period. These ranged from policy submissions to research findings and strategic plans. Connecting these documents with the insights from the 28 in-depth interviews and existing literature was enlightening. This process not only validated the findings from my interviews but also brought a richer, more nuanced narrative to the forefront. Moreover, this documentary analysis proved to be more than just supplementary; it was foundational in corroborating the interview findings, memory work and reinforcing my theoretical framework. By weaving together these various strands of evidence, I built a comprehensive view of the social and political landscape that informs LGBTQ+ youth policies over extended periods of time (Table 1.1).

Autoethnographic and memory work

I apply autoethnography to my research because it allows me to connect my personal experiences as a queer person and queer activist with larger cultural and social issues. This method fits naturally with queer identities

Table 1.1: Participant profile

Politicians	DCYA	Department of Education and Skills		
Number of participants	2	1		
Public service	DCYA	Department of Education and Skills	The Equality Authority	HSE
Number of participants	2	1	1	1
Civil society	LGBTQ+	Mainstream Youth	Media	
Number of participants	9	1	2	
Participants in LGBTQ+ youth services during the time period who are now adults	Transgender	Gay	Lesbian	Bisexual
Number of participants	2	2	2	1

Total: 28

such as my own, which challenges rigid norms and embraces the fluid and evolving nature of identity. Through autoethnography, I can tell stories that don't always conform to traditional expectations but reveal deeper truths about navigating life as a queer person.

For me, autoethnography is a way to reflect on my own experiences while also questioning societal norms. It gives me the space to share stories that are personal, honest and sometimes uncomfortable – stories that might not have clear resolutions but hold meaning. These narratives help me explore the challenges and joys of living authentically in a world that often values conformity over individuality.

I carried out this work over many years, through journaling (a practice I developed as a reflective youth worker in the early 2000s), through analysing these journals and through conscious written memory work. In 2016, I asked equality expert and friend Patricia Prendiville to interview me on the topics of this book. I felt that Patricia, who has such deep knowledge of the Irish and international LGBTQ+ rights movement, was the ideal person to direct this conversation, which was held over three hours, recorded, transcribed and analysed.

By combining autoethnography with qualitative interviewing and documentary analysis, I aim to tell stories that inspire change and bring attention to voices and experiences that are often overlooked. This approach isn't just about sharing my journey; it's also about challenging harmful systems and encouraging others to do the same. By integrating interviews, documentary analysis and autoethnographic and memory work, I aimed to do more than just map out the policy landscape. I sought to enrich the ongoing dialogue on policy development, community engagement and the impact of societal attitudes about young people. This approach revealed the power and necessity of diverse methodologies in capturing the complex realities of policy making and its impact in real-world contexts.

Thematic analysis

I decided to approach the work using a thematic analysis due to its flexibility, its rigour and its compatibility with the methodology (key informant interviews, documentary analysis and autoethnography). While my work on Ireland's LGBTQ+ youth movement spans over 20 years, my active analysis of the information used in this book also spanned over a decade. Analysis of interview data began by listening back to the recordings and then through the transcribing of each interview. The time spent in this process allowed for a deep familiarity with the data ahead of the next stages of analysis. With the help of computer-assisted qualitative data analysis software, I used Braun and Clarke's six-step approach (2006) to identify themes and patterns which form the basis of the analysis present in this book.

I was conscious of relational ethics – including informed consent, safeguarding participants' anonymity. To various degrees, I have personal relationships with the research participants. In a relatively small country and LGBTQ+ and policy field, I must respect interviewees' integrity as well as the personal relationships involved. Due to these relationships, it is possible that interviewees could share information they might not have shared otherwise. To safeguard against overexposure, I have worked vigorously to ensure anonymity and to reflect on my position in relation to participants throughout.

Theoretical framework

This book is motivated by a central concern for the lives of LGBTQ+ young people. As such, it draws on concepts such as stigma and oppression with a view to articulating how the exclusions experienced by LGBTQ+ young people are felt in daily life. Significantly, these concepts also apply to other excluded social groups and so I believe have a strong transferability to other contexts.

The work is, however, primarily focused on the relationship between civil society and government in the development of public policy, and as such, public policy and governance theory provide the central governing concepts for the inquiry.

To develop the theoretical framework underpinning this book, I have therefore brought together three distinct areas which are not traditional bedfellows but which I believe provide the most authentic schema that reflects the core landscapes of inquiry for this work. They are:

- Literature in relation to LGBTQ+ young people, with a particular focus on Irish specificities. This includes the concepts of stigma and oppression as they relate to cultural and structural barriers faced by LGBTQ+ young people and equality and human rights as they relate to approaches to overcome these barriers.
- Literature about how Ireland is governed – including the roles of public administration (such as the civil and public service) and civil society – and how these different actors contribute to the development of public policy.
- Public policy theory and frameworks (how public policy is traditionally made) to develop pathways to linking research findings and theory and a platform for presenting the findings.

This theoretical framework was developed in this way to bring together core ideas that intersect in the consideration of LGBTQ+ young people in Irish public policy and the role of civil society advocacy in advancing their rights. In bringing these ideas together, gaps in existing knowledge quickly emerged, which informed how I would write the book (Table 1.2).

Table 1.2: Theories and concepts

Area	Concept	Essence
LGBTQ+ young people		
	Social memory	Social memory is a concept used to explore the connection between social identity and historical memory. It asks how diverse people come to see themselves as a social group with a shared history (French, 1995).
	Decolonisation	Decolonisation involves identifying colonial systems, structures and relationships and working to fundamentally change these systems.
	Haunting	Haunting is positioned within social theory that highlights how past violences are embedded in contemporary life, influencing the conditions and consciousness of those living in the present. Personal biographies are intertwined with larger social structures so that haunting can illuminate these connections, revealing how individual experiences are linked to broader historical and social processes.
	Queer joy	'Queer joy is a powerful emotion that sustains the fight for recognition and equality for LGBTQ+ people, especially in the face of challenges like gender-based violence and discrimination. But it's also bittersweet because it acknowledges the struggles faced by the community while celebrating advancements towards a more just and equal world' (Wilson, 2024).
	Queer futurity	In Muñoz's terms, queer futurity is the utopian impulse embedded in queer collectivity: the hope that new ways of being, doing and relating exist just over the horizon. As such, it hinges upon an insistence on potentiality and affect and may offer a radical mode of resistance to a fearful and anxious present (Stielau, 2015).
	Intersectionality	The concept of intersectionality describes the ways in which systems of inequality based on gender, 'race', ethnicity, sexual orientation, gender identity, disability, class and other forms of discrimination 'intersect' to create unique dynamics and effects. All forms of inequality are mutually reinforcing and should therefore be analysed and addressed simultaneously to prevent one form of inequality from reinforcing another.
	Stigma	Stigma is when someone sees another in a negative way because of a particular characteristic and/or identity, such as race, disability, sexual orientation or gender identity. Stigma towards queer youth remains an important feature of societies in which heteronormative and cisgender identities remain dominant.
	Oppression	Oppression is the unjust and often violent use of power over a group of people. It is structural and rooted in societal norms, habits and institutional rules. It only targets members of specific communities, such as the LGBTQ+ community.

Table 1.2: Theories and concepts (continued)

Area	Concept	Essence
	Human rights	Human rights emphasise the inherent dignity and the broad spectrum of everyone's rights. These rights include both civil and political rights as well as economic, social and cultural rights, which are aimed at promoting a dignified life for everyone (Crowley, 2015). The application of these rights follows the principles of universality and non-discrimination, key tenets enshrined in the Universal Declaration of Human Rights.
	Equality	The concept of equality, especially as it relates to LGBTQ+ young people, encompasses a broad scope, striving not just for non-discrimination but for the actual betterment of living conditions through the equitable distribution of resources, power and recognition. This approach is rooted in activism, which mobilises and organises community responses to inequality. It often emerges from urgent needs and seeks to address systemic inequalities embedded within social and political structures (Crowley, 2015).
Governance		Governance involves managing a nation's complex affairs through collaboration among governments, public agencies and civil society. Jessop (2004) defines it as the task of steering diverse yet interconnected systems, emphasising the challenge of coordinated action.
Public administration		
	Agenda setting framework	Kingdon's framework for public policy agenda setting focuses on how issues gain governmental attention. He categorises the process into three streams: the problem stream, identifying issues that demand action; the policy stream, where solutions are formulated; and the politics stream, where political dynamics influence agenda setting. These streams may independently flow but converge during 'policy windows' – opportune moments that elevate issues to the agenda if conditions are right (Kingdon, 2003).
	Advocacy coalition framework	Advocacy Coalition Framework considers long-term processes of policy makers and diverse actors. Central to this theory is the belief system that binds coalitions of actors, ranging from policy makers to activists, who navigate policy changes over time. This framework appreciates the fluidity of coalitions and the strategic adaptations they undergo in response to shifting political landscapes (Sabatier and Jenkins-Smith, 1988, 1993).
	Narrative policy framework	Narrative policy framework emphasises the storytelling aspects of policy debates, asserting that the success of policy initiatives often hinges on the compelling nature of the stories woven by its proponents. This approach

(continued)

Table 1.2: Theories and concepts (continued)

Area	Concept	Essence
		examines how policy narratives are constructed and their impact at different levels of policy engagement, from individual decision makers to broader cultural perceptions (McBeth et al, 2017).
	Policy community	Policy community describes the ecosystem of actors who influence policy development, including not only policy makers and lobbyists but also academics and media personnel. These communities are often tightly knit groups who share a common language and set of concerns, although they may hold opposing views on specific issues (Pross, 1995; Pal, 2014).
	Problematising	Problematising is a process advanced by Carol Bacchi on how public policies are often responses to 'problems' that are not objectively given but are framed by specific political, cultural and historical contexts. This perspective invites a critical examination of how issues are represented and the underlying assumptions that guide these representations. It challenges the traditional view of public policy as merely solving problems, instead proposing that policy itself constructs problems in particular ways (Bacchi, 2012; Foucault, 1984).

Book structure: organising framework

This book is organised around a central message and purpose, with nine connecting chapters that build to develop a model to support the central purpose. Figure 1.1 illustrates the organising framework for this book.

Overall message and purpose

The book's overall aim is to share learning about how an oppressed social group – LGBTQ+ young people – moved from being erased from national public policy ('unmentionable') to being a central concern of public policy. I want to share my experience and that of 28 other people, which demonstrates that LGBTQ+ youth civil society drove this dramatic policy shift, and engage you in a model which I have developed for how self-organised minority communities can effect such change. The message is that there are non-elite, non-mediated ways for minority communities to effect public policy changes when certain conditions are in place.

Figure 1.1: Organising framework

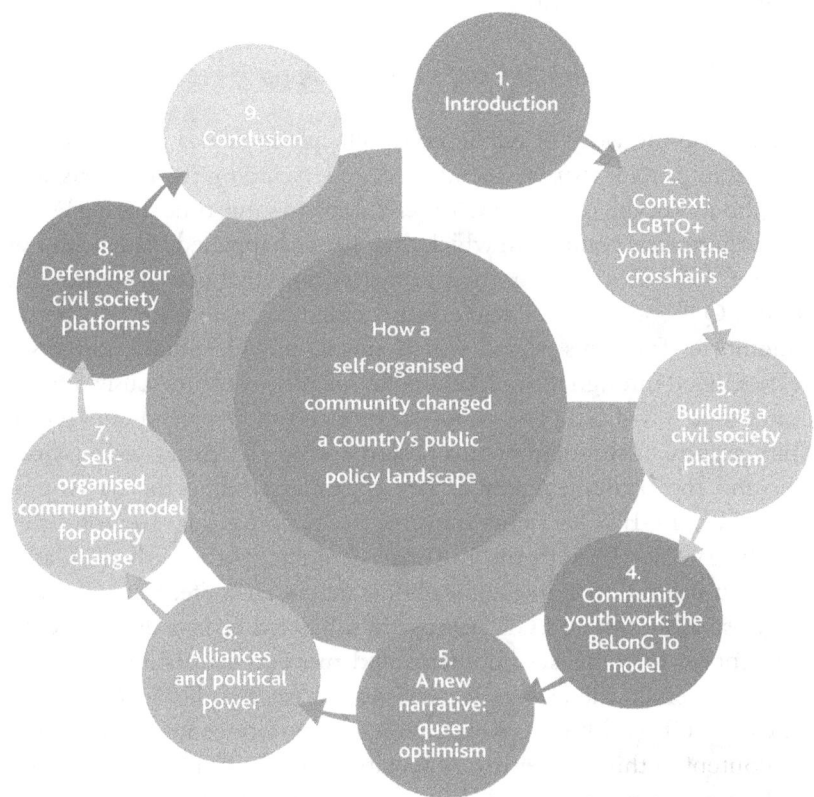

Introduction – Chapter 1

In the Introduction, I 'lay out my stall' on how I am going to discuss, analyse and make useful the significant subject matter of this book. To do this, I introduce you to myself and my positions as a queer person, a queer social justice activist and a queer writer. I talk about my aspirations for this book – for it to be useful to other advocates for social justice on their journeys to improving public policy relating to specific but interconnected marginalised communities. I discuss the methodology I used to gather and analyse a great deal of data over many years and how I combine qualitative interviewing, documentary analysis and autoethnographic analysis to bring to life how real-world policy change can happen for very stigmatised communities. I highlight the gaps in literature which I aim to fill, including the focus on self-organised minority communities in policy making and the leading contribution of LGBTQ+ youth civil society in the progress of both LGBTQ+ rights and young people's rights overall. I further presented the theoretical framework which underpins this book, its key concepts and the structure of the book itself.

Context: LGBTQ+ youth in the crosshairs – Chapter 2

In order to do the work of public policy change itself and to engage in this book, it is important that we spend time understanding the contexts we are talking about. For this reason, in Chapter 2, I spend some time sharing both the social and historical contexts in which this change happened. This begins with a timeline (1993–2015) of significant interventions that provoked movement on LGBTQ+ youth rights, while I also begin to share with you personal key memories from this period which aim to provide unique insights and were developed through the autoethnographic processes previously discussed. I demonstrate how LGBTQ+ youth were placed at the epicentre of the anti-equality argument throughout this period and argue that an understanding of this and the battle against it is key to understanding the development of the whole LGBTQ+ rights movement. In doing this, I emphasise the extraordinary role played by the Christian churches (particularly the Catholic Church) in institutionalising homophobia across Irish life, including in the country's schools, where LGBTQ+ were subjected to brutality. I also draw your attention to some key moments and movements before 1993 which were key drivers in the change we will discuss (such as David Norris's legal cases, early LGB youth groups and LGB community centres). While much of the content of this chapter is very specific to the LGBTQ+ community in Ireland over a particular period, I finally invite you to 'take away' some key insights and see how they can apply to other contexts, times and communities.

Building a civil society platform – Chapter 3

In this chapter, I invite you to engage with the notion of 'self-organised communities' and what it really means for communities pushed to the margins to speak and act for themselves. While this is language often used, in reality marginalised communities too often have limited and mediated access to power holders, which serves to limit their own power to effect change for their communities. Here I talk about building an authentic community-organised advocacy platform, and how, while it experienced much opposition, it served to provide great legitimacy because it resulted in a community speaking directly to civil servants, politicians and others about the urgency for change. I talk about the process of also gaining legitimacy through building a rigorous research evidence base, framing issues within accepted frameworks, all of which allowed LGBTQ+ civil society to progress policy issues and indeed challenge the very processes of policy making in fundamental ways.

Community youth work: the BeLonG To model – Chapter 4

This chapter opens with the voice of Danielle, a trans and neurodiverse activist who began her advocacy through LGBTQ+ youth civil society at a very complex time in her life. Her reflections offer a deep insight into what was happening for young people at this time and provide a springboard for a discussion about the role of critical youth and community work in setting policy agendas. I talk about how critical consciousness raising and providing direct advocacy opportunities had a huge impact on many young people (such as Dani) who could see that their oppression could be turned into action for justice and whose day-to-day realities shaped complex long-term advocacy strategies. These strategies were often driven by organisations with the capacity to 'play the long game' and place each win and setback within a broader vision that was developed through providing space to listen and strategically plan. In this way, these processes allowed for LGBTQ+ youth issues to be integrated into multiple mainstream policies – at a time when the same was not always happening for LGBTQ+ adult issues – and where activists were planning for periods of ten years or more. I argue that because youth and community work is the often invisible and misunderstood quiet process that happens behind the scenes, formal education and history academics have misinterpreted much of the policy gains which happened during this period. I argue that the emergence of an academic 'counter narrative' that frames LGBTQ+ youth and community interventions on homophobic and transphobic violence as somehow damaging to LGBTQ+ themselves fails to understand, and indeed aims to further erase, the impact of LGBTQ+ youth themselves in designing advocacy for social justice.

A new narrative: queer optimism – Chapter 5

In this chapter, I explore how focusing on optimism and narrative change has been crucial to reshaping public perceptions and policy. By reflecting on key campaigns and initiatives, I describe how we challenged harmful narratives and created spaces that allowed young people to see themselves as belonging and thriving in Irish society. The chapter begins with the context of growing up LGBTQ+ in Ireland during a time when stigma and repression defined the lives of many. Against this backdrop, advocacy efforts prioritised celebration. Documentary projects like *Growing Up Gay* brought the realities of LGBTQ+ youth and their families to wider audiences, exposing the country at large to societal changes. I go on to examine how advocacy initiatives sought to reframe the experience of being LGBTQ+ in Ireland. This involved creating opportunities to celebrate milestones, foster joy and develop resilience in young people. Events like the 'Gay Prom' and campaigns such as Stand Up! Support Your LGBT Friends are discussed as pivotal in shifting the focus from harm to empowerment, providing vital visibility and affirmation. I analyse how rather than meeting opposition head-on, advocacy efforts often centred a positive, inclusive vision that reframed the debate. This strategic optimism enabled us to bypass entrenched biases and create momentum for change. Using the narrative policy framework, I analyse how optimism and storytelling were instrumental in influencing policy and changing attitudes among politicians, civil servants and the general public.

Alliances and political power – Chapter 6

This chapter examines the strategic alliances and political engagement that reshaped public policy on LGBTQ+ young people in Ireland and contributed to the success of the Marriage Equality Referendum. It explores how advocates worked within complex systems in the youth work, education, media and political sectors to promote equality, often navigating resistance to achieve progress. A key focus is on BeLonG To's strategic contributions to the Marriage Equality Referendum. By framing marriage equality as essential to the dignity and safety of LGBTQ+ young people, the organisation helped neutralise opposition narratives and broaden public support. Its partnerships with teachers, school leaders and children's rights organisations amplified this framing, ensuring LGBTQ+ young people were central to the campaign. BeLonG To's work mobilised new voters, influenced national messaging and demonstrated how sustained advocacy can build momentum.

Self-organised community model for policy change – Chapter 7

This chapter outlines an original framework for how civil society can shape public policy, focusing on the experiences of LGBTQ+ youth. Drawing on analysis of the extensive data collected for this book, I examine how marginalised communities navigate and influence legislative processes. Civil society emerges as a critical force, translating collective vision and values into policy outcomes. The model introduced is grounded in practical experience and theory, building on frameworks like Kingdon's agenda-setting theory and the narrative policy framework. It emphasises civil society's central role in framing issues, fostering coalitions and driving narrative shifts to shape policy agendas. LGBTQ+ youth civil society in Ireland provides a key case study, transitioning from marginalisation to mainstream inclusion. This progress resulted from sustained efforts in community development, narrative transformation and strategic advocacy. LGBTQ+ youth organisations invested in building relationships, infrastructure and public understanding, dismantling stigma and achieving transformative outcomes for young people. The model highlights the relationships between civil society, politicians and public servants, showing how trust and collaboration enabled policy breakthroughs despite institutional resistance. These partnerships offer lessons for navigating today's constrained civil society space while advancing justice and equality. By reflecting on these dynamics, the chapter provides a strategic blueprint for sustaining civil society's critical role in creating social justice-based public policy.

Defending our civil society platforms – Chapter 8

In Chapter 8, I also make a case for the protection and growth of civil society and space for communities to openly advocate for their rights at a time when such space is under attack. Here, I discuss how governments are curtailing advocacy and damaging this vital space by silencing legitimate criticism and using conditional funding. I further address the growing issue of extremist far-right actors promoting an anti-civil society agenda as a way to curtail the rights of minority groups and how global geopolitical trends and the often inexplicable decisions of private funders further make these vital spaces precarious at a time when they are most needed.

Conclusion – Chapter 9

In the concluding chapter, I reflect on the lessons from LGBTQ+ youth civil society in Ireland, highlighting how community organising, rooted in queer young people's lives and long-term strategy, achieved real gains by reshaping public narratives and tangible public policy. However, the progress made remains precarious, with anti-LGBTQ+ movements globally wielding significantly greater resources to undermine civil society and weaponise disinformation. Looking ahead, I outline a vision for civil society advocacy that prioritises addressing systemic injustices within public institutions, building coalitions and prioritising excluded voices. Activists can challenge the unequal resources between justice movements and their opposition while defending hard-won rights. This chapter offers suggestions for navigating these challenges, rooted in long-term strategy, collective action and the dogged pursuit of social justice.

Figure 1.2: Sinéad O'Connor, RTÉ *Late Late Show*, 1990

Source: RTÉ Archive

Figure 1.3: Parade float (Kevin and Anthony, Dublin Pride, 2006)

Source: BeLonG To – LGBTQ+ Youth Ireland

Figure 1.4: Image of an early BeLonG To at Dublin Pride

Source: BeLonG To – LGBTQ+ Youth Ireland

2

Context: LGBTQ+ youth in the crosshairs

Here I invite you to reflect on the oppressive society where widespread homophobia and transphobia abounded and the particular focus that religious and conservative forces placed on LGBTQ+ young people when it came to denying rights to the LGBTQ+ community as a whole.

I start with a timeline of significant events and developments for LGBTQ+ young people over the period of 1993–2015. I developed this timeline based on the data I collected over many years, and I am struck by how different it is from other LGBTQ+ cultural and historical timelines for this same period. For me, this says a lot about the absence of LGBTQ+ youth and youth advocacy from a growing body of Irish LGBTQ+ writing. It also speaks to the difference it makes when advocates who were embedded in the pursuit of social justice, who know the strategies used, intimately tell the stories. I hope this timeline will be useful to future authors and indeed will be incorporated into their considerations of LGBTQ+ history and advocacy in Ireland.

Timeline for LGBTQ+ developments that impacted LGBTQ+ young people in Ireland (1993–2015)

1993: Decriminalisation

Ireland embarked on a pivotal journey towards equality with the decriminalisation of homosexuality. This landmark court ruling effectively liberated LGB individuals from the threat of legal prosecution, allowing them to embrace their identities boldly and openly. It served as the cornerstone for subsequent activism and legislative advancements.

1998: Equality Employment Act

The enactment of the Equality Employment Act marked a watershed moment, outlawing discrimination in the workplace based on sexual orientation. Its introduction was a clarion call for inclusivity, illuminating the path towards ensuring that every employee, regardless of their identity, could thrive in a fair working environment, reflecting society's evolving attitudes towards LGB rights.

2000: Equality Status Act

The Equality Status Act arrived on the scene, broadening the spectrum of legal protections against discrimination. By prohibiting bias not just based on sexual orientation but also on grounds such as gender, race and disability, this legislation reinforced the commitment to an inclusive society that recognises and celebrates the richness of intersecting identities within the LGBTQ+ community.

2003: Founding of BeLonG To

The founding of BeLonG To brought about a new era of advocacy for LGBTQ+ young people in Ireland. As a Department of Education-funded organisation, it provided essential supports and safe spaces for queer youth, forging a community and developing a wide advocacy platform for LGBTQ+ equality.

2003: National Youth Work Development Plan

This plan recognised gay and lesbian young people in youth work for the first time. Although a small mention, it was the first, and it was purposefully included so as to be built on in the coming years.

2004: 'So Gay' campaign

The launch of the 'So Gay' campaign marked the first concerted effort to address homophobic bullying within schools. By engaging students and teachers for the first time, the campaign opened the conversation about homophobic and transphobic bullying in schools. It was also important that it was entirely written and designed by queer youth as this set the expectation that queer youth themselves had the agency to change the education system.

2005: Teacher Training Programme Development for Social Personal and Health Education (SPHE)

In partnership with BeLonG To, the Department of Education's SPHE programme established the first teacher training programme focused on LGB issues. This training was widely delivered by committed SPHE coordinators, aimed at equipping teachers with the relevant knowledge and tools.

2005: Reachout suicide prevention strategy

The Reachout National Strategy for Action on Suicide Prevention shone a spotlight on the mental health crises facing LGBTQ+ people, explicitly addressing their heightened risks of suicide and self-harm. This was the first major government strategy to mention LGBTQ+ young people and resulted in major government investment in the LGBTQ sector.

2006: Homophobic bullying seminar at Trinity College Dublin

The first significant seminar on homophobic bullying was convened at Trinity College by the Children's Research Centre and BeLonG To, gathering key stakeholders – including international academics, advocates and community organisations – to discuss research findings and evidence from LGBTQ+ young people. This event catalysed further engagement with the Department of Education on the imperative to combat bullying and foster safer climates for LGBTQ+ students.

2006: Stop Homophobic Bullying campaign

In a partnership with BeLonG To, the Equality Authority launched the Stop Homophobic Bullying campaign, which amplified efforts to confront homophobic and transphobic violence in schools. This initiative provided resources for parents, educators and students. Of great significance is that this campaign brought key education stakeholders – the National Association of Principals, the National Parents Council, teachers trade unions – together to support LGBTQ+ young people for the first time, opening the door for decades of partnerships.

2006: Founding of Transgender Equality Network Ireland (TENI)

The establishment of the TENI represented a critical advancement for the transgender community. This organisation provides vital support to the trans community and is an extremely successful advocate for policy change – such as the introduction of the Gender Equality Act in 2015.

2007: Marriage Equality organisation established

The formation of Marriage Equality provided a robust platform for advancing the campaign for same-sex marriage in Ireland. This dedicated advocacy group mobilised public support and ignited a movement that would eventually lead to the enactment of marriage equality in Ireland in 2015 following a huge referendum campaign.

2008: National Network of LGBTQ+ Youth Services launched

BeLonG To's National Network of LGBTQ+ Youth Services was officially launched by President Mary McAleese. The network was built to bring LGBTQ+ youth supports to queer young people across the country. In 2003, there was one LGBTQ+ youth group in the country; by 2015, this had risen to over 30, and by 2024 there were over 60 groups – providing a significant infrastructure in small towns and often giving birth to other local LGBTQ campaigns and Pride parades.

2008: Gay and Lesbian Equality Network (GLEN): 'Valuing visibility: an exploration of how issues of sexual orientation arise and are addressed in post-primary schools' (and work to 2016)

This was the beginning of a vital series of research reports and manuals from GLEN, which work directly with the Department of Education and key stakeholders to mainstream LGBTQ+ equality in schools. As part of their advocacy over the coming years, they produced indispensable guidance for school boards, school counsellors, school principals and school management bodies. As well as being important tools to change schools, GLEN's work also brought the Department of Education and often conservative stakeholders on an equality journey.

2009: Report of the Commission to Inquire into Child Abuse (the Ryan Report)

The commission investigated systemic child abuse in Irish institutions, particularly Catholic-run residential schools, revealing pervasive abuse including physical, sexual and psychological harm, facilitated by a culture of secrecy and government negligence. The horrors revealed in this report galvanised support for the protection of children. It was the focus of a successful campaign for enshrining children's rights in the constitution and the development of specific child protection legislation and a state agency. LGBTQ+ youth advocates supported this work and framed the violence experienced by LGBTQ+ young people in state and religious schools as child protection issues to be dealt with within the new frameworks.

2009: Supporting LGBT Lives research study

The Supporting LGBT Lives study provided crucial insights into LGBTQ+ mental health and well-being. Carried out by the Children's Research Centre in Trinity College and commissioned by GLEN and BeLonG To, with the support of the National Office for Suicide Prevention. This research highlighted widespread isolation, harassment and violence towards LGBTQ+ young people and extremely elevated levels of self harm and suicidality among this community.

2010: Stand Up! LGBT Awareness Week launched

Stand Up! LGBTQ+ Awareness Week was launched, becoming an annual event promoting inclusion and solidarity within schools and more broadly within communities. This campaign aimed to empower young people and adults to challenge homophobia and transphobia and create supportive environments. Ireland's longest running queer rights campaign, Stand Up! still takes place in primary and secondary schools and within communities across Ireland annually.

2010: Growing Up Gay aired

The two-part television series *Growing Up Gay* premiered on national broadcaster RTÉ, bringing to light the experiences of real LGBTQ+ youth in Ireland. By showcasing personal narratives, the series played a vital role in normalising what it meant to be young and LGBTQ+. Its reach was of great importance (one in five of the country's population watched it), and it had a major ripple effect in young people coming out and asking for youth support.

2010: Launch of LGBT Asylum Seeker and Refugee Project

BeLonG To initiated the LGBT Asylum Seeker and Refugee Project, aimed at providing support to LGBTQ+ people seeking international protection in Ireland. This project illustrated the intersection of LGBTQ+ rights and refugee issues, underscoring the vulnerabilities faced by those fleeing persecution due to their sexual orientation or gender identity. Its significance lies in the large number of people who got support and in its impact on influencing people's understanding of intersectional identities.

2010: Civil Partnership Act

The Civil Partnership Act was enacted, granting legal recognition to same-sex couples and providing many of the same rights and responsibilities as marriage. This landmark legislation was a milestone in the journey towards marriage equality, ensuring that same-sex couples could enjoy legal protections in their relationships.

2011: Government commitment to tackle homophobic bullying

The coalition government formed by Fine Gael and Labour committed to addressing homophobic bullying in its programme for government. This political will represented an important acknowledgement of the ongoing challenges faced by LGBTQ+ students, signalling governmental accountability in upholding the rights of queer youth.

2011: Cloyne Report

The publication of the Cloyne Report, which investigated clerical sexual abuse, prompted a national conversation about the separation of church and state in Ireland. The Taoiseach's statement regarding this separation underscored the need for systemic change, including the review of policies impacting LGBTQ+ rights within religious contexts, including religiously owned schools.

2012: 'Stand up' becomes the most viewed Irish public awareness video ever

BeLonG To's 'Stand up to homophobic bullying' video reached over 2 million viewers on YouTube, reflecting a growing public appetite for dialogue on LGBTQ+ youth issues. By harnessing social media, the video prompted discussions around homophobia and transphobia and showcased the resilience of young people standing against discrimination. As of 2025, the video has been translated into over seven languages and viewed over 6 million times online.

2012: International Day Against Homophobia and Transphobia

On the International Day Against Homophobia and Transphobia, BeLonG To representatives spoke at the United Nations Educational, Scientific and Cultural Organization in Paris and participated in the Department of Education and Skills Anti-Bullying Forum. This platform elevated Ireland's commitment to global advocacy for LGBTQ+ young people

2012: Development of 'Growing up LGBT in Ireland' SPHE curriculum

The collaboration between the Department of Education, HSE, BeLonG To and GLEN led to the development of the 'Growing up LGBT in Ireland' SPHE curriculum. This comprehensive framework provided the manual and training for LGBTQ+ issues to be taught directly to students in schools.

2012: ShoutOut organisation was founded

This LGBTQ+ peer-led organisation committed to improving life for LGBTQ+ people by sharing personal stories and running educational programmes within schools across Ireland with great reach and impact.

2013: National Action Plan on Bullying

The National Action Plan on Bullying emphasised the legal obligation of schools to combat both homophobic and transphobic bullying. By mandating support for LGBTQ+ students, this plan represented a proactive approach to safeguarding the well-being and rights of LGBTQ+ young people within educational settings – both schools and informal education settings.

2013: European Union (EU) Presidency LGBT Youth and Social Inclusion Conference

The EU Presidency LGBT Youth and Social Inclusion Conference took place at Croke Park, culminating in the Dublin Statement, which highlighted the importance of inclusion for LGBTQ+ young people across Europe. This event, created in partnership between BeLonG To, the Department of Children and Youth Affairs (DCYA) and the European Commission, again illustrated a commitment to championing LGBTQ+ rights on a global stage.

2014: Better outcomes, brighter future

The National Policy Framework for Children and Young People 2014–20, titled 'Better outcomes, brighter future', included specific commitments to improve the life experiences of LGBTQ+ young people. This framework recognised the importance of intersectional approaches in policy design, addressing various dimensions of disadvantage and discrimination. LGBTQ+ young people are included throughout the influential framework, demonstrating the importance of 'equality mainstreaming' within policy development.

2015: National Youth Strategy 2015–20

The National Youth Strategy 2015–20 built upon previous initiatives, incorporating the needs of LGBTQ+ youth into broader youth development plans. This strategic framework aimed to empower young people including LGBTQ young people at each step, to resource youth work and to develop new youth public policy.

2015: Marriage Equality Referendum and Act

The Marriage Equality Referendum was a historic moment in Irish history, with a majority voting in favour of legalising same-sex marriage. Following this referendum, the Marriage Equality Act was enacted, symbolising a culmination of years of advocacy and activism for equal recognition of LGBTQ+ relationships.

2015: Gender Recognition Act

The Gender Recognition Act of 2015 allows trans people over 18, and those aged 16–17 through a longer process, to legally change their gender and name, obtain a gender recognition certificate and apply for a revised birth certificate. It is a self-identification process.

2015: Introduction of the LGBT Safe and Supportive Schools model

The LGBT Safe and Supportive Schools model, developed by the HSE Health Promotion Donegal and BeLonG To and tested in schools, was introduced to equip schools with comprehensive 'Whole School Community' tools and guidance to build equality, and support for LGBTQ+ students throughout the academic year, within schools and in their communities.

2015: 'Connecting for life'; Ireland's national strategy to reduce suicide 2015–20

The 'Connecting for life' strategy sought to address mental health and well-being among vulnerable populations, explicitly including

LGBTQ+ people. By recognising the specific challenges faced by the community, the strategy aimed to reduce suicide rates and improve access to mental health services tailored to LGBTQ+ people, and specifically LGBTQ+ young people.

2015: The Equality (Miscellaneous Provisions) Act

The Equality (Miscellaneous Provisions) Act was passed, further strengthening the legal framework protecting against discrimination on various grounds, including sexual orientation and gender identity in schools. It is of particular significance as it protected LGBTQ+ teachers from discrimination in hiring and progression in state-funded schools with a religious ethos (most schools).

LGBTQ+ history is often told through major events, but as I mentioned I am interested in what happened to make these events possible – the seemingly smaller moments which turned out to have a major effect on the shape of our journey. With this in mind, I share with you a personal memory of one such moment that had a significant ripple effect in my early days of advocacy at BeLonG To.

Memory: 'Church Anger As Gay Campaign Targets Schools'

I was sitting shell shocked, in Cornucopia vegetarian café in Dublin city centre early on a Monday morning with my phone, notepad and a copy of the previous day's *Sunday Times* in hand. The newspaper carried the front-page headline 'Church anger as gay campaign targets schools'. It was 2004, just one year after we had opened BeLonG To, and the campaign they were talking about was ours. In truth, there wasn't even a campaign yet, we had just received some funding to develop a programme and a possible campaign with LGBTQ+ young people. I was working with the amazing artist Almha Roach and a highly motivated group of young people who wanted to 'do something about schools'.

The young people I was working with had identified school as a dangerous place for them to be, a place of violence, stigmatisation and hurt that I knew ran deep and resulted in trauma that many in our community spent a lifetime trying to recover from. I myself went to an all-boys Catholic school and experienced regular violence from the school principal. The violence was often ritualised. He would drag me up to the altar at school mass to beat and shame me for not being masculine or sporty enough, thinly veiled ways of saying 'gay'.

Listening to the stories of these young people in 2004, I could see that schools, particularly religious schools, were still riddled with homophobia and transphobia. In that first year of working in youth service, the brutality experienced by young people was vividly revealed through three programmes.

First, we introduced the young people to Playback Theatre, a form of improvisational performance, based on Theatre of the Oppressed. Young participants overwhelmingly chose to act out scenarios based on violence they had experienced in school. The programme, run by the extraordinary drama therapist Sinéad Moloney, allowed young people to safely raise dangerous issues, ones they could never speak about outside of the context of the youth service. This tough work ignited an incredible amount of peer support, as the young people helped each other to overcome fear and shame. Following this, a week-long exchange with an LGBT youth service in Manchester brought up several issues. Routine practice for youth exchanges, participants were asked what medication they needed to take on the trip. Of the 12 young people, seven were taking prescription medication for depression and/or anxiety. The fact that 60 per cent of the young people I was working with were taking medication for anxiety/depression (a reality that was borne out by later research), and the resulting conversations it allowed me to start, fundamentally changed my understanding of what it meant to be growing up LGBTQ+ in the early 2000s. Finally, that year I completed my master's dissertation on body image and young gay men (Barron and Bradford, 2007) which I had begun while working at a gay men's health service. This also allowed me to spend many hours in conversation with young people, and violence at school emerged as a central concern, particularly connected to sports, as well as aggressive masculine identities and their impact on young people's self-image.

That year of intensive youth work made one thing very clear to me: we had to do something about schools.

Back in Cornucopia that Monday morning, the last thing I had wanted was for us to be on the front page of *The Sunday Times*. It seemed like everything we were warned about when setting up BeLonG To was coming to pass. Voices from both inside and outside the community had cautioned us not to work with under 17 year olds (17 is the age of consent in Ireland), and under no circumstance should we mess with schools, most of which were maintained by the Catholic Church, advice many of us dismissed as conservative, old-fashioned and a result of (internalised) homophobia. We won the battle around age by arguing that only targeting young people over 17 would put us out of sync with every other state-funded youth service, that the proposition of only working with over 17 years olds was itself homophobic and would likely provoke rather than prevent further homophobic backlash. We were determined to establish BeLonG To in accordance with the same parameters as other mainstream organisations, and we even adapted the policies of other friendly services.

The fear of the Catholic Church among our advisory group was, however, well founded, and there was no quick fix for this. The brutality with which the church has treated the queer community has left deep scars on us individually and as a group.

Confronted with that headline on that Monday morning, I had no template from which to work, no playbook to follow. But I put one foot in front of the other and began what was to become our first defiant pushback against the Church.

I immediately got on the phone and called the National Parents Council, the National Youth Council and the Union of Students in Ireland. I had built up a relationship with these groups, and I knew I could ask for their help. That day, the Department of Education (who funded BeLonG To) called to talk about a complaint they had received about their funding of the organisation. A few days later, I went to meet them to discuss the complaint, which was a thinly veiled homophobic attack dressed as concern as to why the state was funding an LGBT organisation which was at odds with certain Christian moral codes. After my initial worry and a discussion of equality legislation, it became clear that they were asking me to help them frame a response that was supportive of our work.

The point we all galvanised around was a simple one: these were real young people telling us real stories about what was happening to them in school. We had a duty to respond and do what we could to make sure all young people were safe and respected in school. By mid-week, all the national bodies I had called, as well as the Department of Education, had issued statements in support of BeLonG To's schools campaign – the one that didn't even exist yet! In the Dáil, the government robustly defended funding BeLonG To, based on the script I developed with Department of Education civil servants. In the face of what could have escalated into a serious crisis, we sowed the seeds for how to defy the hegemony of the Catholic Church when it came to LGBTQ+ youth. The following year, the youth programme had developed into a national campaign in schools. It was called So Gay! The materials were written by young people for young people, supported by a range of national mainstream bodies, and it was launched at the Equality Authority, the state's independent equality watchdog.

The reason for using this story is to highlight clearly how LGBTQ+ young people have always been in the crosshairs of the religious and socially conservative forces which long held an unequalled sway over public opinion, media and public policy. I also tell you it to capture a key, little known, point at which we began to build a comprehensive pushback against these forces.

In an interview for this book, a campaigner for marriage equality said, 'I would have given up fighting for marriage equality in the morning in favour of making schools safe places for gay kids. School was a place that the state, by law, required young people to go to experience violence and humiliation. Gay kids were experiencing state-funded violence.' As my own experiences can attest, this violence was inflicted from both peers and teachers in many instances. It is a violence that was carried out of the classroom, into the halls and playgrounds our LGBTQ+ young people inhabit. It is a violence that follows them into their communities, and frequently into their homes.

Opponents of LGBTQ+ rights have long focused on children and young people. The argument about young people and morality was epitomised by Family Solidarity, a Catholic lay advocacy group, originally established in 1983 to campaign for the eighth amendment to the constitution, which banned abortion in Ireland until it was repealed by referendum in 2018. Advocating against the decriminalisation of homosexuality, they stated in their 1990 manifesto *The Homosexual Challenge:* 'If the laws against homosexual acts are repealed and the age of consent were made the same for all, then the lawmakers would give a clear message to the young: Homosexual behaviour is normal and acceptable and society does not mind which alternative you choose' (Dunphy, 1997, p 254). Here opponents to law reform present homosexuality as a threat to 'traditional family values', which they describe as Judeo-Christian. Strikingly, across many campaigns against the inclusion of LGBTQ+ people in public policy, opponents place 'the young' at the centre of the debate. This is an effort to harness moral panic around children and young people.

The same moral panic was invoked in *The Sunday Times* article I mentioned earlier, when the Bishop of Achonry and member of the Council for Education of the Irish Episcopal Conference, Thomas Flynn, argued: 'I am not sure there are many teenagers who are gays ... I would be afraid that young people who feel different from their peers, for whatever reason, would identify with this campaign even if they are not that way inclined' (McDonald, 2004). The 'fear' that Bishop Flynn refers to is based on a twofold stigmatisation of gay men, in particular: (1) that gay men are sexual predators who lure young people into having sex, and (2) that proximity to queer people can turn a 'normal' teenager into a queer teenager.

With LGBTQ+ youth being a primary focus for those opposing LGBTQ+ rights in general, many of the people I spoke with felt that LGBTQ+ young people occupied the intersection of discrimination, particularly in an increasingly diverse country. As one civil servant put it: 'Because to move forward progressively on an LGBTQ+ youth issue is harder than on an LGBTQ+ adult issue. There's a double whammy of stigma and stereotyping.'

This 'double whammy' is really about being both LGBTQ+ and legally a child. This restricts LGBTQ+ young people's economic independence and geographic mobility, key factors that would help members of the community to avoid homophobia and transphobia. Generations of LGBTQ+ people left home, and indeed the country, to come out safely. This option is not available to teenagers. Their political participation was also restricted, as under 18 year olds cannot vote and have limited political influence. This suspension in time, accompanied by a widespread belief that being LGBTQ+ was a choice and one that could only be made by an adult, left queer youth in the impossible position that their very existence was denied. As advocates for queer youth, we were left in this bizarre position that we had to contend with these now completely debunked notions – that we were advocating for a phantom community. I remember, and recalled in an *Irish Times* article, how important our relationship with Emily Logan, Ireland's Ombudsman for Children was. She came to BeLonG To in the early days of her role and from 2004 referred to 'LGBT young people' – not 'young people who might be LGBT', or 'young people who felt they could become LGBT' which was the norm in official parlance at this time.

A number of key points which re-emerge throughout this book and that I ask you to keep in mind are:

- the predominance of Christian churches, which maintained aggressively anti-LGBTQ+ positions across Irish society and institutions;
- the influence of those churches in the design and delivery of education to children and young people, including through teacher training and the direct delivery of education to children and young people;
- the deep and widespread stigma attached to those of us queer people who worked with and advocated for LGBTQ+ young people and the challenges we had to face to advance progress;
- the dehumanising position that LGBTQ+ young people faced, where their actual existence was denied, a narrative which allowed homophobia and transphobia to flourish across their lives – in school, at home, in community groups, because it was all located in an abstract space, just the rough and tumble of growing up, victimless jokes as no one was actually young and LGBTQ+;
- the early strategic importance of engaging in deep advocacy with influential national bodies and how this helped to change the narrative on what the lives of LGBTQ+ were really like and what needed to happen to overcome the widespread discrimination they were experiencing.

Let's step back further in time – the history that haunts us

It is important to ground our exploration in the historical context that has shaped LGBTQ+ youth experiences in Ireland – a context characterised by a complex interplay of legal, societal and institutional dynamics against the backdrop of Ireland's unique postcolonial and religious heritage. It is also helpful to feel the 'haunting' that comes from the recurrence of stigma and oppression down through the generations. Queer histories mean so much to our community because we have been written out of mainstream history so often. For example, we grew up not knowing that Roger Casement, revered Irish revolutionary, or Gráinne Mhaol – iconic Irish pirate queen – were queer. These histories are also contained in our bones as a community because the oppressions and violences recur and reappear as hauntings down through the generations. The violences, the oppressive laws and school curriculums, the stigma and shame and the erasure itself – from the canon of histories and from our own family and geographical community's stories – they repeat and they reinforce.

Ireland's stance on LGBTQ+ rights, influenced by its history as a postcolonial state that inherited British laws criminalising homosexuality, was markedly out of step with its Western European counterparts. Notably, the 1861 Offences against the Person Act and the 1885 Criminal Law Amendment Act were direct impositions from British rule, which Ireland retained well into the late 20th century. These laws positioned Ireland alongside Eastern European and former Soviet countries in terms of the timeline for decriminalisation, highlighting a conservative approach to LGBTQ+ rights and the low starting point we had for the hard climb ahead.

Writers have reflected on how defining sexuality in terms of reproduction helped create homophobic cultures. Mexican author and activist Gloria Careaga Pérez suggests that the drive to categorise sexuality as a reproductive function (as opposed to being about pleasure) has led to LGBTQ+ people being defined – in moral, medical and state terms – as sinners, mentally ill and perverts (Careaga Pérez, 2014, pp 143–9).

Homosexual acts were criminalised in differing ways in British laws from the time of Henry VIII until 1967. In his history *Coming Out*, Weeks (1997) maintains that this emphasis on the nuclear family continued to be important in post-war Britain and 'by its nature, must exclude homosexuals except as aberrations' (Weeks, 1977, p 157).

Article 44.1.2 of the Irish constitution (1948, which was first published in 1937) read: 'The state recognises the special position of the Holy Catholic Apostolic and Roman Church as the guardian of the Faith professed by the great majority of the citizens' (Ireland, 1948). As Tom Inglis (1998) puts it:

> The power of the Catholic Church meant that it structured not just the religious life of the Irish people, but their social, political and economic life as well. Consequently, the strategies through which Irish Catholics struggled to gain cultural, social, political, economic and cultural capital were linked in with living a good Catholic life. (Inglis, 1998, p 37)

Although the fifth amendment to the constitution, which removed this article, was passed by referendum in 1972, the fact that the position of the

Catholic Church was enshrined in the constitution delineates the Catholic Church's formidable influence over Irish societal norms and policy directions. Despite the 1972 amendment, the Church's dominance, particularly in the educational realm, perpetuated a societal ethos often staunchly at odds with LGBTQ+ identities and rights.

This influence continued far beyond 1972 in the education system. To this day, the Catholic Church continues to own and assert control in the region of 90 per cent of primary and more than half of all secondary schools nationwide (Byrne and Devine, 2017). This long history and exercise of ownership have led some to comment that the Catholic Church views 'control of schooling as its prerogative', and that the main function of the Irish education system was the 'inculcation of religious ideals and values' (Coolahan, 1981 in McCormack and Gleeson, 2010).

The adverse impact of this dominance on LGBTQ+ youth cannot be overstated. The ramifications of Catholic teachings in schools on the well-being of queer youth is extensively documented (Barron and Bradford, 2007; Higgins et al, 2016). This includes widespread teaching that homosexuality was a sin, the strict policing of gender roles (as embodied in dominance of single-sex schools and single-sex school uniforms) and the teaching that being transgender is against nature and not accepted by the church. Violence towards LGBTQ+ young people in Christian schools in Ireland – from both teachers and students – has been repeatedly captured in research (DCYA, 2017; Higgins et al, 2024). In a major national study conducted as recently as 2024, 49 per cent of LGBTQ+ young people reported personally experiencing anti-LGBTQ+ bullying in school and 69 per cent report witnessing it (Higgins et al, 2024). In this same report, participants suggested that less religious influence in school would make schools safer. Suggestions included less focus on religion, the removal of religion from the curriculum, the removal of church from management of the school and the removal of all religion from the school: 'Religion is far too ingrained in Irish public schools. It has no business there, especially when certain religious ideologies openly threaten the safety and comfort of LGBTQI+ people' (19, woman, bisexual, ID 1305 in Higgins et al, 2024, p 115).

So many Catholic ideals, values and teachings are at odds with fundamental aspects of LGBTQ+ identity. Scholars have written extensively on the impact of Catholic teachings on the health and well-being of LGBTQ+ young people in our schools, a site of much of the focus for advocacy for policy change which is discussed in this book (Lynch and Lodge, 2002; Norman and Galvin, 2006; Barron and Bradford, 2007; Minton et al, 2008; Mayock et al, 2009; Higgins et al, 2016).

For those of us who grew up in pre-decriminalisation Ireland (pre-1993), the invisibility of LGBTQ+ identity was striking. In both Cork and Dublin, gay and lesbian community centres emerged in the late 1970s and early

1980s; however, it is reasonable to say that in a pre-internet era, awareness of these centres was limited. It is also important to reflect on the impact of the HIV/AIDS crisis which both cost the lives of many in the LGBTQ+ community and which further stigmatised gay identity. The first diagnosis of HIV in Ireland occurred in 1982, and the first organised community response occurred in 1985, with the formation of Gay Health Action (RTÉ, 2017). Nolan and Larkan (2015) maintain that Ireland at the outbreak of AIDS was a 'sex-negative' culture in which the 'procreative script' prescribed by Judeo-Christian beliefs viewed sex as 'dirty, sinful, and wrong' except within marriage for procreation. This was a period of 'culture war in which the forces of conservatism and liberalism clashed' (Nolan and Larkan, 2015, p 5). The eighth amendment to the constitution, which recognised the equal right to life of the pregnant woman and the unborn foetus, was overwhelmingly voted in favour of in a referendum in 1983, when 66.9 per cent of voters approved the insertion of the amendment, which created some of the most restrictive abortion laws in the world and, with the exception of Malta, the most restrictive in the EU.

The policing of women's sexuality, and its devastating impacts, was further amplified in 1984 when 15-year-old schoolgirl Ann Lovett died together with her new-born baby as she gave birth at a grotto at Granard, County Longford. The tragedy received huge media attention. Later that same year, the body of a baby boy was found on a beach in County Kerry. This event saw the launch of a major police investigation involving what was claimed to be 'one of the most comprehensive police investigations into the morals and lifestyles of transgressive, especially single, women who were potentially, or known to be, sexually active' (Inglis, 2002, p 8; Mayock et al, 2007).

Two years earlier, in 1982, Declan Flynn, a gay man, was murdered in Fairview Park in Dublin. A group of five teenagers were arrested for the murder. The judge in the case heard that they had wanted 'to clear our park of what we call queers', and they had been 'queer-bashing for about six weeks before and had battered 20 steamers' (McDonagh, 2020, p 24). They were found guilty only of manslaughter. The judge ruled that this 'could never have been a case of murder' and handed down a five-year suspended sentence, allowing the convicted to walk free from court (McDonagh, 2020, p 24). In response to the injustice of the sentencing, a large march of lesbian, gay, women's and rights groups from Dublin city centre to Fairview Park happened in March of 1983, an action of protest and visibility, ten years before decriminalisation, described by some as 'Ireland's Stonewall' (Murphy, 2018).

In 1982, Jack Marrinan, general secretary of the Garda Representative Association, stated that the 'values of society had taken a plunge in recent years with people like homosexuals and pro-abortionists demanding rights' (McDonagh, 2021, p 55), and 'the murder of Charles Self resulted in several hundred individuals from Dublin's gay community being interviewed by the police, resulting in considerable upset and fear among many gay men whose sexuality had become known to family and friends as a result of the police's actions' (McDonagh, 2020, p 23).

This was less than two years since David Norris's unsuccessful case seeking declaration from the state that sections 61 and 62 of the Offences against the Person Act 1861 and section 11 of the Criminal Law (Amendment) Act 1885 were inconsistent with the Irish constitution under article 50. In a judgment that was vocally adherent to Judeo-Christian principles, this case was dismissed in the High Court in October 1980 as was his subsequent appeal at the Supreme Court on 22 April 1983. Again referencing the state's close relationship with the Christian faith, homosexuality was described by Chief Justice O'Higgins as 'morally wrong … potentially harmful to the institution f marriage' (O'Kelly, 2004).

However, by 1988, the social and political climate in Ireland had begun to shift, and attitudes towards sexuality in general, and homosexuality to a lesser extent, were becoming fractionally more progressive, especially under the influence of broader European integration. This change in sentiment provided the backdrop for Norris's eventual success when he took his case to the European Court of Human Rights. The court ruled in his favour, declaring that the Irish laws criminalising homosexuality violated the European Convention on Human Rights, marking a historic victory for LGBTQ+ rights in Ireland and prompting the Irish government to decriminalise homosexuality in 1993.

European institutions, like the EU and the Council of Europe (CoE), have been instrumental in embedding LGBTQ+ rights into their frameworks. Landmark cases like *Dudgeon v United Kingdom* (1981) and policy shifts such as the Amsterdam Treaty's anti-discrimination provisions showcase Europe's legal leadership. Advocacy networks, particularly the International Lesbian, Gay, Bisexual, Trans and Intersex Association-Europe, have capitalised on these structures to professionalise and influence policy (Ayoub and Paternotte, 2019).

While European institutions advanced LGBTQ+ rights, the Irish state's inaction and hostility sent a starkly different message. The actions of the Gardai (Irish police) and courts sent a clear signal that in the eyes of the state, gay people were not protected from harm, and indeed further that the state was willing to harass and put gay people's lives at risk. As stated, opposition to LGBTQ+ rights has long focused on children and young people.

The forces of conservatism seemed to prevail until 1993, focusing much attention on sexuality and maintaining a moral code excluding women's sexuality and gay people. It is very noteworthy that 'key milestones' and 'turning point' histories of LGBTQ+ rights in Ireland skip almost the entire period which this book focuses on. For example, 'Here's a short history of the battle for LGBT rights in Ireland', published in The Journal online newspaper in June 2018, lists key event number five as 'Decriminalisation' in 1993 and number six as 'Civil Partnership' in 2010. The erased 17 years, I argue, are where much of the key change happened in real terms.

Early supports for LGB young people

From 1979 to 1993, Ireland's LGB youth worked to carve out a space within the broader gay liberation movement, navigating a landscape shaped by legal, cultural and social barriers. The establishment of the National Gay Federation (NGF) Youth Group in 1979 marked a major moment, bringing visibility and connection for young lesbian and gay people at a time when institutional and cultural support was scarce. While the movement faced limitations, the efforts of key individuals like Bernard Keogh, teenager Dermod Moore and his mother Phil Moore exemplified the courage and resilience of those who drove change.

The NGF Youth Group arose to address the absence of spaces for Ireland's gay youth to connect, organise and explore their identities. The Hirschfeld Centre in Dublin became a vibrant hub for community building, offering young people a safe space to meet and share experiences. Keogh, a central NGF leader, championed the inclusion of under 21s, emphasising the need for peer support and spaces where young LGB people could develop their confidence and sense of belonging.

In 1982, the group secured affiliation to the statutory Dublin youth service (Comhairle le Leas Óige) and received a modest 'start-up' grant. As it happened, the youth officer for that part of central Dublin was Maurice Devlin, himself an elected member of NGF's administrative council. To avoid conflict of interest and because of the potential for controversy given the legal and political climate, Maurice ensured that other staff colleagues handled the application and conducted the relevant assessments. Both the director and assistant director of the youth service visited the youth group. Nonetheless the recognition and funding were predictably condemned by a number of politicians, including those on educational and youth service committees, and in 1986 support for the group was terminated despite it continuing to meet all the criteria for funding. It was also twice refused membership of the National Youth Council of Ireland (NYCI), highlighting the prevalence of homophobia in Irish youth work at the time.

Devlin's involvement in supporting the LGBTQ+ youth movement was to continue in a number of ways, including as a long-time educator on the professional youth and community work programmes in Maynooth University and as a director for many years of BeLonG To.

Tonie Walsh, co-producer of the Gay Youth Congress of 1985, former president of the NGF and curator of the Irish Queer Archive, recalled how the NGF hosted the world's second 'Gay Youth Congress' in Dublin in 1985, the precursor to the International Lesbian, Gay, Bisexual, Transgender, Queer and Intersex (LGBTQI) Youth & Student Organisation (IGLYO), saluting the others who were involved in that important initiative:

> I recall the National LGBT Federation's pivotal role in championing the needs and aspirations of queer Irish youth at a time in the late 1970s and throughout the 1980s, when addressing those needs and aspirations was hugely problematic, even considered taboo. The establishment of Irish's first lesbian and gay youth group in 1980, followed by a significant submission to the National Youth Policy Committee of 1984 and the subsequent world congress together paved the way for a more urgent and nuanced approach to LGBTQ+ youth in Ireland.

The NGF's Youth Group founding documents reveal a set of activist and movement-building objectives which went beyond providing safe space and included:

- To achieve for young gay women and men, fully equal rights, status, and respect as their heterosexual counterparts.
- To promote by education and example a greater understanding and acceptance of gay people in society in general, and by social agencies, medical, educational and legal institutions in particular.
- To seek from educational authorities the implementation of programmes of education in personal and sexual relationships. In which factual and unbiased information regarding the incidence and nature of homosexuality is presented. (Documents from collection of Professor Maurice Devlin)

The extraordinariness of this documentation lies in the time in which it was written – long before decriminalisation and at such an early stage in the gay rights movement in Ireland, in the oppressive context and climate in which the NGF Youth Group was established and against which it consciously and actively fought.

In its 1990 report 'Equality now for lesbians and gay men', the Irish Council for Civil Liberties (ICCL) highlighted how in 1985 the NYCI refused associate membership to the NGF's Youth Group. In 1988, Senator David Norris, speaking at the NYCI General Assembly in Wexford, criticised the NYCI's continued refusal to accept the NGF's Youth Group as a member (McAleer, 2018, p 56). In 1992, the NGF's youth group was accepted into the NYCI, following a two thirds membership vote in favour of acceptance, which, according to McAleer (2018, p 62), 'was a significant marker in NYCI's history and the start of a change in youth politics'.

Parental involvement through groups like Parents Enquiry, spearheaded by figures such as Phil Moore, added a critical dimension to the movement. These parents not only provided direct support to their children but also engaged in public advocacy, challenging societal prejudices and broadening the conversation around lesbian and gay rights. Moore's public appearances, including debates on national television, shifted public opinion and showcased the strength of family solidarity. This alliance between young activists and their parents emphasised the centrality of family in Irish society and became a model for how to build broader support for LGB issues.

While the decriminalisation of homosexuality in 1993 marked a milestone, the activism from 1979 to 1993 revealed both achievements and challenges. The NGF Youth Group's work laid a critical foundation for future progress, demonstrating that young LGB people were active agents of change, not merely passive beneficiaries. Their efforts to create inclusive social spaces and organise events like the international conference were radical acts that reshaped Ireland's cultural and political landscape. However, these achievements also underscored the need for more robust systemic advocacy to address the structural barriers that continued to marginalise LGB youth. This period of activism highlighted the importance of sustained and inclusive youth advocacy – the need to support young people as leaders in their own liberation (McDonagh and Kerrigan, 2021).

In the early 1990s, Junior Larkin and other young people coordinated a queer youth group in Dublin under the sponsorship of Gay Switchboard. It was known as the Dublin Lesbian and Gay Youth Group, and it provided a vital safe space for queer young people. One former member, queer artist and activist Jaime Nanci, reflected fondly on their time at this youth group:

> I read about it in the back of a copy of *Gay Community News* I found in our local library, which was my first safe space. I took the bus from Dundalk to Dublin, secretly. Of course it was terrifying but it was really a lifeline, at 16, to walk into a room where there were other people like me. After so many years of isolation? It was life changing. And one of the friends I made that first day is still part of my chosen family.

Suzy Byrne, who was centrally involved in GLEN's successful campaign for decriminalisation in 1993 and in the running of *Gay Community News*, supported Junior's work. Together, and against the odds, they hosted an international conference of the IGLYO in Dublin 1994. The conference was funded by the European Commission and the CoE. (Suzy was then elected to the board of IGLYO from 1994 to 1998.) Suzy and Junior also wrote *Coming Out: A Book for Lesbians and Gay Men of All Ages* (1994) – the first Irish book of its kind.

Reflecting, for this book, on this time of great change, Byrne said:

> The supports for young people were informally provided by their peers. They were supported by other voluntary groups within the community who knew how important it was that there was peer-led support and information provision. Around that time queer youth issues were raised in the wider youth work sector but it was difficult to get heard until decrmininalisation happened and even then there continued to be significant homophobia in youth work and informal education.

Joan O'Connell was a member and then coordinator of the LGB youth group called OutYouth, which evolved from the NGF group, between 1998 and 2003. Joan, who did extraordinary work over these five years, spoke with me for this book. She said:

> The existence of a peer-led social group for young LGBTQ+ people was my starting point, in effect. It offered a place outside pubs and clubs which would likely have been an overwhelming introduction to my new communities. Before BeLonG To, we relied on smaller, informal groups like OutYouth. They were lifelines – places where young LGBTQ+ people could connect and find support without fear of judgement. These early spaces didn't have the funding or visibility of later organisations, but they were built on a profound understanding of what community meant, laying the groundwork for everything that followed. OutYouth provided friendships, supports, information and networks for so many, at a time when for a young person living at home, coming out still involved a very real risk of being thrown out and left with nowhere to live.

Joan, as the coordinator of OutYouth, worked with us to establish BeLonG To, something she says she is also still proud of. She recalled:

> I remember hearing about a young person in their mid-teens who had been dropped off and collected from a BeLonG To meeting by their parent. This, to me, was a real milestone, one which demonstrated that something was changing in Irish society, whether to do with acceptance or removing secrecy and shame, or both.

The 1998 'OutYouth report', written by Dr Carol-Anne O'Brien at NEXUS Research for Gay Switchboard Dublin, Gay HIV Strategies and the Eastern Health Board, shined a light on the incredible work of the lesbian, gay and bisexual youth group while highlighting the challenges they faced. OutYouth, which was coordinated by Fergus Ryan at this time, provided a lifeline for LGBTQ+ young people, offering safe spaces to connect, come out and find support. However, the report identified pressing issues, including volunteer burnout, limited resources and the unmet needs of young people facing bullying, family rejection and homelessness.

To address these challenges, the report called for immediate investment in professional support, including a part-time youth worker, and stronger partnerships with statutory and voluntary agencies. It also recommended specialised training for youth workers, teachers and social services, alongside efforts to integrate LGBTQ+ issues into mainstream services like schools and health systems.

Ultimately, the report offered vision and both tangible immediate action and long-term strategies to support LGBTQ+ youth. It called for sustainable funding, systemic inclusion and educational campaigns to ensure that LGBTQ+ young people could feel safe and empowered.

The establishment of BeLonG To in 2003 marked a significant shift, formalising grassroots work towards LGBTQ+ advocacy.

The Irish education system: where queer kids went to learn fear and shame

This profound impact of criminalisation and stigmatisation on LGBTQ+ young people's experiences persisted after decriminalisation, with calls for action in the 2017 nationwide consultation highlighting the need for the removal of religious patronage in schools and hospitals. Legislative changes, such as the removal, in 2015, of section 37.1 of the Equality Employment Act 1998 and the 'baptism barrier' in 2018 (which had allowed state funded schools with a particular religious ethos to discriminate in their admissions process against children who were not of that ethos), reflect progress yet underline the ongoing struggle against discrimination and stigma. Irish studies have consistently shown that homophobia and transphobia remain endemic in schools, with LGBTQ+ young people disproportionately vulnerable to early and prolonged drug use.

In 2011, Ruairi Quinn, then Minister for Education and Skills, established the Forum on Patronage and Pluralism in the Primary Sector. This move came amid growing scrutiny of the role of religious groups, particularly the Catholic Church, in education. The advisory group's report, led by Professor John Coolahan, highlighted the need for diversity in Ireland's primary education system and suggested transferring some Catholic schools to other recognised patrons (Coolahan et al, 2017). Primary schools in Ireland, which serve children aged four to 12, are mostly 'voluntary schools'. They are privately owned, predominantly by Catholic religious communities, parishes or boards of governors. They adopt a Catholic ethos and promote the Catholic faith, yet they receive state funding. Although the secondary school sector is fractionally more diverse, the influence of Christian, particularly Catholic, doctrines remains significant.

Many have critiqued the 'integrated curriculum' in Catholic primary schools, where religious ethos permeates all subjects, not just religion classes. O'Mahony argues that this curriculum design, coupled with the denominational nature of the school system, significantly restricts some parents' and children's ability to exercise their religious freedom, leaving them without genuine school choices due to an ineffective system of opting out of religious instruction (Hyland and Bocking, 2016).

The pervasive Catholic ethos also extends to employment practices in schools. Until a legislative change in 2015, schools were allowed to prioritise hiring and promotional practices that align with their religious ethos, effectively legalising discrimination against openly LGBTQ+ people. This policy underscored the challenges faced by LGBTQ+ teachers, who risked penalties up to and including losing their job if they disclosed their sexual orientation or gender identity, and in turn, to this day, robs LGBTQ+ young people of vitally needed role models. This reflected the Church's severe stance on gender and sexuality as expressed by figures like Cardinal Ratzinger, later Pope Benedict XVI (Ratzinger, 1986 cited in Norman and Galvin, 2006).

Moreover, the Catholic school ethos has been linked to higher instances of homophobic and transphobic bullying, with teachers feeling that their school's ethos hinders their ability to effectively combat such behaviour (Norman and Galvin, 2006; Barron and Bradford, 2007; Minton et al, 2008).

Undeniably, the Catholic Church's influence on Ireland's primary education system has been monumental, affecting curriculum, school choice and employment practices. Efforts to diversify this influence remain crucial to ensuring that schools frespect and uphold the rights and freedoms of everyone who attends them or works for them. This influence continues to be profound today, and its traumatic impact on generations continues to be felt by older queer adults (Reygan and Moane, 2014).

Pushing back against religiously dominated institutions: early organising for LGBTQ+ young people

In 1990, the ICCL report 'Equality now for lesbians and gay men' addressed the elephant in the room: the moral panic evoked by opponents of LGBTQ+ rights when it came to young people. The report stated:

> We unequivocally accept that society must have laws to prevent the sexual coercion of any young person, and we also accept that a common age of consent in relation to sexual activity should be determined for all young people. Moreover, we do not advocate special rights or privileges for young lesbians or gay men. *What we vigorously stand for are their rights, as Irish citizens, to equality with their heterosexual peers in treatment, protection and respect.* (ICCL, 1990, p 22, emphasis added)

This ground-breaking report, published three years ahead of decriminalisation, also advocated for a range of LGBTQ+ rights:

- Young lesbians and gay men, as Irish citizens growing up in Ireland, should enjoy equal rights with their peers. As citizens, they should be protected against discrimination in all aspects of their lives, school, work, youth clubs, and so on.
- They have the right to expect representation and recognition on national youth bodies and in the youth services generally.
- Young lesbians and gay men have a right to explore and to enjoy sexual relationships at the same age as their heterosexual peers.
- All young people have the right to expect the support and facilities of an environment which enables them to develop into mature adults. Being lesbian or gay should not be an excluding criterion. (ICCL, 1990, p 34)

While the LGBTQ+ movement became increasingly organised and influential, it would be reasonable to suggest that until 1993 the forces of conservatism, closely linked to Catholic social teachings, were winning the culture war, which focused much of its attention on sexuality – ensuring that women's sexuality (beyond procreation) and gay people had no place within the moral code of the time (Inglis, 1998; Reygan and Moane, 2014).

The legacy of criminalisation and stigmatisation has immeasurably affected LGBTQ+ young people in Ireland, persisting well beyond the decriminalisation of homosexuality. This enduring impact was highlighted in a 2017 report from a nationwide consultation with LGBTQ+ youth, which detailed persistent discrimination, bullying and harassment, and contained a strong call from young people for the removal of religious patronage in schools and hospitals, alongside a broader demand for the separation of Church and state (DCYA, 2017, pp 7–10). This is very much a 'haunting' for our queer community and for us as queer people. Homophobic and transphobic violence and its impacts being passed down from generation to generation causing harm throughout our lives as so many of us try to make it just stop – for this to be the last generation to experience it.

Legislation supported these discriminatory practices until relatively recently. In addition to the sanctioned discrimination against LGBTQ+ teachers mentioned earlier, the so-called 'Baptism Barrier' permitted schools to favour children baptised into their faith and was not removed until 2018. This affected not only non-religious children but also those from minority religions and children of LGBTQ+ parents who, reasonably, would not baptise their children into a hostile religion (EQUATE, 2017; Barron, 2018; Finnegan, 2018).

The consequences of discrimination and stigma are not only pervasive but also deeply damaging. Studies from Ireland and around the world have consistently found that homophobic and transphobic attitudes are rampant in schools, significantly affecting the mental and emotional well-being of LGBTQ+ students (Norman et al, 2006; Barron and Bradford, 2007; Minton et al, 2008; Mayock et al, 2009; Higgins et al, 2016). These hostile environments have also been linked to higher risks of early and prolonged substance abuse among LGBTQ+ youths (Sarma, 2007).

In the early 2000s, even before social media, LGBTQ+ young people navigated multiple identities and faced various forms of discrimination. Youth, as an identity, is often celebrated for its idealism, but young people are also subject to numerous constraints, including legal limitations and social discrimination. Young people feel targeted by stereotypes and prejudiced treatment. In the early 2000s, Maurice Devlin described the Irish media's portrayal of young people's sexuality as overwhelmingly negative – marked by alarm, dismay and a fear that something sinister is affecting 'our youth', thereby threatening the fabric of society. This portrayal was not only common in both broadsheets and tabloids but also laden with gender biases and a sexual double standard, framing young people broadly as societal 'problems' using similar rhetorical strategies (Devlin, 2003, pp 111–12).

Young LGBTQ+ people often face challenges at various other intersections, which may include poor mental health, poverty, class inequality, homelessness, addiction, violence, racism, sexism, ableism and limited access to education and health services. These issues are frequently exacerbated by persistent homophobia and transphobia. Indeed, LGBTQ+ youth are more likely to encounter prejudice, discrimination and violence compared to their adult counterparts. They frequently endure multiple layers of prejudice and injustice, such as young lesbian Travellers facing unique challenges, or LGBTQ+ youth living in economic poverty (Barron, 2013, p 36). In the early 2000s, BeLonG To engaged in training and outreach to youth services in working-class parts of Dublin where some young people experienced extreme poverty. The outcome was a large number of referrals of young people to the organisation, which really influenced our work. We began providing bus fares and food at group meetings as we understood early on that young people could not afford to travel to a group and often came hungry. It was so important to us that queer young people living in poverty had access to queer youth services, something which instilled a significant class analysis in the work, which was further reflected in a significant number of incredible staff members from working-class communities.

Pursuing social justice when your community is unmentionable

In the context where LGBTQ+ young people were 'unmentionable' in public policy, the LGBTQ+ community had to find ways to frame these young people's needs and concerns in a way that others could understand.

To this day, minority community and grassroots groups have to do this, and for the queer community this has been exhausting. When our concerns were dismissed by mainstream civil society, the government or academia, we often had to 'translate' our movement for social justice into bite-sized frames that could be understood. In this way, nimbly adopting and pushing the boundaries of acceptable frameworks was a core strategy. In the next chapter, I focus on the 'how to' of building an LGBTQ+ civil society platform in order to do this translation. I will look at the processes and risks involved, as well as the need for renewed support for community-led civil society to advocate freely for the rights of communities pushed to the margins.

Five takeaways

1. Recognising LGBTQ+ communities as perpetual targets of extremists

The chapter illustrates how LGBTQ+ people, particularly young people, have historically been placed in the crosshairs of societal, religious and political forces. From moral panics to targeted discrimination, LGBTQ+ people have long been scapegoated during periods of cultural or political dominance by conservative forces and at times of change. This enduring reality is insufficiently acknowledged in broader historical narratives, leading to a failure to understand how deeply systemic these patterns of marginalisation are. As activists, we can recognise and confront the longstanding targeting of LGBTQ+ communities, particularly young people, ensuring that these patterns are named, documented and addressed as part of the fight for equality.

2. The critical role of historical context in advocacy

This chapter spoke about how understanding the historical backdrop of LGBTQ+ oppression in Ireland provides crucial insights into contemporary challenges. The systemic abuse and neglect of LGBTQ+ young people in schools, public institutions and policy frameworks didn't arise in isolation but was deeply shaped by decades of institutional control and societal resistance to difference. By connecting present struggles to historical causes, activists can better identify and dismantle the roots of inequality.

A thorough understanding of historical context can equip activists to craft strategies that do not just address symptoms but challenge the systemic ideologies that perpetuate harm.

3. The power of exposing failures in state responsibility

Historically, the Irish state's neglect and hostility towards LGBTQ+ young people sent a clear message that their lives were disposable. Schools failed to protect them from violence, and policies often excluded their needs entirely. However, by exposing these failures, advocates have managed to create leverage for change, holding institutions accountable for their inaction. Advocacy strategies can include exposing the failures of institutions in meeting their duties, turning these shortcomings into opportunities for systemic reform.

4. Combatting the weaponisation of morality against LGBTQ+ youth

As the chapter shows, LGBTQ+ young people have often been the focal point of moralistic arguments designed to undermine their rights. Campaigns claiming to 'protect children' have historically been used to justify discrimination and block progress, while simultaneously portraying LGBTQ+ identities as dangerous or immoral. These tactics rely on deeply rooted cultural fears that resonate widely if left unchecked. Activists today must proactively counter the weaponisation of morality against minority communities; we need to foreground safety, fairness, equality to disavow a resurgence in the repressive and violent use of morality by bad actors against minority communities.

5. The importance of documenting LGBTQ+ histories for advocacy

LGBTQ+ histories are often overlooked or deliberately erased, leaving the contributions and struggles of past generations underrepresented. This chapter highlights how the marginalisation of these histories has weakened public understanding of LGBTQ+ oppression and resilience. Documenting and preserving these stories is essential, not just to honour past struggles but to equip current and future advocates with the tools they need to push for change. We can prioritise documenting and amplifying LGBTQ+ histories to ensure they serve as a source of inspiration, evidence and guidance for future advocacy.

Figure 2.1: *Gay Community News* youth issue 2007 'Look who's talking!' cover

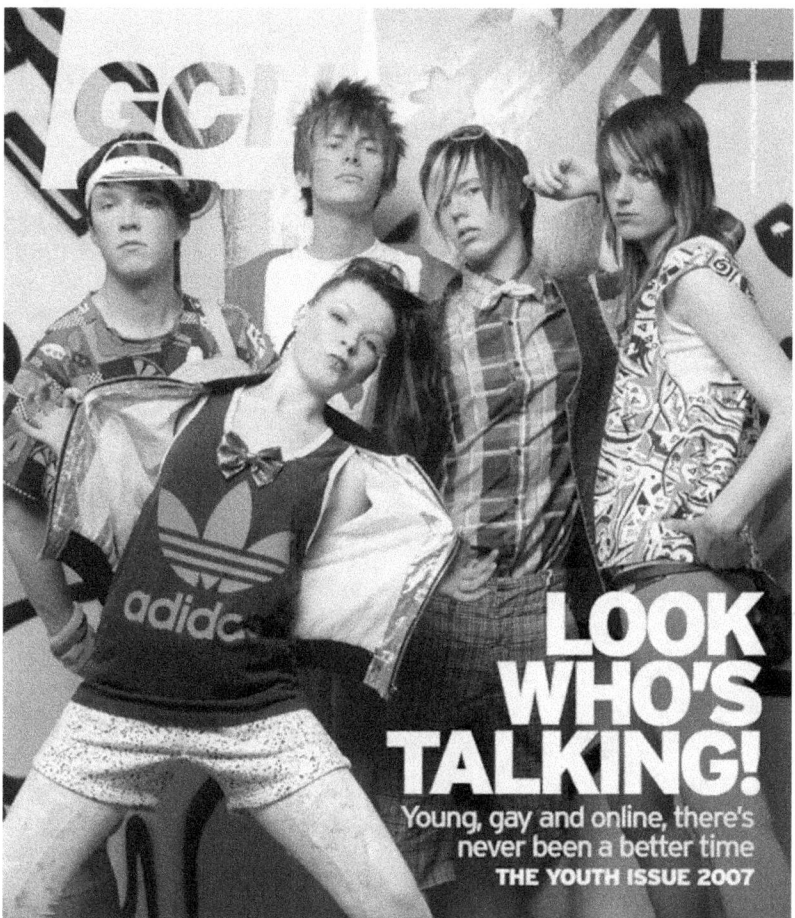

Source: Gay Community News, Dublin

Figure 2.2: *Gay Community News* youth issue 2006 'Generation next' cover

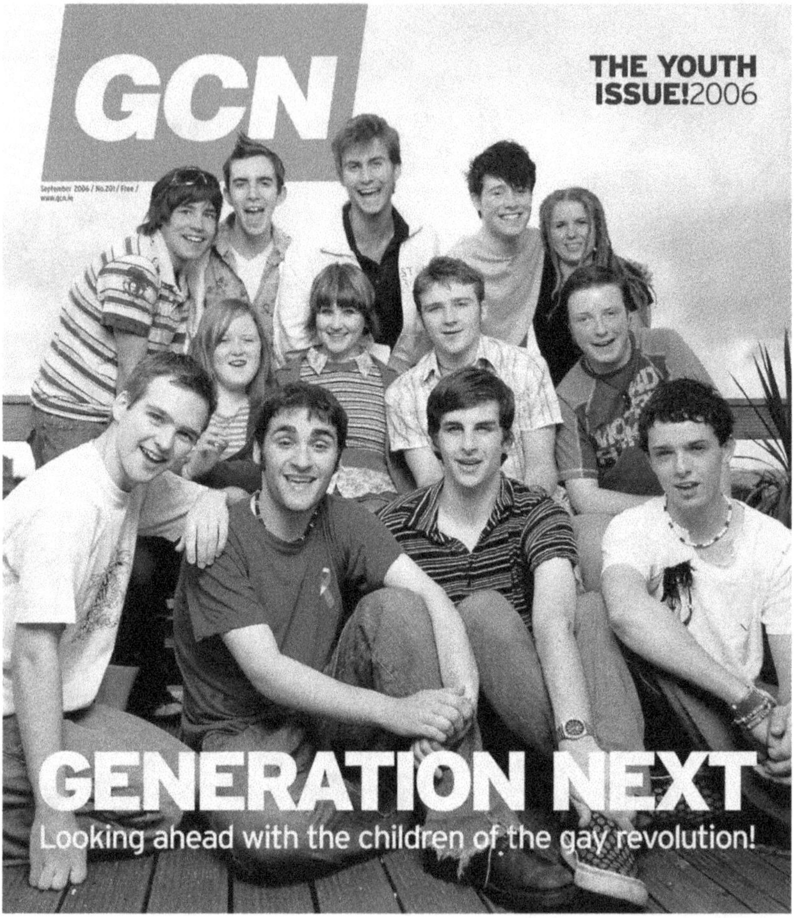

Source: Gay Community News, Dublin

Figure 2.3: International Day Against Homophobia & Transphobia

Source: BeLonG To – LGBTQ+ Youth Ireland

Figure 2.4: BeLonG To 'Key principles for working with LGBT asylum seekers and refugees' (2011)

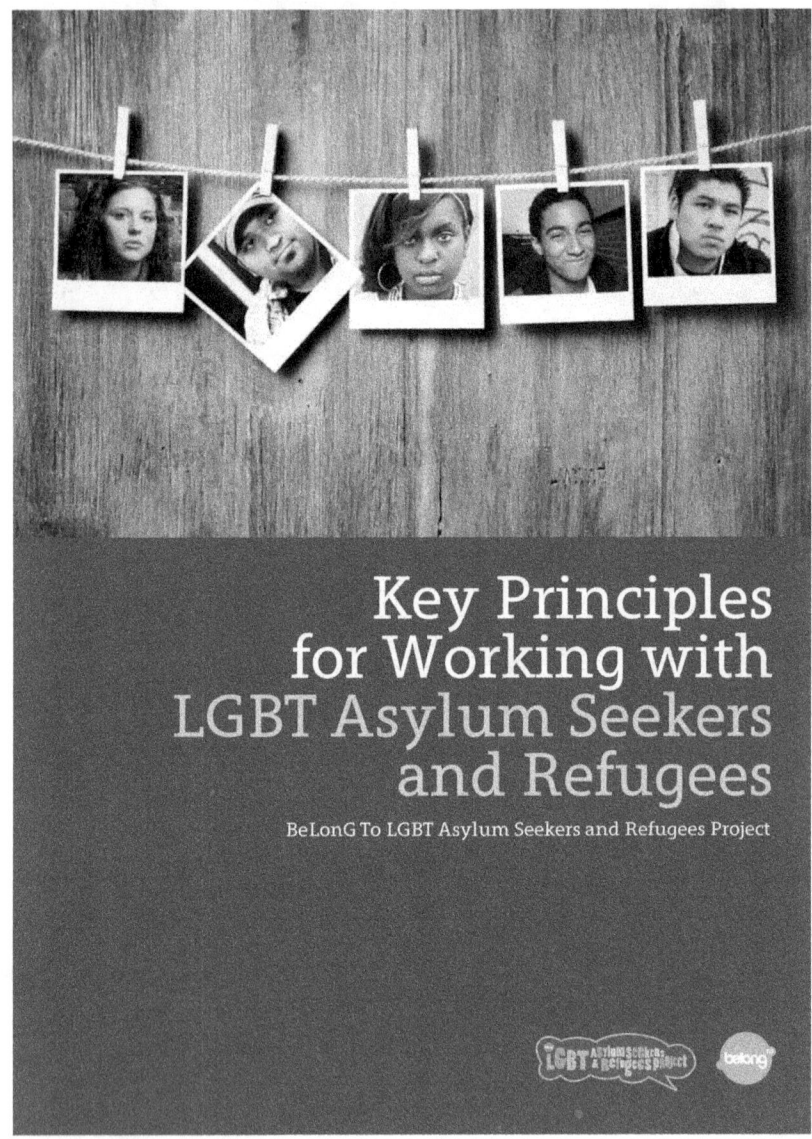

Source: BeLonG To – LGBTQ+ Youth Ireland

3

Building a civil society platform

The current chapter and the next three chapters work closely together. In these four chapters, we are diving deeply into the creating, direction and analysis of an agile, energetic and quick-thinking LGBTQ+ youth civil society that had the imagination and resources to both plan long term and adapt quickly in shifting sands. It is the story of BeLonG To and our work to urgently change Irish society because the young people we worked with everyday were often living through unbearable conditions. We were able to work on many issues and fronts at the same time – supporting queer young people in violent situations directly, working with queer young people to develop their political analysis, creating opportunities to campaign, campaigning, lobbying and engaging in a huge programme of changing what it meant to be LGBTQ and young in Ireland. These chapters delve into the behind the scenes of this work over many years. I do so purposefully – to draw out learnings which I am committed to making useful to other activists and advocates from marginalised and minority communities in the hope that they will be useful to future advocacy.

In this current chapter, I invite you to engage with the notion of 'self-organised communities' and what it really means for communities pushed to the margins to speak and act for themselves. While this is language often used, in reality marginalised communities too often have limited and mediated access to power holders, which serves to limit their own power to effect change for their communities. Here I talk about building an authentic community-organised advocacy platform, and how, while it experienced much opposition, it also served to provide great legitimacy – resulting as it did in a community speaking directly about the urgency for change to civil servants, politicians and others. I also talk about the process of gaining legitimacy through building a rigorous research evidence base, framing issues within accepted frameworks, all of which allowed LGBTQ+ civil society to progress policy issues and indeed challenge the very processes of policy making, underpinned by a dogged determination to speak and act for ourselves. This chapter, along with Chapter 8, greatly informs why I place civil society at the core of the 'Civil society model for social justice policy change' which I present in Chapter 7. In this section, I incorporate the voices of people I interviewed, ensuring their reflections and analyses are given the space and attention they deserve.

I begin with a reflection of my own.

Memory: One day, everyone will have always been for this

I had travelled to the International Association of Suicide Prevention Conference in Killarney Conference Centre in beautiful County Kerry in the South West of Ireland, with my friend and colleague Ciaran McKinney, the Director of Community Development at the Gay and Lesbian Equality Network (GLEN). It was 2007, and it was a huge conference. To this day, it happens annually in different parts of the world, and this was the first time for Ireland to host it. Ciaran and myself were invited by the National Office for Suicide Prevention to host a table about the LGBTQ+ community and suicide prevention in Ireland. For anyone who has been to these sorts of huge conferences, hosting a table is like 'a foot in the door' – you really want a place on the main stage, but you understand that it's a process, and in this case it was an international conference with experts from around the world. I know that the National Office for Suicide Prevention, and its Director Geoff Day – who was a steadfast champion of our work – had to really advocate for us to be there.

Having said that, with our 'no small tables' internal mantra it was somewhat deflating that we were the only representation from the LGBTQ+ community there – just Ciaran and myself and our little table 'down the back'. No speaker spoke about our community from the main stage and I was confronted a few times each day with homophobia and with the narrative that young people were being pushed into suicidality because of the lack of religion (nothing could be further from the truth for the young people I worked with). By the last day, I was tired and frustrated. We had been advocating for the need for support for LGBTQ+ young people and for structural changes in the systems they engaged with (including religious ethos schools) for four years now. I had visited too many young people I deeply cared about in hospitals, seen too many self-harm wounds, had to intervene in too many schools and families. Those four years (2003–7) of advocating for suicide and self-harm prevention had been formative but so difficult. There were others in the field who clearly did not want an LGBTQ+ community voice. I remember vividly being at a suicide prevention meeting at parliament, where after I spoke a senior politician audibly whispered to his colleague 'here we go, the gays are taking over'. We had collated an abundance of international research, held a high-profile international seminar at Trinity College, ran two national campaigns, designed teacher training with the Department of Education and indeed secured LGBT people as a named focus population in the National Action Plan for Suicide Prevention – yet we were coming up against such resistance and a narrative that there was no proof of the link between homophobia/transphobia and suicidal ideation among young people.

Then in Killarney, for the closing keynote address, President of Ireland Mary McAleese took to the stage. In a speech that was greeted the following day with the front page headline: 'President Mary McAleese today called for a national change in attitudes to end the bullying of gay people', the President spoke to the assembled international audience about 'an undercurrent of both bias and hostility which young gay people must find deeply hurtful and inhibiting'. She went on to make the powerful statement: 'Homosexuality is a discovery, not a decision, and for many, it is a discovery which is made against a backdrop where, within their immediate circle of family and friends as well as the wider society, they have long encountered anti-gay attitudes which will do little to help them deal openly and healthily with their own sexuality.'

In her precise and powerful speech, she foregrounded the link between homophobia/transphobia and suicidality. My heart was pounding with a mix of emotions. I felt that the young people I was working with were really being seen and heard and our community was seen and heard. I felt a pride of sorts that it was the first citizen of Ireland – a country still clawing its way out from under the yoke of colonial and religious bigotry – who was proclaiming this link to the world. It was the beginning of a powerful relationship with President McAleese, her family and colleagues, who would go on to launch our national network of LGBTQ+ youth groups the following year, and of course make her most powerful interventions eight years later in the Marriage Equality Referendum at a BeLonG To Yes event in May 2015. The tide was turning, and the rights of LGBTQ+ young people were moving in the public and political conversation from violence and erasure towards visibility and defiance.

I present this story about President McAleese's intervention at the International Association of Suicide Prevention Conference in Killarney because it speaks to both the frustration of building an unpopular civil society platform and the joy that occurs in those moments when that platform becomes accepted as legitimate and one that decision makers have to sit up and listen to.

In the years surrounding this event, LGBTQ+ advocates dedicated significant effort to framing LGBTQ+ youth rights in ways that resonated with broader societal and policy frameworks. They also worked to build a strong evidence base demonstrating the state's obligation to support these young people. This was challenging, as the accepted frameworks often did not fit and we had to find, or often did not find, ways in. We also had to challenge conventional policy making. For example, at times policy makers wanted to listen to 'experts' such as doctors, academics and psychiatrists rather than to the LGBTQ+ community itself. The process of policy making also sought conventional research which preferred quantitative numbers-driven data which was not ethical or possible for a largely hidden population.

Other events and social changes which impacted on LGBTQ+ youth visibility

It is also vital to our understanding to appreciate that the Irish LGBTQ+ civil society platform was not somehow detached from broader international and national progressive changes that were occurring at the same time.

In Ireland, as I will talk further about in a later section, the rigorous uncovering of brutal and criminal institutionalised child sexual abuse (as highlighted in the Ryan and Cloyne Reports), and on bullying and youth mental health, helped create an environment and a language in which to talk about some of the experiences of brutality that LGBTQ+ young people had and were facing in Irish schools. These foci, as awful as they were, made it possible to talk about the obligations of the state to protect LGBTQ+ young people from harm and to further promote their visibility as part of the country's ongoing reckoning with the secrecy and shame that enabled religious and state institutions to carry out horrific abuse of children and women.

At the same time, in a very different way, globally the LGBTQ+ community became a connected community via social media, which really started taking off in the early 2000s with Friendster in 2002 and Myspace in 2003. By the mid to late 2000s, platforms like Facebook (2004 to Harvard students, opened to the public in 2006), YouTube (2005), Twitter (2006), and Instagram (2010), had made it a mainstream part of our lives. The LGBTQ+ community has long been recognised as an early and innovative adopter of internet technologies, leveraging the digital space to build community, find connection and challenge societal norms that often marginalised them in offline spaces. By the late 1990s and early 2000s, dating and social networking platforms such as Gaydar (1999) emerged, integrating the burgeoning capabilities of GPS and the internet to help users connect with others nearby. The community's pioneering approach to digital technology was deeply tied to necessity: with limited visibility in mainstream media and significant societal stigma, the internet became a tool for empowerment. As detailed in the Slate article 'When AOL was GayOL' (Auerbach, 2014), queer tech enthusiasts and developers played a central role in shaping these platforms, ensuring they met the unique needs of LGBTQ+ users. This engagement with technology was driven by a recognition of its potential to circumvent traditional barriers to connection, advocacy and representation. For many, discovering online communities marked their first experience of belonging (Auerbach, 2014).

Leading with legitimacy

Among the people I spoke with, the role of civil society in initiating and driving policy change was highlighted repeatedly. Anna Quigley, who has been involved in community activism in the Dublin's North Inner City since the 1980s and was a Dublin City Councillor and Chairperson of BeLonG To, said: 'Civil society organisations – they're always the drivers of change; it's very rare for change to come from within the system. At certain points, you can have key champions within the system, but it's almost always the NGOs who drive the issues.'

Tied to this initiation is the issue of legitimacy – who has the authority to speak on behalf of a particular community? It is clear that we drove an agenda whereby the LGBTQ+ community would not be spoken about any longer, and that we would take our own space. To do this, we heavily employed the truism of 'those closest to the struggle are closest to the solution', and that communities pushed to the margins had to have the space to voice their own issues and solutions. As Mary Cunningham, Executive Director National Youth Council of Ireland, whom I interviewed for this book, put it:

> If BeLonG To hadn't been there to lead the way, paving the path for others to follow, much of what we've achieved wouldn't have been possible. No other organisation would have taken on these issues, and even if mainstream organisations had been committed to doing so, they wouldn't have had the legitimacy needed to address them effectively.

This 'authenticity' that came with LGBTQ+ civil society groups being from and of the community they advocated for was something we had to work hard at framing – it was not naturally accepted in an environment of erasure – but it became a positioning that was both ethically correct and strategically significant.

CIVICUS World Alliance for Citizen Participation maintain that 'legitimacy refers to perceptions by key stakeholders that the existence, activities and impacts of Civil Society Organisations are justifiable and appropriate in terms of central social values and institutions' and that 'an organisation is legitimate if it makes sense, has respectable people, competence and knowledge of the topic (organisational Curriculum Vitae)' (Civicus, 2010).

A contributor to this book who is a senior civil servant spoke about the legitimacy of LGBTQ+ civil society groups in terms of competence and knowledge:

> I believe BeLonG To's LGBTQ+ work was built on real expertise, creating a vital space to explore social justice approaches grounded

in equality principles. True commitment to social justice requires critical self-reflection and a willingness to challenge both oneself and others. Without that interrogation, I'd argue, people don't belong in this space.

This analysis was further built on by a civil servant I spoke to when she said:

> I think the approach BeLonG To took in terms of always having that focus on the young person in the context of a bigger society and a focus on what needs to change in that society so these young people are in a better place. That identification of where the change needs to happen in the broader policy arena was clear.

This validity, borne from analysis and a refusal to have LGBTQ+ voices erased or mediated through others in the policy community and academia, had many layers. When it came to addressing the rights of LGBTQ+ young people, it became vital to develop opportunities where LGBTQ+ young people spoke directly to power for themselves. Doing this purposefully and safely was part of a process of consciousness raising and politicisation of young people. Anna Quigley, whose son attended BeLonG To, remarked on the importance of the organisation's approach to youth work:

> Because I know when my son went, young people weren't met with this message, 'we're going to help you with your problems', which could easily have been the approach. But it was that the young people don't have any problems, it's the world around you that needs fixing. And you can work with us to do that.

It is striking that so many of those I spoke to – government ministers, journalists, civil servants, those who were LGBTQ+ young people during this period themselves – could recall how an advocacy platform was being built whereby queer young people's own voices were authentically foregrounded. Brian Finnegan, previously editor of *Gay Community News*, and current Communications Director at the International Lesbian, Gay, Bisexual, Trans and Intersex Association-Europe said:

> What struck me during that march with the young people was not just their courage to stand up and say, 'We're gay, and we won't accept this', but they had the facility to organise and communicate with one another to make it happen. In that moment, it became clear to me that this was more than just engagement – it was empowerment. I suddenly understood BeLonG To's work on a deeper level; it was about creating

the conditions for empowerment, enabling young people to take control of their own advocacy and stand up for themselves.

Organised visibility for queer young people was also recollected by a civil servant who spoke with me:

> I remember the launch of the campaign and the participation of BeLonG To members, quite powerfully all right. And it was very meaningful. People were really participating and sadly, that's a little bit rare in the professionalised world of community and voluntary work. And I'm not saying, BeLonG To wasn't professional, it was professional, but it was professional to the extent that it could also live with the chaos and the reality of people's lives.

Brian Finnegan, recalling his engagement with BeLonG To while he was editor of *Gay Community News*, said:

> I believe that it played a momentous role in that change ... in that, it has professionalised the idea of youth engagement and youth groups and the spreading of youth groups across Ireland, the connectivity of youth groups to each other across Ireland – spearheading that movement of youth groups. It is all part of one piece – it's a movement up, it's a movement of people upwards.

Much of this movement building relied on the physical development of a network of LGBTQ+ youth groups across Ireland. These were physical spaces, often within local community or youth centres, where queer young people could meet with youth workers, and out of which they could campaign and link in with other young people from around the country through a network managed by BeLonG To.

Building the infrastructure for LGBTQ+ community youth work

The development of an infrastructure of LGBTQ+ youth work projects began with support from the Health Service Executive's (HSE) National Office for Suicide Prevention for the express purpose of tackling isolation among LGBTQ. BeLonG To's (2008) strategy noted:

> Since early 2007 BeLonG To has been working to support the development of designated LGBT youth groups outside of Dublin. This work has been carried out through using BeLonG To's 'Start-Up Pack', which is a manual for good practice of establishing and sustaining a group. It contains a step-by-step guide and an accreditation scheme.

Once a group is established it works with BeLonG To on gathering evidence of Quality practice in 6 areas. When this is completed successfully, they become part of the BeLonG To Network of LGBT youth groups. (BeLonG To, 2008, p 35)

Between 2003 and 2015 the number of LGBTQ+ youth groups in Ireland grew from 1 to over 30.

In addition to building the physical network of youth projects through which LGBTQ+ young people could connect and voice their issues, LGBTQ+ civil society had to frame these issues in accessible ways for others, and to invest heavily in building a robust evidence base. This involved learning how to work within the public policy-making process and learning how to push its parameters.

Framing LGBTQ+ young people's issues for public policy change

Framing the issues faced by gay and lesbian people after decriminalisation was enormously challenging for civil society groups, particularly in an environment where the legitimacy of gay and lesbian identities was not widely accepted. The interviews I conducted for this research were vital in helping to understand the full spectrum of needs and, more importantly, rights that LGBTQ+ communities needed and deserved to live in a fairer society. Having first-hand accounts helps paint a full picture of the challenges faced by civil society groups. As Eoin Collins, the extraordinary LGBTQ+ rights activist and leading figure in the Gay and Lesbian Equality Network (GLEN), said in interview with me:

> At that time [early 1990s] we were searching for policy windows to make the case for the acceptance of a lesbian and gay identity. Decriminalisation was about removing the criminality of sexual relations between men, but gay identity is about much more than that – it's about life, about how your whole being is affected. That's what we were trying to communicate.

The first step in this acknowledgement of identity was naming it. This was the early stage of making erased identities visible. It was so important on the journey. As Niall Crowley, equality expert and former chief executive officer (CEO) of the Equality Authority said:

> One of my first meetings while at the Equality Authority focused on key issues raised by LGB civil society. They said 'We want you to explicitly include gender, marital status, family status and sexual orientation.' On the surface, it seemed like a small ask, but in reality,

it was deeply significant. Reflecting on the battle to have LGB people named in the Social Partnership Agreement helps explain to me why this was such an important concern.

People I spoke to who were involved in developing an Irish equality infrastructure and also focused on finding ways of framing LGBTQ+ rights spoke about 'shoehorning' and uncertainties about how to present their issues so that they would fit with accepted policy narratives. This practice of taking advantage of all opportunities while at the same time scrabbling for the right framing and narrative is a key feature of this time in the 1990s.

One such accepted policy framing was, understandably, poverty. The Combat Poverty Agency, together with GLEN, published the report 'Poverty, lesbians and gay men: the economic and social effects of discrimination' in 1995. Reflecting on work at this time, Collins said:

> It was shoehorning, and I don't think it was accepted by some people at all. And even now, it's a stretch because lesbian and gay people are a large population group rather than being a group where all people are poor. So, what we had tried to do was build the human rights aspect to poverty, that poverty impacts even more severely on lesbian and gay people who were already poor, and then increase the risk of poverty for those who are, for example, coming out and might lose their jobs. I suppose it was radical at the time of bringing in a much stronger focus on the causes of poverty and the structure that actually creates poverty.

This focus on the causes of poverty was something which other minority communities shared with the LGB community at this time. Again, Collins reflected:

> There was a parallel process going on as well, which is the kind of coalition building if you like – Pavee Point [Traveller and Roma organisation] and GLEN and disability groups were coming together, creating common cause, and that was all generated by the more radical elements within each movement who wanted to move towards an equality and human rights agenda.

Another perspective that shifted somewhat from the traditional 'poverty model' was community development. As Dr Oonagh McArdle explains, in Ireland, community work and community development – often used interchangeably today – have been state funded since the late 1980s as a way to tackle poverty and inequality (McArdle, 2020, p 4). This approach is rooted in a unique discipline and ethos, dedicated to working professionally and collaboratively with communities to drive social change, promote inclusion and achieve equality (Ad hoc Group, 2008, p 12).

Reflecting on this work in the 1990s, Collins discussed how community development became an area of focus of LGB advocacy. It was an area where there was government resourcing, and many other areas (such as education, mental health, partnership rights) were not yet on the agenda in Ireland:

> We focused on community development because, at the time, it was the only real option. Once equality legislation was passed, there was a sense of having reached a milestone – marriage equality wasn't even on the radar, as it wasn't a reality anywhere in the world. We were trying to figure out what progress could be made in Ireland, and community development was the only space where tangible change seemed possible.

A major change happened at the end of the 1990s and in the early 2000s. Ireland's progressive equality legislation (the Employment Equality Act 1998, the Equal Status Acts 2000) had a huge impact on the LGBTQ+ community's ability to advocate for change

As Collins put it:

> The Employment Equality Act was much easier to achieve than decriminalisation. Decriminalisation challenged deep-seated ideologies and was harder to argue for, especially since it revolved around discussions of sex – something Irish society found awkward to address. By contrast, the Employment Equality Act was more straightforward. It was harder for people to openly say, 'gay people should be sacked', even if some felt we shouldn't be included at all.

Equality legislation provided the framing to work with LGBTQ+ young people in the 2000s

The Equal Status Act 2000 was significant in the development of interventions to support LGBTQ+ young people, including in the development of LGBTQ+ youth services and actions to combat homophobic and transphobic bullying in schools.

As one senior civil servant from the Department of Education who provided BeLonG To with its initial funding put it:

> The Equal Status Act was a key justification. Without it, [BeLonG To] likely wouldn't have stood out among the many other applications we received. This was the basis for their inclusion in the 2003 funding allocations. When reviewing the Equal Status Act of 2000, we

recognised the department's responsibility to support minority groups, which influenced the decision to allocate funding.

The Equal Status Act also became a crucial tool for addressing homophobic and transphobic violence in schools. As one public servant explained to me, while there were champions in the Department of Education and in schools, they needed a mandate to act: 'It's not that they didn't want to do it,' he says, 'but the Act gave them a lever to say, "We have no choice." It allowed them to frame it as a requirement rather than personal enthusiasm, which made it a much stronger argument.'

The lever provided by the Equal Status Act was discussed in *The Irish Times* in October 2006, in an article on the BeLonG To and Equality Authority campaign 'Making Schools Safe'. In that feature, the CEO of the Equality Authority, Niall Crowley, was quoted as saying that victimisation on the grounds of gender or sexuality was prohibited under the Equal Status Acts:

> A person who is responsible for the operation of an educational institution must ensure that any person who had a right to be there is not harassed or sexually harassed … the responsible person will be liable for the harassment or sexual harassment unless he or she took reasonable, practicable steps to stop it. (Irish Examiner, 2006)

Everyone I spoke to, from LGBTQ+ young people themselves to government ministers, described experiencing or discovering the extent of homophobic and transphobic bullying in Irish schools at this time. In many ways, it can be seen as the defining policy issue for LGBTQ+ young people during this period.

The emerging evidence of the extent of homophobic and transphobic violence in schools created a strong sense that action needed to be taken to support LGBTQ+ young people in those spaces.

Bullying held deep significance within the LGBTQ+ community. Finnegan, formerly of *Gay Community News*, explained their strong support for addressing school bullying: 'In 2003, ten years after decriminalisation, the issue of youth and bullying was personal for me because I was badly bullied as a kid. I felt driven to give it a voice – not just for myself but for others experiencing the same.' They also reflected on the community's support for BeLonG To: 'BeLonG To resonated because we've all been young and alienated, especially in rural areas. We grew up on a monochrome, overtly oppressive island, and so many of my contemporaries were severely bullied at school.'

The extent to which homophobic and transphobic bullying resonated with broader society is reflected in a number of media articles from the time. Of particular note is the reporting of a speech from President McAleese, at the launch of a network of LGBTQ+ youth groups (a year after her address on suicide discussed earlier). An *Irish Times* article from October 2008 reported that 'the President also made the link between her own experience growing up with sectarianism in Belfast and homophobia, saying that the two were first cousins. "Nobody should have to suffer because of their sexual orientation in this country"' (Irish Times, 31 October 2008a).

Bullying was a pressing issue for young people, particularly in the LGBTQ+ community, and it served as a relatable and actionable 'policy hook' supported by existing legislation. Crowley explained:

> If marriage was the issue, schools were the battleground. That's why the 2008 Stop Homophobic Bullying in Schools Campaign was so crucial. Schools were, and likely still are, steeped in homophobia. The Equal Status Act applied, and I believed homophobia was illegal, but we couldn't get cases filed under it. Bullying became the way to address it.

The changes in legal and policy context were not immediately obvious to the education system, and it took time and effort from civil society, including seminars, research, toolkits, campaigns and submissions, to get the message across. This work served to crystallise an understanding of the modern context, and by 2013 schools' legal obligation to prevent homophobic and transphobic bullying was made explicit through the Department of Education's Action Plan on Bullying and mandatory guidelines ('Anti-bullying procedures for primary and post primary schools', Department of Education and Skills, 2013b). These procedures have a legal basis in the Education and Welfare Act 2000, and all schools are obliged to implement them. Schools must include homophobic and transphobic bullying in their definition of bullying and must document and report on such incidents. Importantly, schools are also obliged to 'take proactive, educational and preventative measures to create school cultures that are safe for LGBTQ+ young people'.

One senior civil servant who was involved in developing the Action Plan on Bullying and mandatory guidelines noted: 'Schools knew they needed to do this. The case was well made. What the plan and procedures did was to move the discussion from "we should do this" to "we have to do this now".'

Framing the issues as 'bullying' marked a shift in how LGBTQ+ young people were addressed in Irish public policy. It provided the legal framework for the government to require schools to support them. It was never about creating a victimised narrative for LGBTQ+ youth but about both addressing a reality and, crucially, about extending legal protections and obligations to them.

Mental health and well-being

As a result of the advocacy of LGBTQ+ groups, LGBTQ+ people were named as an 'at-risk' group requiring additional intervention from the state in the area of suicide prevention in 'Reachout: national strategy for action on suicide prevention 2005–2014' (BeLonG To, 2005).

The relevant sections of the strategy read:

> Marginalised groups often experience discrimination and can be vulnerable to self-harming behaviour. Such groups include lesbians, gays, bisexual and transgender people, asylum seekers, homeless people and the traveller community ... according to the BeLonG To Youth organisation lesbians, gays, bisexual and transgender people are more likely to be medicated for depression and are more likely to engage in alcohol misuse, drug abuse and deliberate self-harm. (BeLonG To, 2005)

In turn, two actions were included in the National Strategy:

- determine the risk of engaging in suicidal behaviour associated with belonging to a marginalised group;
- develop services, supports and information/education resources to improve mental health and well-being and reduce any increased risk of suicidal behaviour among marginalised people. (HSE, 2005, p 37)

The strategy committed the government to funding LGBTQ+ services and researching suicidality in the community, creating a lever for systemic change. As one public servant explained:

> Even if the HSE dismissed government policy, you could point to it and say, 'Well, it's policy.' It gave us the leverage to push back and initiate broader conversations. Getting that section on the LGBTQ+ community into the policy document was a real breakthrough – it sounded like 'motherhood and apple pie', but it opened the door to much bigger discussions.

In 2005, the first major national strategy to include LGBTQ+ young people focused significantly on mental health. David Carroll, former Executive Director of BeLonG To, explained: 'We were working with young people who were self-harming, and I know too many LGBTQ+ people who have contemplated suicide. That inclusion in 2005 was so important – it meant the issue was being taken seriously and brought support that would never have existed otherwise for queer youth.'

An increasing mainstream recognition of the mental health impact of homophobia and transphobia is evident in media coverage of the issue. One article from *The Irish Times* in 2009 refers to my contribution to the Oireachtas Committee on Health, which stated:

> BeLonG To, a national service for gay and transgender young people, said a significant minority of young LGBT people were at risk of self-harm and suicide, largely because of the stress associated with prejudice and discrimination. 'The Oireachtas committee report clearly recognises the risks for LGBT people and for people from marginalised groups.' (Irish Times, 11 June 2009)

Advocacy from LGBTQ+ civil society groups led to sustained mental health-focused investment in the LGBTQ+ community. Between 2005 and 2015, the HSE's National Office for Suicide Prevention invested over €2 million in LGBTQ+ organisations, becoming one of the largest funders in the decade leading-up to the Marriage Equality Referendum, greatly increasing its capacity.

Notably, the HSE also funded BeLonG To 'to provide a national voice' for LGBTQ+ young people, enabling the development of a broader youth advocacy platform. Framing issues through suicide prevention and mental health promotion allowed for deeper engagement and advocacy, giving LGBTQ+ youth seats at influential decision-making tables for the first time.

This marked a shift, with the LGBTQ+ community finding meaningful positions within established frameworks to address the challenges faced by queer youth. At a time when LGBTQ+ youth were at the centre of a culture war – contending with socially and politically entrenched Catholic dogma and hostile education systems – it's vital to remember the radical social justice agenda we were striving to implement.

Hand in hand with framing queer young people's issues in ways that could be heard by politicians and others in civil society, we needed to build a strong research base to provide a robustness to the demands.

Building the evidence base

Building a solid evidence base is key to driving policy change. As a community under constant attack, we knew the urgency of acting and focused on research that could genuinely improve the lives of queer young people. In the early years of the organisation, we facilitated many academics to do their work – mainly as there was a dearth of Irish queer youth research, and we expected that this facilitation would be beneficial. While some was, much wasn't, and it became clear that the demands, particularly from university students, were unhelpful for the young people. By 2006, we set out to avoid academic voyeurism and endless discourse analysis that didn't lead to real change. At BeLonG To, young people and our team created a research ethics code, asking academics to show how their work would directly benefit LGBTQ+ youth. We asked questions about how the work would be used by the researcher or the university to create policy change. Tired of being treated as exotic subjects expected to relive our traumas, we set the bar high – and more often than not, we said no to researchers and focused on partnering with institutions who could carry out the research we needed to drive our policy agenda. This effort was key to developing practical, informed policy solutions that gradually improved the status of LGBTQ+ young people in public policy.

Early stage evidence in the 1990s and the need to change the rules of the game

Research was an area which posed serious issues for LGBTQ+ civil society groups in the early 1990s, requiring a reframing in the understanding of how minority communities are researched. As Collins put it:

> Civil Society groups were dealing with the civil servants who kept saying, well, you show us the numbers and we'll put protection in place. Our point was always, well you put the protections in place and then we'll show you the numbers because you're not going to see the people until they're safe and protected.

Here we can see how LGBTQ+ civil society groups needed to make visible to others the discrimination and stigma they experienced, so as to be able to bring about change. To do so, however, they had to challenge taken-for-granted processes, such as the process of data gathering itself, which was fraught with biases that disadvantaged highly stigmatised and erased communities. LGBTQ+ advocates had to, in Bacchi's sense, 'problematise' policy making and question the rules of engagement and seek to alter them so as to be able to progress policy change (Bacchi, 2009).

Notwithstanding this considerable challenge, civil society groups did gather evidence on the realities for LGBTQ+ people in Ireland. This largely began in 1995 with the report 'Poverty, lesbians and gay men: the economic and social effects of discrimination' (Combat Poverty Agency and GLEN/Nexus, 1995). This report provided the evidence for the Equality Authority to establish an LGB task group which produced 'Implementing equality for lesbians, gays and bisexuals' (Equality Authority, 2002).

Evidence to act in schools

The power of research led by LGBTQ+ civil society really showed in work with the Department of Education. Reflecting on efforts to tackle homophobic and transphobic bullying in the Action Plan on Bullying (Department of Education and Skills, 2013a), one civil servant at the Department of Education said to me: 'We did our homework – there was plenty of evidence showing LGBT bullying was a real issue, even in primary and early secondary schools. We'd pulled together years of research, and it made all the difference. We could stand behind everything we said, and all that work really paid off.'

LGBTQ+ civil society dedicated significant energy to exposing the realities of homophobic and transphobic bullying in schools, building a strong Irish evidence base. Crowley emphasised the importance of this research: 'Homophobia and transphobia were so rooted in schools. Management didn't want to engage, so we needed policies and legal obligations to mention LGBT people. The research was everything – it exposed what young people had been telling us for years and showed just how bad it was.' The research didn't just confirm what people knew – it broke the silence and gave the justification needed for policy changes.

The first public event in this work to build the evidence base for policy change in the Irish education system was a seminar on homophobic bullying held in Trinity College Dublin in 2006. This seminar was held as a partnership between BeLonG To and the Children's Research Centre at Trinity College and brought together Irish education stakeholders and international experts. This seminar deepened the work of the Children's Research Centre at Trinity College in the area, and that centre would later carry out a significant study into the experiences of LGBTQ+ youth in Ireland. The seminar also provided a platform for BeLonG To to develop a relationship with the Social, Personal and Health Education (SPHE) Support Service of the Department of Education. SPHE went on to co-design the first Department of Education lead teacher training programme on LGBTQ+ issues. This programme was delivered to many hundreds of teachers in the coming years. At this time, BeLonG To began to support a number of key research projects. These included a study with the School of Education in Trinity College, who explored the experiences of homophobic bullying among LGBTQ+ young people themselves (Minton et al, 2008).

The case to act on drug use and policy

The fight for LGBTQ+ inclusion in public policy has always been about addressing the interconnected challenges faced by our community. Drug policy and mental health are two areas where this connection is particularly clear.

The inclusion of LGBTQ+ people in the Dublin North Inner City Drugs Task Force Strategy, and later in the National Drugs Strategy, was driven by ground-breaking research. As one drug policy reform advocate explained:

> I heard the North Inner City Drugs Task Force was supporting BeLonG To, funding them to work with LGBTQ+ young people and carry out research. This put pressure on the National Drugs Strategy because it was the only task force specifically funding an LGBTQ+ organisation to do drugs-related work – and the research showed why. That moved us all to understand the issues.

In 2007, with support from the Department of Community, Rural and Gaeltacht Affairs, BeLonG To published the report 'Drug use amongst lesbian, gay, bisexual and transgender young adults in Ireland'. The research revealed that 65 per cent of LGBTQ+ young adults in Ireland have used drugs, with 60 per cent reporting use in the past year. Factors such as isolation, bullying and lack of support contribute to higher rates of depression, anxiety and substance use compared to their non-LGBTQ+ peers. Notably, 42 per cent reported using drugs weekly or monthly. The findings call for targeted, culturally competent interventions, peer-led outreach and inclusive policies to address these disparities and support LGBTQ+ youth effectively (Sarma, 2007).

As a youth worker in 2003, I saw this first hand. Young people would share stories about their drug use, often as part of a broader crisis – leaving school early, being arrested or struggling with mental health issues. This research wasn't about discovering something new; it was about showing others the urgent realities we were already too painfully aware of. By 2018, BeLonG To became one of the few organisations advocating for the full decriminalisation of drug users, continuing its commitment to addressing the root causes of harm in the LGBTQ+ community, including stigma, shame and criminalisation.

Mental health: evidence to build support

The connections between drug use, bullying and mental health became even clearer with the 2009 'Supporting LGBT lives' study, a landmark piece of research on mental health and well-being funded by the HSE's National Office for Suicide Prevention. Co-commissioned by BeLonG To and GLEN, it highlighted the devastating mental health impacts of homophobia and transphobia: 'Those who experienced homophobic bullying and/or lack of acceptance by significant others as a consequence of their LGBT identification were particularly susceptible to depression, self-harm, and/or suicidality' (Mayock et al, 2009, p 37).

This research became a cornerstone of advocacy for LGBTQ+ youth, influencing policy change and even shaping the core messages of the 2015 marriage equality campaign. Journalist Anna Carey's book *BeLonG To Yes: Voices from the Marriage Equality Campaign* reflects how messaging about the mental health impacts of homophobia and transphobia played a pivotal role in building public support (Carey, 2015).

Both drug policy and mental health advocacy revealed the same urgent need: to address systemic issues that harm LGBTQ+ young people. Whether it's addiction or suicidality, these struggles don't exist in isolation – they're deeply tied to experiences of exclusion, rejection and erasure. By grounding our work in evidence and amplifying the voices of those most affected, we were pushing for an expansive policy response for queer youth – one that demanded a multitude of policy changes.

This work demonstrates how constructive and effective community organisation and civil society advocacy has been for LGBTQ+ rights in Ireland. When we reflect on this period of change, the freedom of civil society to engage with the government and to hold the government to account was so valuable. This draws into question increasing measures to limit the capacity and influence of an independent civil society and how retrograde such movement has been.

Five takeaways

1. Building legitimacy to drive meaningful change

This chapter highlights the necessity of legitimacy in building an advocacy platform that shifts social and policy norms. BeLonG To established its credibility by amplifying the lived experiences of LGBTQ+ youth while grounding their advocacy in robust legal frameworks like the Equal Status Act. By operating at the intersection of evidence and authenticity, the organisation challenged entrenched biases in policy making and reframed LGBTQ+ youth issues as a concern for the government. As activists, legitimacy is a strategic tool for our advocacy. It is earned through consistent representation of the real lives of our communities and alignment with legal and policy frameworks – this combination can create influence and power.

2. Harnessing policy windows through strategic framing

LGBTQ+ youth civil society aligned its goals with policy priorities already on the national agenda, such as suicide prevention and anti-bullying strategies. This strategic framing allowed LGBTQ+ youth issues to gain traction within established policy initiatives, bypassing resistance from gatekeepers. Activists can seek policy windows that allow them to frame their objectives within broader public concerns, creating opportunities for action that might otherwise remain inaccessible.

3. Rigorous evidence as an advocacy cornerstone

This chapter underscored the power of data and research in advocacy, leveraging rigorous studies to substantiate its claims. Evidence such as mental health statistics, case studies and surveys on bullying ensured that advocacy efforts could withstand scrutiny and counteract opposition arguments. This evidence-driven approach validated the work and built trust with policy makers, creating the case for systemic change. As activists, prioritising robust evidence to back up our advocacy can feel frustrating, sometimes making a case that is already obvious, but recognising that data can be a persuasive force in breaking down institutional resistance can be key to protecting and promoting the rights of our communities.

4. Overcoming resistance through strategic persistence

Resistance, both overt and covert, was a recurring challenge in BeLonG To's advocacy journey. However, the organisation's strategic persistence – paired with data and alliances – allowed it to keep LGBTQ+ youth issues on the agenda. For example, the eventual inclusion of LGBTQ+ issues in national suicide prevention strategies reflected years of sustained pressure, showing how persistence can dismantle entrenched prejudices over time. As activists from minority communities, resistance is an inevitable part of advocacy, and we can approach it with the long view that systemic change often requires relentless engagement over long periods.

5. Civil society as an engine of advocacy innovation

The chapter demonstrated how civil society can drive change by positioning itself as both a disruptor of outdated systems and a builder of new ones that free societies from prejudices and voice the rights of minority communities. BeLonG To's leadership in coalition building, outreach and evidence-driven policy work illustrates how civil society organisations fill gaps in governance and elevate marginalised voices. Their success in forming cross-sector alliances, from local minority groups to national advocacy bodies, shows how civil society, when supported and informed, leads social change. Civil society's capacity to innovate and collaborate is critical for addressing systemic inequalities. As activists, we should see ourselves not as peripheral actors but as central architects of change.

Figure 3.1: 'Oh be nice!!', Jamie O'Brien

Source: BeLonG To – LGBTQ+ Youth Ireland

4

Community youth work: the BeLonG To model

This chapter opens with the voice of Danielle, a trans and neurodiverse activist who began her advocacy through LGBTQ+ youth civil society at a very complex time in her life. Her reflections offer a deep insight into what was happening for young people at this time and provide a springboard for a discussion about the role of community youth work in setting policy agendas. I talk about how critical consciousness raising and providing direct advocacy opportunities had a huge impact on many young people (such as Danielle) who could see that their oppression could be turned into action for justice and whose day-to-day realities shaped complex long-term advocacy strategies. These strategies were often driven by organisations with the capacity to 'play the long game' and place each win and setback within a broader vision that was developed through providing space to listen and strategically plan. In this way, these processes allowed for LGBTQ+ youth issues to be integrated into multiple mainstream policies (at a time when the same was not always happening for LGBTQ+ adult issues). I argue that because youth and community work is the often invisible and misunderstood quiet process that happens behind the scenes, formal education, history and policy academics have misinterpreted much of the policy gains which happened during this period. I argue that the emergence of an academic 'counter narrative' that frames LGBTQ+ community youth work interventions on homophobic and transphobic violence as somehow damaging to LGBTQ+ young people themselves fails to understand, and indeed aims to further erase, the impact of LGBTQ+ young people themselves in designing advocacy for social justice. This chapter forms the basis for 'community youth work' being a core element for the 'Civil society model for social justice policy change' presented in Chapter 7.

Memory: Danielle's speech

The following memory is from Danielle, a trans woman whom I was fortunate to meet in 2006 when she was a teenager and I was her youth worker. Danielle changed my life and my advocacy in fundamental ways. At the time of writing this book in 2025, Danielle is an organiser with Neuro Pride Ireland. She made the following speech at the tenth birthday of IndividualiTy, a group for trans young people at BeLonG To. This speech is included without edits with Dani's permission.

> Hi everyone!
>
> Some of what I'm going to say is very difficult, but I want to tell you about the history of this wonderful group, and the only way I can truly do that is with honesty. If anyone needs to talk, BeLonG To Staff are here, and so am I.
>
> My name is Danielle Lavigne, I'm an administrator with Bi+ Ireland Network, and ten years ago, I helped co-found IndividualiTy.
>
> To see how this group has evolved in the ten years since, it fills me with a kind of joy and relief that I can't begin to explain. But I'll try.
>
> When I first came to BeLonG To, I was technically still too young to be there, but they still helped me. Michael Barron would meet with me and I would hang out in the café in Outhouse. Sometimes I would go to the groups: there was the larger group for everybody, and there was BeLonG Teen. It was scary and it was difficult, because I'm a very shy [autistic] person, but it was as close as I could get to people who were like me. But there weren't any openly trans kids there.
>
> Over the course of my teen years, I became severely mentally ill, as mental health professionals refused to treat my body dysphoria, but I fought so hard. My psychiatrist refused to give me hormone blockers because I wasn't 18, the age the College of Psychiatrists of Ireland recommended against international best practice.
>
> Eventually, after a suicide attempt, I ended up in psychiatric hospital for a number of months. I was referred to it to assess my gender dysphoria, and they treated me like my life wasn't as important as those of the other kids on the ward. They psychologically abused me, and tried to repress my gender as much as they could, because they said, parents would be upset if I 'turned any of the kids gay'. I eventually turned most of them, of course, but I don't like to brag.
>
> While I was there, Michael Barron would visit me and attempt to help. During my stay, he asked me if I would be interested in setting up a trans group within BeLonG To, and I was. On leaving the institution, I had meetings with David Carroll about setting up a group that I hilariously called The T Titans, which was definitely funny the 52nd time I said it.
>
> We met with young folks involved with TENI [Transgender Equality Network Ireland], and we set down language which we tried to make as inclusive as possible. We probably didn't succeed at being perfectly inclusive, but that's why we never stop, isn't it? Eventually, it was time to begin the group in earnest.
>
> I remember having so much fun some fortnights. We would dance in the arcade, we would watch videos, we would talk about our dysphoria,

we would talk about our parents and families, we would share in a way we never got to do before. And we came up with a name. The T Titans sadly didn't get picked, nor did the Transformers, but IndividualiTy, with a very important Capital T, was born.

We were a family. A family that made adorable information leaflets, but a family nonetheless. Some remain family to this day.

I had left school due significantly to transphobic bullying before I was hospitalised, and I began homeschooling. BeLonG To helped try to find me a new school, along with the Department of Education, but most schools refused to take me as a girl, at least not without the approval of the school's parents. The fight for schooling scared me off trying to go to school, but it led BeLonG To to fight harder for everyone else. The Ombudsman for Children at the time, Emily Logan, took my case to the Minister for Education and told her to write to every school and tell them that they must accept trans students. [The minister may never have done this, but she was at least told to.]

Meanwhile, my psychiatry team set up the first conference on trans youth treatment, with my situation, and one other, as case studies to be presented. I was not allowed to attend, but again, Michael Barron was my advocate, and was able to attend. The upshot was that if I was really good, and attended my homeschooling, they would let me have hormone blockers. Dangling treatment in front of a vulnerable trans teen in order to control me, in retrospect, was not an ethical practice, but it was a small victory.

Eventually they allowed me access to an endocrinologist who also refused to treat me, until I fought hard enough that she gave in after threats of legal action. It wasn't until I was transferred to adult endocrinology that I could start hormones at the age of 16.

I tell you all of this, because it's a part of your history. At the time, it didn't feel like we were making history, but when barriers were put up at every turn, all we could make was history. And BeLonG To was one of the few organisations run by adults who were kind when most adults were nothing but cruel.

Those adults who were cruel to me and to other members of IndividualiTy, were afraid of facing themselves, and their own discomfort with the gender binary. If these young people wouldn't be constrained, then perhaps they had wasted their lives trying to fit into rigid boxes themselves.

I find myself now an adult, and I see kids who are feeling everything I have felt. Who have stayed up at night feeling like there's something wrong with them. Who have anguished over how to tell their parents. Who never saw anyone like them on TV or in movies. [LGBTQIA+ representation has slowly blossomed in children's media, but the threat that it may again be restricted is ever present, as has happened in many countries.]

I see all of this and then I see IndividualiTy, where young people get to go and see themselves reflected in society. Where you don't have to be afraid. Where you don't have to be on guard every second. Where you don't have to worry about that look that says, 'What are you?'

And I didn't make that space. You did. You did it by being bold enough to say, 'This is who I am, and I'm going to be that person in the world.'

When IndividualiTy started, it was usually less than a handful of people each fortnight. Now it's over 70 trans and non-binary folks. That's 70 people who have each other's backs, which isn't even to mention the other BeLonG To members. I couldn't imagine an army of that size when I was old enough to attend BeLonG To.

Everyone who is brave enough to stand out and live is an absolute hero, and I don't exaggerate. Every last trans and non-binary person living even a little bit as themselves, is making space for another kid to live with less fear. For another adult to live with less fear. For me to be able to look at my body and not say, 'I was born wrong', but to instead say, 'No one's body is ever wrong. This is my body, and I shaped it. It's not like anyone else's, and it's beautiful.'

That doesn't happen overnight. That takes time. And work. We have had to change not just the minds of everyone around us but our own minds, warped by years of mistreatment.

And we're doing it. You're doing it.

You're pushing for recognition of young people who have every gender and none. You're pushing to have services treat trans, non-binary and intersex people with dignity and respect. You're fighting against transphobia, and biphobia, and homophobia, and misogyny, White supremacy and disablism. You're pushing to Repeal The Eighth and make available free, safe and legal pregnancy care because we all deserve bodily autonomy. You are fighting Direct Provision because no LGBTQIA, straight or cis child should be forced to spend their lives in institutions designed to punish those seeking refuge. [The eighth amendment was repealed in 2018, but the fight for reproductive rights and ending direct provision continues.]

You are so much more than heroic. You're real, and you're alive, and you are saving lives every day just by being counted. You are leaders.

But you're also dealing with stuff that hurts. And I know it hurts. And you deserve love, and understanding, and kindness, and a better world. And we will make it better. Together.

Thank you.

(Danielle, 2017, at the Ombudsman for
Children's Office in Dublin, Ireland)

Danielle and I remain close friends and champions of each other's activism. I was present in the Ombudsman for Children's Office in Dublin when she made this speech and asked her for a copy of it then, and to include it in this book now for a number of reasons. First, Danielle's story is of historical significance. She was the youngest person in Ireland to transition, and she demonstrated Herculean strength in taking on health and education systems which were deeply opposed to her achieving what she did. Second, I asked her if I could include it as a commentary on the power and effectiveness of critical youth and community work as a force for change. For Dani, the support and doggedness that BeLonG To provided was central to her battle for recognition, respect and rights. BeLonG To placed her voice and rights central to engagement with institutions who were demonstrating a callous disregard for her. It was a humane and human rights position for the organisation to maintain over years of engagement with these institutions, and one that would ultimately prove successful in supporting Dani to receive the care and recognition she needed.

Further, the organisation's work to support Dani, and other trans and non-binary young people to organise collectively as a trans project – IndividualiTy – demonstrates the simple yet radical approach to embodying the principle of 'those closest to the struggle are closest to the solution'. IndividualiTy have made a very significant contribution to Irish society, including through joining with TENI to advocate for the progress of the Gender Recognition Act 2015 and for its review in 2018 (Gender Recognition Act 2015). Further, for Danielle, after she moved on from BeLonG To and IndividualiTy, she applied what she learned about social justice and advocacy to her continued work for equality for trans and neurodiverse people.

Community youth work

A political approach to community youth work was the approach taken by BeLonG To, which sought to raise critical consciousness and provide advocacy opportunities, enabling young people to channel their oppressive experiences into collective action for justice.

Back in 1984, in what was a dark time for Ireland in many ways, the National Youth Policy Committee made the extraordinary statement that

> [i]f youth work is to have any impact on the problems facing young people today then it must concern itself with social change. This implies that youth work must have a key role both in enabling young people to analyse society and in motivating and helping them to develop the skills and capacities to become involved in effecting change. (National Youth Policy Committee, 1984, p 116)

This longstanding vision for community youth work's potential role in social change resonates with the approach taken by LGBTQ+ civil society in Ireland. The influence of community youth work practice on the development of LGBTQ+ youth-inclusive policies is clear. Its significance arose from the use of a particular radical social analysis approach.

BeLonG To was developed by people who came from a variety of youth, community and social justice work positions. We explicitly incorporated a motivation to drive 'social change' into the organisation's documentation, training and other materials (BeLonG To, 2008).

In keeping with this impetus, from its establishment we adopted a 'critical social education' model of community youth work. The intention of this model is to support young people to take actions to improve their and other young people's lives.

As Hurley and Treacy put it:

> The foundation of the [critical social education] model of youth work is that if young people can be made critically aware of their social and political situation they will be motivated and mobilised to seek change within the structures of institutions that impact negatively on their life situations. This emphasis on youth work contributing to social change enters youth work and young people into the political arena. (Hurley and Treacy, 1993 p 41)

Interviewees suggested that youth empowerment and social analysis contributed considerably to advocacy for policy change. Since its establishment, BeLonG To has delivered youth empowerment training programmes and supports to young people to exercise agency and voice, in keeping with its vision of '[a]n Ireland where Lesbian Gay Bisexual and Transgender (LGBT) young people are empowered to embrace their development and growth confidently, and to participate as agents of positive social change' (BeLonG To annual report, 2012, p. 6).

The significance of youth work as a professional practice also emerged from those I spoke with. This is of particular significance when considered beside the 'moral panic about youth' which opponents of LGBTI+ rights engaged in, as highlighted earlier.

Anna Quigley reflected that

> [y]outh work was absolutely crucial because it enabled BeLonG To to do its work, but also I remember at a parents' evening one of the parents kept asking [a youth worker] about her qualifications and she was able to talk about the professional standards that applied to work with young people in a youth work setting.

This approach has a broader historical and practical basis in Irish approaches to community work. Since the 1990's, Irish community work has grown into a distinct discipline, rooted in principles of equality, human rights and collective action. The 'Towards standards for quality community work',(Community Workers' Co-operative, 2008), emphasised tackling structural inequalities – such as those tied to race, gender and class, through collaborative and analytical approaches. Unlike individual-focused services, community work prioritises collective decision making and action, aiming for outcomes that benefit entire communities. It begins by 'starting where people are at' (Alinsky, 1971) but moves towards addressing the deeper systemic issues driving marginalisation (Crickley and McArdle, 2010).

At its core, community work relies on genuine participation, where marginalised voices are empowered to lead and advocate for meaningful change. It is guided by an ethical practice that balances immediate community needs with long-term goals for justice. Practitioners are called to use their influence thoughtfully, building alliances and networks that amplify collective power (Towards Standards Ad Hoc Group, 2008)

In her article 'Rocking the boat while staying in it: connecting ends and means in radical community work', Dr Oonagh McArdle, who carried out research with Irish community workers, offers some salient insights which are transferable to how Irish LGBTQ+ youth and community workers carried out their work. Her discussion of radical community work – grounded in seeking systemic changes through non-violent and participatory methods – is reflected in how LGBTQ+ young people themselves designing participatory responses to homophobic/transphobic violence in school. Further, her discussion of 'radical pragmatism' among community workers who navigate systemic constraints (such as the complexity of the national education system) while staying true to transformative goals (such as achieving an education system which is fully inclusive of young people's sexuality and gender identity) rings true (McArdle, 2020).

In the case of LGBTQ+ youth civil society, radical pragmatism was driven by the urgency created in workers by spending time with queer youth. What is clear from my own and other youth workers' experience is that the exclusion, oppression and violence experienced by young people demanded urgent responses. Youth work practice provided vital direct supports to many young people, and this direct work with young people instilled a passion and a sense of responsibility in youth workers and policy advocates to seek urgent change. This was particularly the case in relation to homophobic and transphobic bullying and mental health support. We had an urgent moral imperative to act.

This imperative was also to get support to queer youth living outside of major urban centres. From 2007 onwards, a considerable focus was put on developing LGBTQ+ youth groups outside of Dublin. It became my primary focus for a number of years – to build a network of support so that young people would not have to travel from across the country to meet other young people in safe youth projects. In 2007, there were LGBTQ+ youth projects in three spaces; today, there are over 40 across the country. It is an exceptional infrastructure in a small country, and one built on the belief that no one should have to leave their area to be part of an LGBTQ+ community.

In addition to building an infrastructure, this was also infused with the principles of radical community work and radical pragmatism. For example, when we initiated the establishment of an LGBTQ+ youth service in Donegal, we engaged with an array of local organisations and government bodies. The regional HSE (a government organisation), regional youth service, police, schools, intercultural project and sports clubs, along with a number of out LGBTQ+ young people, were invited together to discuss what supports could be put in place in the region. Over time, this group became a steering committee, and BreakOut, a queer youth service within the mainstream youth service, was formed. The pragmatism here was to become part of the existing array of stakeholders – ensuring that, even if we moved slowly, what would be established had widespread community and institutional support. Across the country, while the youth groups grew in numbers and locations, the steering groups composed of community pillars expanded their interests into other areas – particularly into making schools better places for queer youth. Over a number of years, the projects born from those early gatherings, while linked to the national body, became independent, locally funded and sustained and driven by local needs.

This radical and pragmatic approach was core to the development of the LGBTQ+ youth policy agenda in significant ways. First, the agenda of BeLonG To was set by the issues which emerged through youth committees within the organisation's structures – including the issues raised by the network of local youth groups. Second, the organisation ensured that politicians and policy makers had opportunities to hear directly from LGBTQ+ young people. These 'organised visibility' opportunities occurred at events, ministerial meetings and meetings with government departments. The effect was to bring decision makers into proximity with LGBTQ+ young people so that they could understand and feel how inequality was being experienced by young people. In addition, the development of a considerable network of LGBTQ+ youth work projects throughout the country, operating through a critical social education model, helped develop a network of young activists. The influence of this became apparent in the Marriage Equality Referendum where LGBTQ+ youth projects in many areas played central roles in canvassing and persuading.

Policy integration for LGBTQ+ youth

These advocacy strategies succeeded in embedding LGBTQ+ youth issues into multiple mainstream policies, often achieving more progress than similar efforts for LGBTQ+ adults during the same period.

The recording of public policy change through the landmark events – such as decriminalisation and marriage equality – can make invisible the changes and movement building beyond and behind these events. Work for the inclusion of LGBTQ+ young people across all these aspects required the transformation of mainstream policy. This in turn necessitated extensive solidarity work, a position that equality is for all, an anti-oppression analysis and an appreciation that young people live at intersections. The reality of the intersectional nature of being LGBTQ+ and young in Ireland at this time necessitated a great deal of coalition building, openness, mobility and complex combinations of issue framing and varying emphasis at different times.

As such, much of the inclusion of LGBTQ+ young people in Irish public policy over this period was within mainstream youth policy, rather than with LGBTQ+ specific policy. As such, it can be overlooked in assessments of LGBTQ+ public policy progress (Dukelow and Considine, 2017, p 370). Some of the most significant advances were in the areas of mainstream education, youth, drugs and alcohol and health policies. This approach can be seen in terms of 'equality mainstreaming' (Equality Authority, 2002) in relation to LGBTQ+ young people – where the drive is that the lives of LGBTQ+ young people are considered within all policies that relate to young people. This approach took dogged work in relationship building and in becoming involved in very fundamental ways in large cross-government policy development to ensure that they contained clear objectives and outcomes for LGBTQ+ and other minority children and young people.

While the 'big-ticket items', which are referenced in social policy anthologies – such as decriminalisation, the Equal Status Act and the Marriage Equality Act – were discussed by the people I spoke to for this book, so were the less visible inclusions – such as the National Strategy for Action on Suicide Prevention (2005), the National Drugs Strategy (2009), 'Better outcomes, brighter futures' (2014) and the National Youth Strategy (2015).

These inclusions follow the path whereby civil society advocacy influences the government's agenda, which then leads to the bringing together of a policy community to develop public policy. The work of civil society to advocate for the Department for Education Action Plan on Bullying and mandatory anti-bullying procedures for schools can be seen to follow this path as illustrated in the process of policy development of the Action Plan on Bullying (Figure 4.1).

In this process, civil society advocated to the political system, which in turn activated the public service to develop policy in collaboration with civil society. This process is commonly used by civil society groups and is familiar to public servants and politicians. It is significant that LGBTQ+ community advocates knew how to 'play the game', used

Figure 4.1: Process of policy development of Action Plan on Bullying

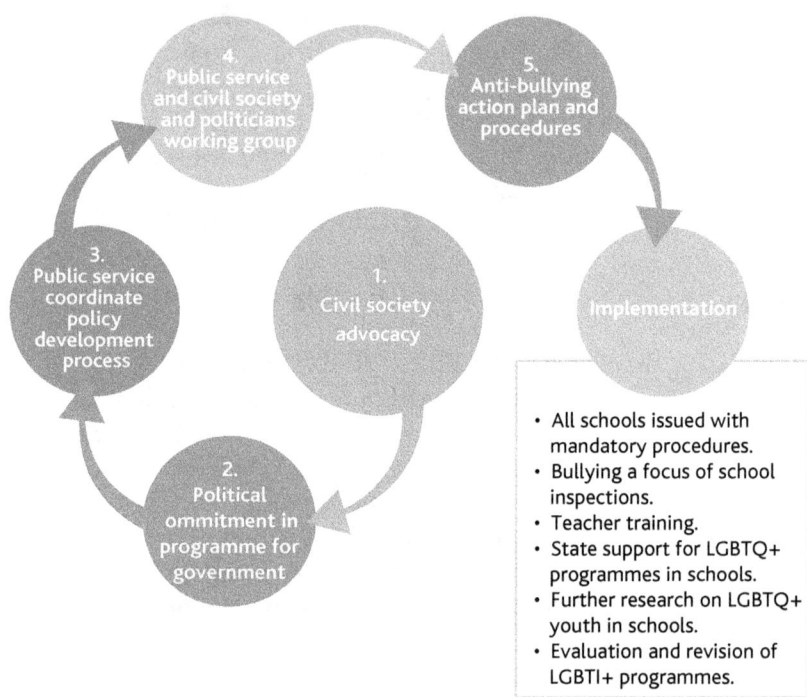

general elections and programmes for government as opportunities and were prepared and equipped to work with the civil service in these processes.

Having advocated for the inclusion of commitments to support LGBTQ+ young people in schools in individual political party manifestos, we achieved a commitment in the programme for government 'to encourage schools to develop anti-bullying policies and, in particular, strategies to combat homophobic bullying, to support students' (Department of Education and Skills, 2013, p 11).

With further advocacy to the new Minister for Education, Ruairi Quinn, and with the deep commitment and drive of his special advisor Neil Ward, a working group was created to develop what became the Action Plan on Bullying. I sat on this small group with LGBTQ+ rights colleagues Dr Carol-Anne O'Brien (BeLonG To), Brian Sheehan (Gay and Lesbian Equality Network [GLEN]) and Sandra Gowran (GLEN). Originally, this group was to focus specifically on homophobic and transphobic bullying (that was the Programme for Government commitment that we had advocated for), but advocacy from other groups late in the day meant that it was expanded to include all forms of bullying. The outcome of this group's work and action plan were anti-bullying procedures, underpinned by legislation, which were the most significant developments in relation to tackling bullying in Irish schools to have been published in 20 years (Foody et al, 2018).

This marked a transition of LGBTQ+ children and young people, and the violence they experienced in the forms of homophobic and transphobic bullying, 'from a position of social and educational invisibility to one of visibility', and an acknowledgement by the Department of Education that homophobic and transphobic bullying were legitimate educational problems which needed to be addressed (Bailey, 2016, pp 35–6).

Strategic, long-term advocacy

Organisations engaged in LGBTQ+ advocacy often employed long-term strategies, integrating wins and setbacks into a broader vision shaped by listening and planning with young people. While knowledge of how to action specific processes of advocacy for policy change is significant, what is more remarkable is civil society's long-term strategic and planned approach. This consciously brought together public awareness campaigns, the building of an LGBTQ+ youth support infrastructure and advocacy for policy change. Of further note are the actions taken by civil society to work with the government to implement the policy change, indicating that the production of policy was not seen as an end in and of itself. In terms of implementation, state investment in LGBTQ+ civil society is an important feature, as is LGBTQ+ civil society's use of such resources to advocate for further policy change, to change attitudes and to provide direct youth work to LGBTI+ young people.

In 2006, the National Office for Suicide Prevention made a significant financial investment in BeLonG To which allowed the organisation to take on a stronger role as 'a national voice for LGBT young people and their issues' (BeLonG To, 2008). The following year, the One Foundation (a philanthropic organisation created by Ryanair founder Declan Ryan) also invested in BeLonG To – for what would become six vital years. The injection of significant financial capacity and time to think and strategise made a huge difference in what was possible.

As David Carroll said to me:

> What happened couldn't have happened without the One Foundation. The amount of time, expertise and money they invested ... to support us to develop long-term strategic plans. The organisation was transformed. Services were doubling annually, and the advocacy work really took off. It was all driven by having spent all that time planning, building communications and political

strategies – long-term advocacy strategy looking at what we wanted for LGBT young people.

BeLonG To produced three ambitious strategic plans over this period for 2005–7, 2007–11 and 2011–13, which contained much of the advocacy for policy change goals which were pursued (Lyons, 2013). The 2007–2011 strategy contained a clear articulation of plans to effect structural and policy change (BeLonG To, 2007). This strategy was visible to those making policy. A civil servant who spoke to me said: 'None of the other special interest groups had the same impact. Maybe they weren't coming to us, just focused on their own piece. BeLonG To, back in 2003, was similar before it developed a clear long-term strategy to engage with us and others.'

The work of LGBTQ+ civil society to improve mental health policy towards LGBTQ+ young people needs to be understood in the context of long-term strategy. This strategy was to reduce isolation, through the development of community infrastructure, increase acceptance, through public awareness and narrative change campaigns, and to improve laws and policies so that the state honoured their rights. Figure 4.2 represents the relationship between direct community youth work, research, strategic planning advocacy for policy change, policy change occurring and it's implementation.

It is vital to acknowledge the decades of work to change the country's views of, and laws towards, LGBTQ+ people in advance of 2003, without which none of this could ever have happened. What has yet to be fully acknowledged in writing about LGBTQ+ rights in Ireland is the pivotal role played by highly focused strategies for change between 2003 and 2015, as illustrated in this diagram. These strategies were carefully crafted and typically included a clear articulation of the organisation's worldview, beliefs and values. They outlined the key issues to be addressed in the coming years, the specific changes being sought, the actions needed to achieve those changes and how progress would be measured. For example, elements of the Action Plan on Bullying from 2013 were already reflected in BeLonG To's 2008 strategy, demonstrating the foresight and intentionality behind these plans and the doggedness in pursuing them of many years (BeLonG To, 2008).

Critique of academic counter narratives

Long-term contributions of youth and community work are often overlooked, misunderstood or erased in formal education and historical accounts, leading to a misinterpretation of how policy gains were achieved. Even further, some academic narratives claim that LGBTQ+ youth and community interventions on homophobic and transphobic violence harmed

Figure 4.2: LGBTQ+ civil society strategic advocacy to improve mental health

LGBTQ+ civil society strategic advocacy to improve mental health

Foundational → Youth work practice → Emergent evidence → Advocacy → Policy change → Resource services / Resource evidence → Ongoing state resource to LGBTI+ community → Strategic planning 2008–12

1980s–90s | 2003–4 | 2005 | 2008–ongoing

Strategic planning 2005–7

Civil society and implementation

- State investment in network of LGBTQ+ youth supports (45 by 2018).
- State support in national LGBTQ+ youth advocacy.
- State support in LGBTQ+ research.
- State support in LGBTQ+ equality campaigns.
- LGBTQ+ civil society work with state to develop further policy including in education, health, youth, drug use.

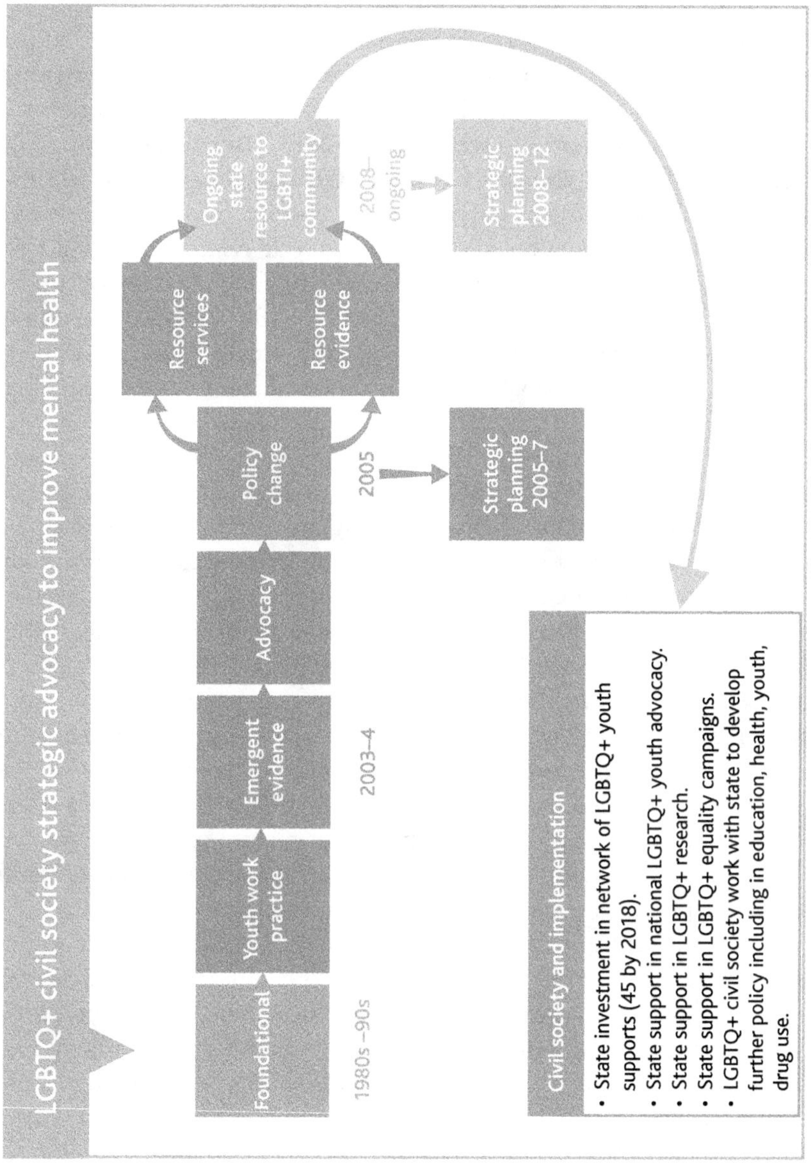

LGBTQ+ young people, including by creating a fatalistic view of growing up LGBTQ+. This perspective fails to recognise the role of LGBTQ+ youth themselves and the LGBTQ+ community in general in designing and driving advocacy for social justice and risks further erasing hard-won self-organised community gains in national policy.

Byran and Mayock (2012) argue that 'the dominant image invoked by many researchers, as well as organisations advocating for LGBTQ+ youth, has been that of an isolated, victimised, and largely powerless young person who is "at risk" of self-harm and suicide' (pp 12–13). Bryan and Mayock (2017) argue that advocacy discourses around LGBTQ+ youth mental health can reinforce what they call a 'suffering suicidal script'. By consistently framing LGBTQ+ young people as vulnerable and at risk, these narratives risk producing a reified script of queer lives as inevitably unhappy or dangerous. This, they suggest, may contribute to negative self-perceptions and limit the possibilities for imagining flourishing queer futures (pp 65–85). While Bryan and Mayock offer a valuable critique of the dominant mental health discourse surrounding LGBTQ+ youth, however, their analysis underestimates the role that LGBTQ+ community organisations play in balancing the imperative to highlight mental health risks, so as to affect policy and practice changes, with efforts to foster resilience, joy, and belonging. While the authors appear to suggest that such organisations' work may contribute to a 'suffering suicidal script' – where repeated messaging around risk creates a reified narrative of LGBTQ+ lives as inevitably unhappy – they offer limited engagement with the lived realities and strategic challenges faced by these organisations. Their analysis risks flattening the complexity of community-based advocacy, which often must navigate between public health messaging and the creation of hopeful, affirming spaces for young LGBTQ+ people.

This book challenges these notions, which I suggest focus on limited literature reviews while ignoring the bigger picture of what the LGBTQ+ community, including LGBTQ+ young people, did to achieve significant social and policy change on many fronts at the same time.

While advocating as a queer person for the rights of the queer community, we have faced attempts to delegitimise both our efforts and our voices, including claims that we caused harm. Such critiques dismiss what the community itself has identified as a priority – addressing the urgent harms it experiences. Tackling these harms is foundational to creating the conditions for healing, safety and liberation. Addressing injustice starts with confronting the harm it causes. To criticise survivors for how they choose to address their lived experiences only serves to perpetuate homophobic and transphobic agendas, rather than advancing equality and justice.

These 'counter narratives' fail to acknowledge the broader equality underpinning of work with LGBTQ+ young people, the reality of the urgencies which present themselves in LGBTQ+ community youth work and schools and the nature of public policy development processes. As Kingdon 1984 outlines, issues become public policy problems when harm is identified and government action is seen to be required, for example in the case of violence in schools. All policy changes have to be framed, and homophobic/transphobic violence and poor mental health were authentic framings which could and did induce important policy responses. But this framing occurred purposefully and within limited policy and professional development environments.

Such counter narratives fail to acknowledge the overwhelmingly colourful, joyous, positive and organised framings of the LGBTQ+ community through LGBTQ+ youth services in local communities, Pride festivals, local community events, families, media and the deliberate growth in social and political representation. It overlooks extensive community youth work during this period – based on equality and anti-oppressive practices and consciousness-raising education. While the next chapter speaks at length about this overwhelmingly optimistic and positive presentation by the queer community itself about what it meant to be young and queer (which, I assert, has been the dominant narrative of this time), challenging the idea that it was a 'dominant' approach to foreground powerlessness and victimisation.

Such policy-focused analysis, when undertaken at a remove from the communities it seeks to describe, can miss the deeper significance of LGBTQ+ civil society's engagement in the education system. This work has not simply been about addressing immediate harms, but about contributing to a broader vision: the building of a radically more inclusive society for LGBTQ+ young people. Crucially, many of the policies and programmes under critique have been shaped directly by LGBTQ+ youth themselves, reflecting their lives and collective agency.

In this light, some critiques risk contributing – albeit unintentionally – to the erasure of the queer community's role in shaping its own future. For many within the community, such framing can feel disorienting, as if the work done to protect and support LGBTQ+ youth is being recast as harmful. The emotional and historical weight of this is not insignificant. It recalls earlier moments when queer communities were blamed for the violence they experienced – for failing to conform, for speaking out, or for the backlash that advocacy sometimes provoked.

At stake here is more than disagreement over policy. What is being overlooked is the long-standing activist tradition that underpins LGBTQ+ engagement in education reform: a movement grounded in a wider mission of addressing structural inequality and, in Crowley's words, 'developing alternative forms of society' (Crowley, 2015, p 5). When this complex and deeply embedded work is viewed solely through narrow policy critique, a dissonance emerges: organisations working closely with LGBTQ+

young people and grounded in community-based practice are portrayed as problematic, with little recognition of the long-term, layered strategies that have guided their work.

Figure 4.3 outlines the interconnections between these strategies and their role in transforming educational settings for LGBTQ+ youth.

When placed in the broader context of LGBTQ+ civil society's determined and sustained work over more than a decade, the tendency to focus only on the 2013 *Action Plan on Bullying* and related procedures can appear reductive. Such framing overlooks both the foundational work that preceded these policies and the significant positive impacts that followed their implementation.

These debates are taking place at a time of increasing hostility and risk for LGBTQ+ communities. Violence against queer individuals, particularly young people, is on the rise (Higgins et al, 2024), and the gains made in educational spaces are being actively challenged. In this context, some of the narratives that have entered academic and policy discourse may inadvertently echo elements of broader global critiques of civil society. In other contexts, such critiques – often termed 'anti-NGOism' – have been used to delegitimise human rights organisations and roll back protections for marginalised groups. While the intentions behind these academic critiques may differ substantially, it remains important to be mindful of the wider political currents in which such narratives circulate.

Now an adult, one early member of BeLonG To who was centrally involved in designing anti-homophobic/transphobic materials for schools in the 2000s reflected:

> Three things stand out to me from that experience: firstly that the elements of this campaign were developed by young people themselves, facilitated by BeLonG To, in an authentic way. It wasn't an outsourced or top-down campaign, and it was all the more effective for that. Secondly: the mere process of engaging young people in such a campaign was in some way liberating in itself, because it showed them that they had agency in shaping their own school environments to become less permissive spaces for homophobic bullying. Thirdly, hundreds of teachers around the country were only too willing to support the message, if given the campaign materials and resources, even if it meant challenging more conservative actors in their schools.
>
> It's hard to understate the change in Irish schools in that time, because in my school of 500 pupils, not a single student was out, and that was typical. In the two to three years that followed, that totally changed – across the entire country. And BeLonG To was a big part of that transformation.

Figure 4.3: LGBTQ+ civil society strategic advocacy in education system

LGBTQ+ civil society strategic advocacy in education system

Foundational work (1980s–2000s)
- 1980s–2000s: LGBT community development
- 1990s: key research reports
- 1998–2000: equality legislation

2003–4
- National youth work (state supported)
- Research and public campaign

2004–7
- Coalition campaign and political support
- Coalition building and teacher training
- Strategic planning 2004–7

2007–11
- Political and institutional advocacy
- Resource: state and philanthropy
- Major public campaign
- Strategic planning 2008–12

2012
- Programme for government
- Working group government and civil society
- Action Plan on bullying and procedures
- Focus on counter narrative

Civil society and implementation
- LGBTQ+ programme – 59% of schools.
- LGBTQ+ state curriculum.
- Teacher training.
- Whole school community manual created and evaluated.
- Research and evaluation of programmes.

Strategic planning 2012–15

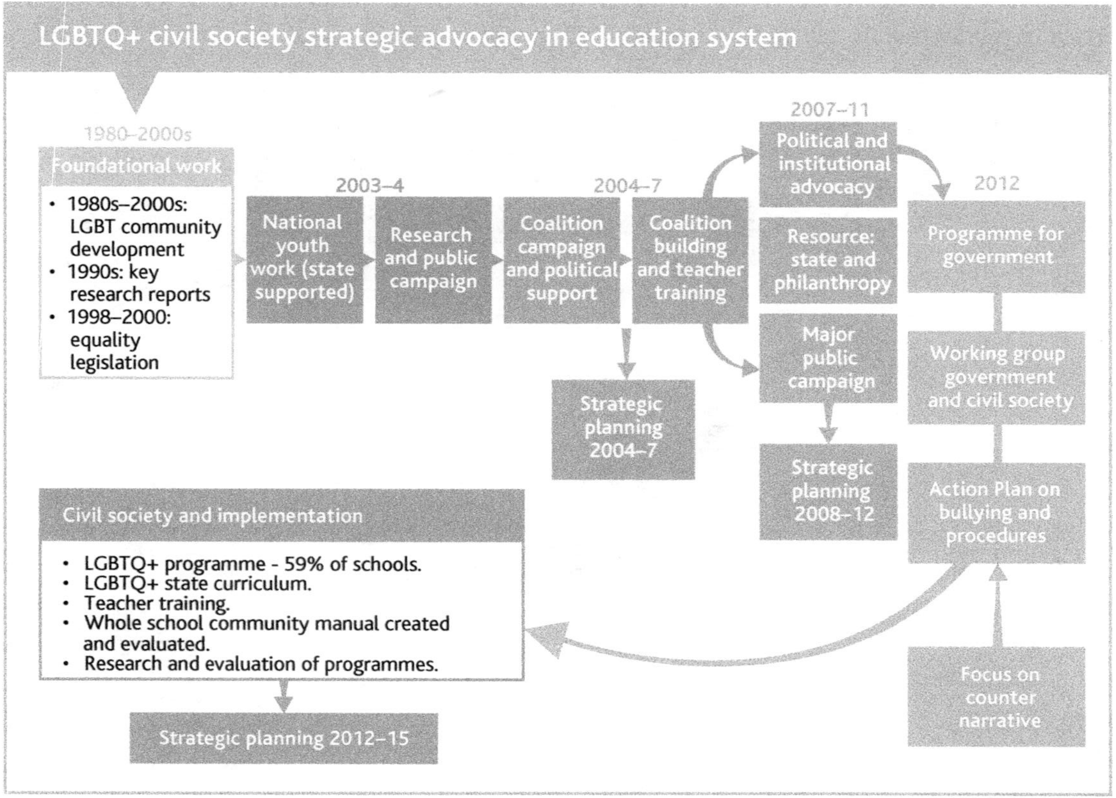

Policy implementation as a key to LGBTQ+ young people's rights

Within anti-bullying and mental health policy, opportunities existed for community empowerment when it came to policy implementation. For example, the National Office for Suicide Prevention resourced BeLonG To to 'provide a national voice' for advocating on behalf of LGBTI+ young people and supported the creation of a network of LGBTI+ youth empowerment projects. It is significant to note that the anti-bullying procedures referenced here refer to *'the promotion of school cultures that are welcoming of diversity;* and the recognition that elimination of homophobic and transphobic bullying will lead to improvements in school climate for all students'. Notably LGBTQ+ civil society used this opportunity to advocate to the Department of Education and Skills to produced *Growing Up LGBT: A Resource for SPHE and RSE*. This resource was developed collaboratively by the Department of Education and Skills, the Health Service Executive, the Gay and Lesbian Equality Network (GLEN), and BeLonG To to support Social, Personal and Health Education (SPHE) and Relationships and Sexuality Education (RSE) in post-primary schools. It provides lesson plans and guidance to facilitate discussions on LGBT identities and issues within the educational curriculum, which was groundbreaking in that it came from government and was a comprehensive official curriculum resource, which was develop in partnership with the LGBTQ+ community itself (Department of Education and Skills et al, 2012).

Further building on this work, The LGBTQ+ Safe and Supportive Schools model outlined in Chapter 2 to this study takes a 'whole school-community' approach to the inclusion of LGBTI+ young people not just in their schools but within their wider community – the antithesis of isolating one negative aspect of young people's identities. These initiatives, while in part responding to the real lifelong impact of homophobic and transphobic violence, presented the solution as being one of empowering young people, civic engagement and challenging heteronormative structures (Barron and O'Hagan, 2016).

A striking feature which emerges from my analysis is the mobility adopted by the LGBTQ+ community in improving the status of LGBTQ+ people, and young people in particular, in Irish public policy. At various moments in time, LGBTQ+ policy responses were being developed towards younger people, older people, drug use, sexual health, mental health, partnership rights (including marriage equality), immigration (including international protection to people seeking asylum), education, child protection, poverty and community development. This study considers these initiatives 'in the round' rather than through isolating aspects of a small number of policy documents.

Reflecting on her time as a participant within LGBT youth civil society during this time, Fiona (cultural activist, former youth project user) shared the following:

> The real magic of BeLonG To, as I remember it in those early days, was how the young people in the group were centred, listened to and taken seriously – both in the regular meetings and on broader campaigns. We were treated as experts of our own experience, given decision-making roles in the organisation and encouraged to dream big about what changes we could make – culturally and policy-wise – to create brighter futures. What made BeLonG To a truly radical group was the solidarity created with other marginalised communities – for example, Travellers and asylum seekers – and their inclusion in campaigns.
>
> At the core of BeLonG To was a deep belief in engaging and empowering young people to make positive changes on issues that affected them. For a confidently opinionated queer teenager, it was a little sanctuary from the Catholic school system which demanded deference to authority (a demand I couldn't fulfil!) and subtly perpetuated myths about the LGBTQ+ community as sinful, lonely, sexually deviant aberrations.
>
> I'm now at the point where my own child is entering secondary school, and I've been so heartened and touched at school open days to see LGBTQ+ posters covering hallways, bathrooms signposted for all genders and LGBTQ+ clubs advertised in prospectuses. I know this is the legacy of the work started by BeLonG To over two decades ago.

Danielle's story at the start of this chapter and Fiona's story here show how BeLonG To became a space for queer young people to find support and create change. For Danielle, it was a lifeline during an incredibly tough time, giving her the chance to build IndividualiTy – a group that created a sense of belonging for trans and non-binary youth. For Fiona, BeLonG To was one of the few places where her voice was valued and her ideas taken seriously, offering a stark contrast to the rigid authority of her Catholic school. Both found a space where they could not only be themselves but also work towards something bigger.

What connects their experiences is how BeLonG To gave them the tools and trust to make a difference. Danielle's advocacy helped tackle systemic barriers, while Fiona's involvement in campaigns built solidarity with other marginalised groups. The effects of their work are still seen today, from more inclusive schools to greater visibility for LGBTQ+ young people.

Their stories tell us that real radical change can start with spaces where young people are supported, heard and empowered within their self-organised community, supported by teams of youth workers which include queer community members who understand at a personal and fundamental level what it is like to grow up queer in their environments.

Five takeaways

1. Centring youth voices as experts in advocacy

The approach described here shows the power of treating young people as experts in their own lives, placing them at the heart of advocacy and policy development. By creating platforms like IndividualiTy (for trans young people) and involving young people directly in designing campaigns and resources, BeLonG To allowed their voices to lead the change. This model reminds us as activists that advocacy is most effective when those closest to the issue are empowered to define the solutions. As Danielle's story demonstrates, supporting young people properly to take ownership of their advocacy helps create leadership and also achieves public policy wins.

2. Radical pragmatism as a path to tangible change

BeLonG To navigated systemic resistance with a balance of radical vision and pragmatic strategy. This meant working within existing systems – like schools, local government bodies and health services – while maintaining transformative goals, such as making education genuinely inclusive of LGBTQ+ children and young people. The success of the BreakOut LGBTQ+ youth project in Donegal, built through collaborative partnerships, highlights the importance of working with stakeholders to create sustainable change. This pragmatic yet ambitious approach offers a valuable lesson for us as advocates for social justice – systemic change requires both patience and a dogged commitment to long-term goals.

3. Intersectionality as a core principle of advocacy

By integrating solidarity with other marginalised communities, such as Travellers and people seeking international protection, into community youth work, the LGBTQ+ community demonstrated the power of intersectional advocacy. Addressing overlapping systems of oppression expanded the reach, relevance and vision of the work and raised young people's expectation about what equality was. For activists, this underscores the importance of building coalitions across movements, recognising that collective action is more impactful in achieving systemic change.

4. Transforming crisis into opportunity for policy change

BeLonG To's ability to frame urgent issues like homophobic and transphobic bullying as opportunities for systemic reform shows the strategic value of responding to crises with proactive advocacy. Securing government commitment to tackle homophobic bullying and producing the Action Plan on Bullying (2013) is a prime example of how civil society can use policy windows to push for meaningful change. As activists, we can note that crises often reveal systemic weaknesses, and addressing these with evidence-based solutions can lead to long-term policy shifts.

5. Challenging counter narratives to protect community-led advocacy

The critique of LGBTQ+ youth work as perpetuating 'suffering suicidal scripts' highlights the ongoing need to speak back to counter narratives that undermine grassroots advocacy. BeLonG To's success in embedding LGBTQ+ youth issues into national policy demonstrates the importance of countering such claims with evidence and lived experience. As minority community activists, we can remain vigilant against efforts to erase minority community-driven efforts from policy discussions and recognise that these critiques often reflect systemic resistance to marginalised voices gaining influence. Upholding the agency and leadership of those most affected is essential to sustaining progress.

Figure 4.4: Michael Barron as Dublin Pride Grand Marshall 2010, and husband Jaime Nanci

Source: Paula Geraghty, photographer

Figure 4.5: Donegal LGBTQ+ Pride parade rainbow flag

Source: Bernie McLaughlin, photographer

Figure 4.6: Michael Barron and Glen Edward McGuinness at Dublin Pride 2009

Source: Author's own

Figure 4.7: The first BeLonG To LGBTQ+ Prom poster

Source: BeLonG To – LGBTQ+ Youth Ireland

Figure 4.8: Gay Prom poster

Source: BeLonG To – LGBTQ+ Youth Ireland

5

A new narrative: queer optimism

This chapter is about the power and use of queer optimism and joy to transform how LGBTQ+ young people were seen in Ireland. It's a story of replacing old, harmful stereotypes with hope, celebration and belonging. At its heart is a simple but radical idea: focusing on what's possible rather than what's wrong. Key events like the TV documentary series *Growing Up Gay* and the national Gay Prom provided much needed positive visibility and empowered LGBTQ+ young people to claim the milestones and spaces they'd been denied and showed others – including parents and older LGBTQ+ people – that a different reality was possible. By embracing joy and community, key aspects of LGBTQ+ youth civil society advocacy could feel uplifting, non-combative and right and just.

But this wasn't solely feel-good work. It was deeply political, influencing public attitudes and shaping policies. Queer optimism became a bridge between the personal and the political, helping Ireland move towards a society where LGBTQ+ young people could see a place for themselves and where politicians and policy makers could picture the society we were working towards – and it was a good one, a future that they could all see themselves in.

Memory: *Growing Up Gay* in rural Ireland

In 2005, I began discussing the making of a documentary series about LGBTQ+ young people with the brilliant filmmaker Aoife Kelleher. The series took years to make, with many late-night discussions with Aoife, Jaime Nanci, Hugh Rodgers and Anna Rodgers. Eventually these discussions came to fruition, and the results aired on RTÉ – Ireland's national television station – in April 2010. *Growing Up Gay* was given a prime time slot and aired over two weeks. It told the story of amazing young people we were working with in BeLonG To and others who were living around the country. It was an extraordinary moment and the first time the lives of real Irish LGBTQ+ young people had been broadcast into people's living rooms so openly and honestly. Each episode was accompanied by a helpline number at the end, with the message – 'if you are affected by any of the issues in this programme please call this number'. The number was simply the BeLonG To office number, and during the weeks after the series aired, we received calls, mostly from parents and young people from all around the country who had seen the series. This ground-breaking nationwide broadcast had opened the door to so many discussions around what it really meant to be LGBTQ+, coming out and many of the big life-changing issues wrapped up in this – often for the first time.

One call I received was from a Donegal man who had been living in London for decades. His question has stayed with me. He told me that he had left Donegal in the 1980s because it was impossible to be gay in Donegal or indeed Ireland at that time. He was one of generations of LGBTQ+ who left the religiously conservative, paralysingly frightening and violent place that Ireland was for LGBTQ+ people in the 1970s and 1980s. He said that after all these years he still missed Ireland, and having seen the TV series he felt some hope and optimism which got him thinking about moving back home. He called to ask if Ireland had really changed this much. We spoke and shared our stories for over an hour.

His story resonated so deeply with me because of my own experience of leaving home and because it got to the very heart and point of what we were trying to do at BeLonG To – to build a society where LGBTQ+ people belonged and where young people wouldn't have to leave home, if they did not want to, because of who they are. To do this, we had to change the narrative about what it meant to grow up LGBTQ+ in Ireland – and this was our strategy for this programme. But how far along were we, and had Ireland moved at all?

The following summer, I was in Donegal with my husband whose father comes from the Inishowen peninsula. We were driving up the main street of Buncrana – a town that we'd come to know well, having spent many long weekends and holidays there. As we drove along taking in the storefronts and trying to spot any changes since our last visit, out of the corner of my eye I caught a glimpse of some young people writing the word 'Gay' on the pavement. My immediate response was to think this was an instance of homophobia, so we had to stop the car and check what was going on and maybe even intervene. We went across the road and, to our delight, found the young man writing the words 'Being Gay is Okay' with chalk on the pavement. Looking back along the street, we saw that there was a whole gang of young people up and down the town's main street writing queer affirmation notes on the pavements and walls. It was the local LGBTQ+ youth group that we had helped set up, along with many of their peers and allies from other youth services and even the local police, who were all out together writing LGBTQ+ positive messages.

That man's call and his questions in 2010 have stayed with me, and I think of him often, about his wondering whether Ireland had really changed that much. If it really was safe to move home. I wonder what his life would have been like had he seen young people and the police out on the streets of the little town he grew up in, on a hot summer's day, writing LGBTQ+ positive messages on the footpath.

Moments like this reminded me why we worked to change the narrative about LGBTQ+ young people in Ireland. Stories like his – of isolation and yearning – made it clear that belonging is essential for survival and dignity.

Further, I tell you this story because, with the establishment of BeLonG To, much consideration was given to how to present LGBTQ+ youth identity to varying audiences. Our primary concern was for what LGBTQ+ young people themselves heard and felt about themselves, but we also needed to work with families, schools, politicians and policy makers.

We set out to present explicitly positive images of LGBTQ+ identity, to begin the work of counteracting narratives of hopelessness and tragedy. BeLonG To's early manifesto stated the desire to be 'an organisation that would present a positive image of what it meant to be LGBT and young – images that would inspire young people sitting in bedrooms and on buses across the country'. This drive to convey an optimistic message was picked up on by Anna Quigley:

> I remember that there was a desire within BeLonG To, to convey positivity, that positive representation, or affirmation and telling positive stories was always important. Right from the very beginning. And definitely, when you think about those early groups in BeLonG To, the need for positivity to counter all of the challenges and the stigma that these young people were facing. The idea that it can't all be doom and gloom that actually this is something that should be celebrated.

Being able to imagine growing up and becoming a queer adult in Ireland was revolutionary – it was an entirely new mindset that needed to be nurtured and scaffolded. We were coming from a place where queer identities were stigmatised, criminalised and violently repressed. The traditional markers of life transitions – heterosexual relationships, marriage, kids, religious rites of passage, safety to become old and wise to your grandchildren – were actively denied queer youth. A huge reimagining of what it meant to be queer and what the future meant needed to happen. It was a global drive, and one which I term for our context as 'queer optimism'.

The term 'queer optimism' is the title of a 2008 book by Michael Snediker in which the author proposes an alternative to a focus in queer theory 'which has privileged melancholy, shame, and the death drive', and which alternatively takes positivity seriously and worthy of consideration (Snediker, 2008, p 3). I deeply believe that taking optimism seriously is vital to working for social justice. If we cannot see a future where justice prevails, if we accept that the barriers put in the way of liberation are insurmountable, if we are unable to extract opportunities from difficult conditions that can seem overwhelming, then we cannot become 'agents of positive social change'. Optimism in the face of oppression is deeply political: it rejects the status quo and enables us to speak up and organise. If we were inviting young people to be political, then we needed to imagine a new future with them.

This imagining had to happen quickly and became deeply connected to creating celebratory queer spaces with queer youth. BeLonG To youth groups themselves were those spaces, and much effort was put into having fun and introducing young people to queer culture and providing space where they could share their cultures – such as anime, gaming and music, which contained so much possibility for a world where being LGBTQ+ could be celebrated. In 2005, a group of queer youth we worked with delivered a performance of animated superhero television show *Teen Titans* on the mainstage of the Dublin Pride Festival, and the following year BeLonG Teeny Bop began, which was a regular alcohol-free teenage queer dance night in various venues around Dublin. Throughout this period, some of Ireland's most beloved drag queens and kings hosted workshops and talks for young people, sharing their artistry and stories. We also organised excursions that opened the door to the vibrant worlds of queer theatre and cinema, giving young people the chance to see themselves reflected in these creative spaces.

All of this was purposeful – to empower young people to imagine and to have the milestones their heterosexual cisgender peers were having – but on their own terms, in their own way.

In this context, the 'Gay Prom', a celebratory ball which took place for three consecutive years in 2008–11 (Irish Times, 2008, 11 October) as of particular importance. The prom, initiated by Enda McGrattan (aka Veda Beaux Reves), while a celebration, was also created because LGBTQ+ young people were most often not allowed by their schools to bring their same-sex partners to their Debs balls. For many, being out in school was not an option, and for many queer kids experiencing daily homophobic harassment, the opportunity to attend their own school Debs ball was removed. There was a strong, focused intent in this work. The work was driven by what is often described as queer joy, 'a powerful emotion that sustains the fight for recognition and equality for LGBTQ+ people, especially in the face of challenges like gender-based violence and discrimination. But it's also bittersweet, because it acknowledges the struggles faced by the community while celebrating advancements towards a more just and equal world' (Langley, 2024). It was a joy I knew first hand from my experience in New York as a young person when I gravitated to a gang of young queers, all with our own traumas, who partied our summer away together.

In her article in the *Irish Times* in 2010, 'What's the difference between the debs and gay prom?', journalist Roisin Ingles answered the question:

Debs: Insecurity, fake tan, big hair.
Gay Prom: Confidence, pride, big smile.

Answering the same question, one young person simply said, 'It's kind of like a Debs, just way bigger and way better.'

For some queer people I spoke to, the shift towards presenting a positive image of what it meant to be young and LGBTQ+ was of great significance due to their own experience of growing up in a previous generation in Ireland: 'When I was growing up, I was an isolated gay boy. I had no sense of community or that I was part of an oppressed group. I thought I was wrong, damaged and that I deserved everything I got'.

The hope allowed for movement building and the generation of policy solutions. This optimism was born out of a place of deep oppression which necessitated both immediate solution finding and creating and holding a long-term vision. This optimism was demonstrated through public campaign messaging. To present this optimistic vision, advocates engaged in a conscious process of 'narrative change', which rejected oppressive stereotypes and, in an equality activist tradition, presented 'alternative forms of society'. An interviewee described this vision as a presentation of a 'new normal'.

As Caoimhe Gaffney, who was an active member of BeLonG To as a young teenager (2004–8) recalled:

> It is hard to overstate how important BeLonG To was for me personally and in finding a voice in civic society. Among the laughter and creative chaos of art and theatre workshops, I gained confidence to step into the world. In 2004, I performed with other members at Dublin Pride – a small, chaotic performance that felt monumental to us. The following year, our group decorated a Pride float, parading down Dublin's main streets, where we often faced harassment. Dressed in feathers and bedazzled masks, I stood in a giant swan, waving to the crowd, feeling happiness and liberation, free of fear or resentment.
>
> I joined BeLonG To at 15, after years of bullying in school and home life. Sundays at BeLonG To were my only happy memories during that time. It was a place where I was accepted, listened to and encouraged to imagine a life I had been told was impossible.
>
> Twenty years later, I remain close to friends I made there. Together, we believed we could change things, and with the youth workers' support, we began advocating for anti-bullying campaigns and speaking to the media and politicians. Discussions were heated but focused; we wanted systemic change, not just for ourselves but to prevent anyone from suffering as we

had. BeLonG To took me from a place of exclusion and victimisation to one where my voice mattered, and I was unafraid to use it.

Cultural activism at BeLonG To

The campaigns during this period were strongly driven by LGBTQ+ young people themselves and partnerships with youth workers and policy advocates, who in turn invited exceptional filmmakers, designers, communications professionals to become involved. There were many campaigns over this time, Figure 5.1 is a non-exhaustive overview of them.

Figure 5.1: Timeline of LGBTQ+ youth campaigns

LGBTQ+ youth advocacy campaigns in Ireland: a timeline (2004–15)

2004 — That's So Gay!
- First queer youth-created campaign into schools and youth centers.
- Delivered affirming messaging for LGBTQ+ youth.
- Defined by significant Catholic Church opposition.

2006 — Making Schools Safe for LGBT Young People
- First campaign supported by a state body (the Equality Authority).
- Larger budget, wider reach.
- Launched by Síle de Valera, granddaughter of Irish founding father Éamon de Valera.

2009–10 — Stand Up! Don't Stand for Homophobic Bullying
- Annual anti-bullying campaign introduced.
- First use of online videos and celebrity endorsements, including Colin Farrell.

2010 — Growing Up Gay!
- Most-watched Irish TV documentary on LGBTQ+ life, directed by Aoife Kelleher.
- Won multiple awards and increased demand for BeLonG To youth services.

2010–12 — Stand Up! Support Your LGBT Friends
- Expanded into Ireland's most-watched civil society PSA (2+ million views).
- Strengthened solidarity and inclusivity in schools and communities.

2012–ongoing — Stand Up LGBTQ Awareness Week
- Department of Education-endorsed campaign.
- Promoted raising rainbow flags and fostering inclusivity.

2015 — BeLonG To Yes: Campaign for Marriage Equality
- Public-facing campaign with election-style posters and voter registration drives.
- Released influential videos highlighting family voting and youth-led engagement.

The LGBTQ+ community's embrace of cultural activism in Ireland was a remarkable fusion of creative imagination, technological savvy and deeply personal advocacy. Historically, many queer people sought refuge in the arts, drawn to creative expression as a means of escape long before they fully understood their identities. This early nurturing of imagination became a unique asset in the fight for equality, providing a wealth of artistic talent, marketing expertise and storytelling skill to design compelling campaigns. As early adopters of social media and digital marketing, LGBTQ+ activists recognised the internet's power to amplify their message, connecting directly with audiences in ways that traditional media could not. This blend of creativity and innovation resulted in initiatives that felt authentic, visually captivating and emotionally resonant, capturing public attention while forging a new narrative about what it meant to be LGBTQ+ and young in the world.

One of the most powerful examples of this creative activism was the Stand Up! Don't Stand for Homophobic Bullying campaign, which debuted in 2009 and evolved in subsequent years. The campaign, designed with young people over a number of years, flipped the typical focus from the bullied LGBTQ+ child to the wider school community, calling on bystanders to stand up and take action. This shift reframed the narrative, positioning the fight against bullying as a collective responsibility and empowering allies to intervene. The campaign's emotional core was brought to life in a series of poignant public service announcements, including a memorable video featuring a young Barry Keoghan – Hollywood star, then a teen actor – portraying a student showing solidarity with his LGBTQ+ friend. This video, with over 2 million views since its initial release, was translated into multiple languages and became a new standard for how to portray queer youth in a non-victimised way. The campaign's impact demonstrated how the community's creative instincts, combined with a keen understanding of social media and its ability to reach people en masse, could inspire a shift in public behaviour and attitudes.

Ireland's relatively small, interconnected society further amplified the power of cultural activism. The old adage, 'one in every family', gained new relevance as increased visibility and openness created a growing network of allies. Colin Farrell's outspoken support, inspired by personal experience with the homophobic bullying faced by his brother Eamonn, became emblematic of this dynamic. His participation in BeLonG To's campaigns and public events brought high-profile visibility to the cause, opening doors to greater media coverage and political engagement. Actors like Simone Kirby and an emerging generation of talent also lent their voices, further embedding LGBTQ+ advocacy in the cultural mainstream. The resonance of this work continued to ripple outward – years after its release, BeLonG To's iconic 'He's gay and we're cool with that' poster gained new life when American pop sensation Lil Nas X referenced it on social media following his own coming out. These moments of cultural connection, fuelled by optimism and imagination, transformed activism into a living, breathing movement that celebrated joy, resilience and the collective power of a community determined to change its world.

At the heart of this work was a deliberate effort to challenge deeply ingrained myths about LGBTQ+ people – what some call 'control mythologies'. It was not just about visibility; it was about rewriting the stories that kept young people feeling erased and unsafe.

Control mythologies and the necessity of optimism

To understand the need for this optimism and narrative change work, it is helpful to see LGBTQ+ young people as an oppressed social group, who were subjected to marginalisation, powerlessness, cultural imperialism and violence (Young, 1990, p 41). Such violence is institutionalised and systematised, for example within the education system, the health system, religious institutions and family structures. This homophobia and transphobia is premised on deeply embedded multi-layered and intersectional stigmas, where, in Goffman's terms, an LGBTQ+ young person has for generations been 'reduced in our minds from a whole and usual person to a tainted and discredited one' (Goffman, 1963, p 3).

Reinsborough and Canning speak of 'control mythologies' that work to support the 'status quo' (Reinsborough and Canning, 2010, p 39) and encourage advocates for social change to engage in narrative change work at the 'point of assumption' to challenge these mythologies at an emotional level and to create new narratives. Fisher argues that such narrative change work is particularly significant when it comes to 'public moral arguments' (Fisher, 1984, p 12). It is clear from a wide array of literature (Barron, 2013; Reygan and Moane, 2014; Nolan and Larkin, 2016), and interviews that LGBTQ+ issues are located within a 'public moral argument' comprising 'control mythologies'. These mythologies include persistent narratives that frame gay men as a danger to children, cast homosexuality as inherently immoral, portray LGBTQ+ identities as contagious or a choice, and claim that visibility or affirmation of LGBTQ+ people undermines society by disrupting traditional gender norms. The sheer weight of these control mythologies can crush people, especially young people in formative years. These are intergenerational community traumas that repeat and repeat.

Analysis of literature, documentation and interviews for this book indicates that LGBTQ+ advocates engaged in narrative change work to challenge these 'control mythologies' in planned, purposeful and strategic manners, and that such work, in turn, influenced the ability of the policy community to improve the status of LGBTQ+ young people in public policy – including in the 2015 Marriage Equality Referendum.

Envisioning and imagination

My research indicates that work to improve public attitudes towards LGBTQ+ people and work for policy change were consciously interwoven throughout the period from 1993 to 2015.

This began with work to have gay and lesbian people's identity recognised. In their 1995 book *Gay and Lesbian Visions of Ireland: Towards the Twenty-First Century*, Eoin Collins, Íde O'Carroll and contributors presented a vision of Ireland, just two years after decriminalisation, in which lesbian and gay people were present, visible, active and contributing. This set a positive and visionary tone for how LGBTQ+ advocates would engage in public discourse over the following two decades. The authors were not 'speaking back to' homophobic arguments but were presenting alternatives. This can be seen in terms of 'radical imagination', which Haiven and Khasnabish argue is essential 'to imagine the world, life and social institutions not as they are but as they might otherwise be' (Haiven and Khasnabish, 2014, p 229).

This approach was continued by BeLonG To in the 2000s, initially through its name – emphasising that LGBTQ+ young people 'belong to' their community and wider society. This approach became visible in the 2006 campaign in partnership with the Equality Authority to address homophobic and transphobic bullying in school, which included a series of posters depicting teenagers in school with the slogan 'She's [or He's] gay and we're cool with that.' The Stand Up! Support Your LGBT Friends campaign was launched in 2009 and further developed this positive narrative. The first (of many) online ads for this campaign was created with a number of well-known young Irish actors. It centred around the line, 'We all have gay friends who stand by us during tough times, so we need to stand by them when they need us too, so stand up – show your support for our lesbian, gay, bisexual and transgender friends.' This simple line dismissed (without directly addressing) a prevalent idea that there weren't many LGBTQ+ people. It presented LGBTQ+ people as active agents (who 'stand by us during tough times') and invites non-LGBTQ+ people to join in the vision for a more inclusive Ireland through the call to action to stand up.

The purposefulness of this approach, referred to by contributors to this book and by BeLonG To documentation, shines new light on this period of social change in Ireland. There can be a tendency to see significant social changes through exceptional events (for example a referendum). There is also a tendency to prioritise well-understood data forms (such as opinion polls) and isolated individual stories over the strategy of the civil society organisations who drive long-term social change strategies.

The BeLonG To strategy published in 2007 identified two connected 'campaigns' for social change. One campaign was described as 'LGBT positive recognition campaign (long term)' to affect policy change in the education system; its objectives were the 'creation of mandatory structures and processes within schools that promote LGBT positive recognition' and the 'inclusion of LGBT people and issues into the broader school curriculum'.

The second was to be a public awareness campaign, the rationale for which was to support and interact with the policy change work:

> The removal of homophobia and transphobia in society and true positive recognition for LGBT young people is ultimately a long-term objective. It is important to establish awareness and recognition of LGBT youth in all settings where young people are likely to engage with their peers and professionals. This will set useful groundwork in terms of gradual changes in the attitudes and behaviours of those working and interacting with LGBT young people. This positive change will also support and help to add public voice to our longer-term work around positive recognition for LGBT young people at the institutional level. (BeLonG To, 2008, p 41)

This strategy, with its clear vision of removing homophobia and transphobia from society and achieving positive recognition for LGBTQ+ young people, was intentionally designed to change public attitudes. By taking real steps, including reshaping how the LGBTQ+ community and its youth were perceived, it focused on and campaigned for a change in public opinion. Over the eight years leading up to the Marriage Equality Referendum, this approach significantly contributed to building a more confident, visible and empowered LGBTQ+ community while taking concrete actions towards increasing societal support for LGBTQ+ equality.

Reflecting for this book on his involvement in early BeLonG To and the changes since, one early member of BeLonG To said:

> When I think of the dramatic changes of that time, I think of the poster campaign BeLonG To launched to stamp out homophobic bullying in schools. The idea was to turn the notice boards of hundreds of schools around the country into LGBT positive billboards. The images and slogans would be developed by BeLonG To members themselves and would feature affirming, uplifting statements. Groups of regular students in uniform, looking straight out of the poster, with text declaring: 'He's gay and we're cool with that.'
>
> What I remember most clearly was my own knee-jerk scepticism that religious school boards, with clerical leaderships, would allow something like this to happen. I doubted that authorities would go along with it, which in itself is revealing about how young people interpret the silence of authorities in these contexts. To call out homophobic bullying and to affirm gay students' dignity and standing,

in these terms, would be to acknowledge that there were out and proud LGBT teenagers walking around the hallways of these schools, and there was nothing wrong with it. 'What if they refuse to put them up?' I asked Michael. 'Maybe they will,' he shrugged, 'but let's see.' It was empowering because it demonstrated to the young people participating that they had standing to advocate for themselves and for recognition in these formal institutions, even if some authorities didn't welcome it.

In the end, a great many schools went along with it. Hundreds of teachers responded enthusiastically and placed the posters prominently in schools. Those few who attacked the campaign only drew attention to the stale prejudice still lurking in parts of the school system, prompting questions about their own role in fostering hostile environments for LGBT young people. The opposition melted away, and the posters went up.

Optimism as a key to effecting policy change

Niall Crowley, equality expert and founding chief executive officer of the Equality Authority, maintains that there is an Irish tradition of equality which

> has a particular engagement with people who experience inequality and their organisations. There is a concern within this tradition about institutional and structural sources of inequality in society. This has involved a focus on social change and developing alternative forms of society. It includes an ambition for a more equal distribution of resources (including income, wealth, jobs and social goods such as education, health and accommodation), status and standing, power and influence and relationships of love, care and solidarity between groups.

To understand the changes in policy for LGBTQ+ young people during this time, the narrative policy framework offers a particularly helpful lens. This framework highlights the crucial role of policy narratives in shaping policy outcomes. As McBeth et al explain: 'Politicians, political strategists, and media reporters understand intuitively that how a story is rendered is as important to policy success and political longevity as are which actions are undertaken' (McBeth et al, 2017, p 173). They further emphasise that policy debates take place on the 'terrain of narratives', spanning both formal settings like parliaments and informal spaces such as media, social media platforms and interest group websites. These narratives influence every stage of the policy process, from decision making to implementation, regulation and evaluation.

In this way, we can see how campaigns of optimistic, hopeful narrative change, in addition to painting a future with LGBTQ+ young people, were actively aimed at policy makers so as to bring them 'on a journey' towards an equality-based destination that they could see. Both politicians and civil servants I spoke to talked about LGBTQ+ civil society's ability to name the desired outcome and to demonstrate it through its campaigns and language. One civil servant I spoke to talked about becoming very emotional when listening to a story about why we developed LGBTQ+ youth groups around the country and why we spoke about a country where no one would ever have to leave their local area because of being LGBTQ+. She shared that she had known too many people in her own life who had left Ireland because they were gay. The very idea that this would not have to happen resonated deeply with her. This civil servant was centrally involved in driving many of the positive policy changes for queer youth for a number of decades.

Much of the policy change that happened during this time happened as part of what was described as 'equality mainstreaming'. 'Mainstreaming' in the context of minority communities is an emotive word. In the LGBTQ+ community, it can evoke ideas and feelings of assimilation – queer people becoming 'the same as' others, losing our community identity and imagination to integrate within the status quo (Vaid, 1995, p 54).

Mainstreaming here refers to equality mainstreaming within government policy development – a well-established process that means taking equality into account in the way the government exercises its functions, including all its policy development. In other words, equality should be a component of everything a government does.

This push to have queer youth considered within the weighty infrastructure of national children and youth policy, on an equal basis as all other young people, was born from the drive to change the narrative about LGBTQ+ youth. It was changing the image from one of a small number of very vulnerable, frightened, invisible, confused young people, to one where LGBTQ+ young people were centrally involved, visible and actively involved, everywhere.

At BeLonG To, I referred to this as the 'no small tables policy'. By this, I meant that when we engaged in networks, consultations, government or civil society discussions representing the needs and views of queer youth, we would only do so at the main table where most power lay. This was borne from experiences of representative bodies and government departments having diversity and equality subgroups with very little influence who reported to a more executive group who in turn made decisions or recommendations. I learned early on how ineffective these processes were, and how in effect they limited or sometimes neutralised the voices of minority communities.

In Belfast in the early 2000s for an all-Ireland meeting of youth organisations, I have never forgotten being told to wait at a small table in a side room while the established generalised youth services met. When eventually invited into the big room with the big table, my input was limited to a few minutes' description of LGBTQ+ youth. Sharing my views and analysis on overall youth policy was not possible. I knew from that moment that to be effective, I needed to be at the big table meetings. What followed was a difficult process of advocacy for why LGBTQ+ young people required mainstream attention and why we would refuse anything else. This work included standing for and being elected to boards of mainstream children and youth organisations and building public visibility and voice through the media. Over time, it became impossible for representative bodies or government bodies to refuse us a seat at the big table. It was a war of attrition and ruffled feathers, but within a few years not having an LGBTQ+ group participating at the big table became inconceivable. We were coming with an ambition for equality and a view of what that looked like.

Reclaiming the youth and family narratives, and their policy implications

As outlined in earlier chapters, opposition to LGBTQ+ rights has long focused on 'moral panic' about young people. Groups such as Family Solidarity campaigned against the decriminalisation of homosexuality in the early 1990s on the basis that it would corrupt young people. Those opposed to anti-homophobic and transphobic bullying campaigns in the early 2000s argued that they risked confusing young people into thinking they were gay. In this context, the act of establishing an LGBTQ+ youth project and public policy advocacy platform can be seen to go to the very heart of the 'public moral argument', while refusing to engage in debates about the legitimacy of LGBTQ+ youth identity.

This optimistic presentation of social and policy change towards LGBTQ+ young people, which didn't 'speak back to' oppressive narratives, can be seen in terms of 'the angel shift' as detailed in the narrative policy framework as opposed to the 'devil shift', where 'actors will exaggerate the malicious motives, behaviours and influence of opponents' (Weible et al, 2009, pp 132–3). With the 'angel shift', advocates foreground the community's ability to solve a problem and de-emphasise the opposition (McBeth et al, 2017). Although we experienced near continuous opposition from conservative Christian groups, we did not highlight that reality in our public statements. We acted like it was just not part of our narrative – like these groups did not exist. This was again an act of radical imagination – speaking from a position of how society should be, not how it was.

This work to shift perceptions of LGBTQ+ young people didn't happen in isolation. It was part of a wider movement of change, as Irish society began questioning the power structures that had long dictated social norms.

Broader cultural shifts away from deference and towards independence

This effort to change the narrative about LGBTQ+ young people aligned with and greatly benefitted from a broader social movement that was shifting away from deference to the Catholic Church and its teachings about LGBTQ+ individuals. As Barry Andrews, former Minister for Children and Youth Affairs, said to me:

> The period of undue deference to religion came to an end. The period of undue deference to political institutions came to an end and, of course, too, the financial institutions, so there was a period where central authority or any received Catholic social teaching were at their most vulnerable. There was real public unrest and a sense that everything was crashing down. I think the atmosphere was very, very positive for social change on issues. The country was fed up with being preached at. The Ryan Report came out and the Murphy Commission Report had come out and there were just endless reports about the inadequacies of child protection, historically and currently, the Church was caught at a minimum speaking out of both sides of their mouth. Something had to give. Yes, it was all awful, but also ripe for social change.

Former Minister for Children and Youth Affair Frances Fitzgerald expressed a similar analysis to me:

> It's a dramatic change, and it reflects a shift in people's view of the Catholic Church as well. People began to feel more independent. The Church's attitude toward homosexuality had marginalised people for so long – it was cruel, and society started to see it as such. Then the [clerical sex abuse] scandals came, fundamentally altering power relationships in our country. It forced us to ask, 'Why have we let this go on for so long? Why haven't we supported these children and young people?'

There is a strong connection between the unveiling of clerical sex abuse and growing support for the LGBTQ+ community, and in particular for LGBTQ+ children and young people. The release of the Cloyne Report in 2011, in the early days of a new Fine Gael–Labour coalition government, provoked an unprecedented response from the Irish state. The report indicated that the papal nuncio, acting on behalf of the Vatican, had refused to cooperate with the criminal investigation.

Taoiseach Enda Kenny's statement on the matter in the Dáil in July 2011 is widely viewed as a turning point in church–state relations. His speech included the following passage:

> This is not Rome. Nor is it industrial school or Magdalene Ireland, where the swish of a soutane, smothered conscience and humanity and the swing of a thurible ruled the Irish Catholic world. This is the Republic of Ireland in 2011. It is a republic of laws, rights and responsibilities and proper civic order where the delinquency and arrogance of a particular version of a particular kind of morality will no longer be tolerated or ignored. (Irish Times, 20 July 2011)

Writing about the significance of this moment, Anne-Marie McAlinden said that

> the Taoiseach's speech during the parliamentary debates on the Cloyne Report … is a defining moment in Irish political and legal history and in the nature of Church–State relations in Ireland, which offers a unique opportunity to make a permanent break with the past. The previous mixed and ambiguous relationship of Church and State in Ireland has taken a new turn and is no longer amorphous or undefined. Over the last few years, since the abuse scandals first began to emerge, the historically indulgent attitude of the State to the Catholic Church has been dramatically reversed. (McAlinden, 2013)

A contributor suggested that the Ryan Report may have prompted a response from the Department of Education: 'I think the department began to realise their duty of care to young people. After the Ryan Report, they became generally aware of the issues in institutions run by the Church, for which they had responsibility.'

A number of contributors to this book felt that efforts to support LGBTQ+ young people in schools and to secularise education were deeply interconnected, part of the same broader push for change.

One political figure reflected on the changing attitudes of civil servants in the Department of Education, indicating that department officials' opinions on LGBTQ+ issues and secularism (interchangeable) were similar to those of the rest of a changing Ireland:

> The homophobic bullying fell into the same category as secularising schools – it was something that had to change, and we were going to change it. When there are champions who are convinced and articulate, it makes a difference. Three or four principal officers, and in two cases assistant secretaries, privately told me they supported my secularism and shared the same view.

Key takeaways
1. The power of reframing narratives positively

The shift from focusing on LGBTQ+ vulnerability to celebrating queer optimism demonstrates how narrative change can drive social change. BeLonG To's approach rejected traditional control mythologies that portrayed LGBTQ+ youth as tragic figures and instead foregrounded joy, possibility and belonging. For activists, this highlights the importance of crafting narratives that challenge oppression and present a compelling and inclusive vision of the future. By presenting an 'angel shift' narrative – where the focus was on the potential for positive societal change – as activists we can invite communities, policy makers and allies to actively participate in what we are working to build.

2. Youth-led cultural activism as a strategy for visibility and empowerment

BeLonG To's emphasis on youth-led initiatives, from the Gay Prom to campaigns like Stand Up!, shows the value of centring those most affected by inequality in advocacy work. This work provided LGBTQ+ young people with the milestones and experiences their peers took for granted while creating spaces to celebrate their identities. This strategic visibility empowered young people to take ownership of their stories. As activists, we can recognise the potential of cultural activism – which is not just a method of raising awareness but is a way in which we can redefine societal norms through celebrating ever-changing non-traditional identities.

3. Imagining and demonstrating an alternative future

BeLonG To's campaigns were not just about countering discrimination – they offered a reimagined vision of society where LGBTQ+ young people thrived. Through its messaging and programming, BeLonG To articulated a 'new normal' that policy makers and communities could tangibly see and support. This work reminds us of the importance of demonstrating solutions alongside articulating problems. A clear, hopeful vision of the future helps to galvanise support by showing what change looks like. For example, presenting a society where no LGBTQ+ young person would have to leave their local community was a powerful call to action for policy makers.

4. Leveraging broader cultural shifts for advocacy gains

BeLonG To's work coincided with – and capitalised on – broader societal changes in Ireland, including a decline in deference to the Catholic Church. This alignment allowed LGBTQ+ advocacy to be heard in a context where many were questioning institutional power structures. For activists, this highlights the importance of recognising and leveraging wider cultural shifts to amplify our work. By aligning their strategies with societal momentum, movements can more effectively address resistance and build support. Connecting LGBTQ+ youth advocacy to the broader push for educational reform and secularism shows the value of positioning campaigns within larger frameworks of change.

Figure 5.2: 'He's gay and we're cool with that' poster 2007 from the Equality Authority and BeLonG To, later used by Lil Nas X to address his coming out on social media

Source: The Irish Human Rights and Equality Commission and BeLonG To – LGBTQ+ Youth Ireland

Figure 5.3: BeLonG To young people James Kavanagh, Esther Twieg and Senator David Norris promote Ireland's first Gay Prom

Source: BeLonG To – LGBTQ+ Youth Ireland

Figure 5.4: 'Stand Up!' poster for LGBT Awareness Week (2012)

Source: BeLonG To – LGBTQ+ Youth Ireland

6

Alliances and political power

This chapter examines the strategic alliance building and political influence that were central in changing Ireland's public policy approach to LGBTQ+ young people. It analyses how LGBTQ+ advocates navigated complex systems in the youth work, education, media and political sectors – spaces often shaped by resistance and exclusion – to promote equality as a guiding principle. This required persistence and a careful understanding of institutional dynamics, enabling advocates to align their goals with those of diverse partners while maintaining a clear focus on LGBTQ+ young people's liberation. The chapter places a particular focus on how politicians who were interviewed for this book understood these relationships and movements. These efforts reshaped the frameworks within which youth and children's issues were understood, moving them from the margins to the centre of national discussions.

Critically, this chapter examines how these alliances directly influenced the successful Marriage Equality Referendum in 2015 – a connection that, to date, has been underexplored. By framing marriage equality as an issue deeply tied to the dignity, safety and futures of LGBTQ+ children and young people, years of groundwork laid within youth and the children's rights sectors proved vital. This framing expanded the coalition of groups supporting the referendum immeasurably and neutralised anti-equality arguments centred on 'protecting' children. The strategic partnerships cultivated in the years prior ensured that these elements of the referendum campaign had credibility and reach. Core to the 'Civil society model for social justice policy change' I present in the next chapter is 'politics and partnerships', which is based on the content of this chapter.

This chapter provides an analysis of how these alliances, including directly with politicians who were interviewed for this book, were rooted in long-term trust building and an acquired understanding of power dynamics – which involves us working with people we don't agree with, where often we find connections are common ground to move together and where sometimes we just have to accept that movement is not possible but that trying is in itself important.

Building alliances in the youth sector

The youth work sector in Ireland has been deeply influenced by the principles of Catholic subsidiarity and by neoliberal governance. This sector operates through two key mechanisms: government funding for youth organisations to deliver services typically handled directly by the state in other countries and collaboration between the government and youth organisations to shape policy and legislation for young people.

The principle of subsidiarity, rooted in Catholic social teachings, holds that 'the state should only have a secondary ("subsidiary") role in providing for people's care, welfare and education' (Devlin, 2008, p 95). This approach shaped Ireland's youth work tradition, where services were historically provided by religious organisations rather than a centralised welfare state. Over time, this model blended with neoliberal practices like subcontracting services, making Ireland's youth work sector unique in its structure and delivery.

By the time BeLonG To emerged in 2003, this system presented significant challenges for LGBTQ+ advocacy. The sector's historical ties to religious organisations, coupled with a lingering resistance to LGBTQ+ inclusion, meant that early efforts to gain acceptance were often met with hostility. The broader education sector presented similar resistance, creating an uphill battle for change.

Having said this, the youth sector was also fertile ground for pushing for a change in the status of LGBTQ+ young people as it was also infused with people with radical thinking, particularly in the area of class analysis. Again, BeLonG To found natural alliances with other minority community youth organisations. Early in this work, the 'Strength in diversity' programme we developed brought young people from the Traveller community at Pavee Point, young people from migrant communities at the Migrant Rights Centre and LGBTQ+ young people at BeLonG To together. It was an extraordinary programme that provided young people from communities that may not have otherwise met opportunities to step into each other's lives, explore oppression together and for intersections to naturally emerge (which included young people coming out as LGBTQ+ and young people coming out as being from the Traveller community). This work also allowed the organisations involved to deepen their advocacy for policy change, and when BeLonG To joined the influential National Youth Work Advisory Committee (which under the Youth Work Act 2001 advised the Minister for Children and Youth Affairs on youth work and youth policy), there were already friendly faces at the table. With the support of the committee and the National Youth Council of Ireland (NYCI), BeLonG To co-produced 'Addressing homophobia: guidelines for the youth sector'. Then Minister for Children and Youth Affairs Barry Andrews said:

> My Office is committed to supporting the youth sector in tackling homophobic bullying and I would urge all youth organisations, youth workers, volunteers and all those working with young people to

commit themselves to addressing and combating homophobia. In doing so, they will be helping to ensure that youth work settings welcome and are supportive of all young people equally. (Office of the Minister for Children and Youth Affairs and BeLonG To, 2010)

A key element of the work in the youth sector was about LGBTQ+ youth civil society being both useful and constructive with both civil society (through training and supporting each other's initiatives) and government (by providing equality expertise in policy development) while not spreading itself too thinly and focusing on how to get the best outcomes as quickly as possibly for the young people on whose behalf we worked.

Building alliances in the education sector

Moving Ireland's education sector to support LGBTQ+ students, in addition to the journey through its religiosity as discussed earlier, required navigating a highly decentralised landscape where the Department of Education wielded relatively limited direct power over how schools operate, if we compare the system to others in Europe. Progress depended on methodically building alliances with key stakeholders across the sector, whose combined efforts helped create meaningful and lasting change for LGBTQ+ young people in schools.

Sandra Gowran, from the Gay and Lesbian Equality Network (GLEN), was instrumental in this work. As a teacher with deep knowledge of the education system, she focused on building trust and relationships across the sector. Her partnership with Dr Carol-Anne O'Brien, Advocacy Manager at BeLonG To, combined expertise in the sector with advocacy and international experience (Dr O'Brien worked for many years in Canada), resulting in initiatives that reshaped how LGBTQ+ equality was approached in schools. Together, they ensured that all education stakeholders – including religious bodies – were brought 'into the tent' and that they were provided with training and specific manuals and support that empowered them to move away from religious and conservatively entrenched positions.

Collaboration with the National Association of Principals and Deputy Principals played a critical role in bringing school leadership into the fold, while the involvement of Education and Training Boards ensured these efforts reached schools across the country. At a regional level, partnerships like those in Donegal resulted in the development of the LGBT Safe and Supportive Schools resource – a ground-breaking whole-school approach championed by Health Promotion within the Health Service Executive in Donegal that has since been adopted nationally. Alliances – spanning teachers, trade unions, school patron bodies, school leaders, policy makers, health professionals and representative bodies – was the slow but vital work in the education system. As former Minister for Education Ruairi Quinn, interviewed for this book, said: 'In order for change to be effective, it has to be bought into by very different groups within the wide landscape that is the education world in Ireland, and once that actually happens, once people buy into it they don't buy out of it again.'

International alliances

Irish queer activists and advocates have a long history of involvement in the international LGBTQ+ rights movement – including Patricia Prendiville being the Executive Director of ILGA-Europe (the very influential European region of the International Lesbian, Gay, Bisexual, Trans and Intersex Association) from 2004 to 2009, to Brian Sheehan being its co-chair in 2012–19 and Suzy Byrne, Roweena Russell and Oisín O'Reilly all being board members of the International Lesbian, Gay, Bisexual, Transgender, Queer and Intersex Youth and Student Organisation (IGLYO) in the 1990s and 2000s. Ireland is a small country, and human rights advocates have long looked and worked internationally, sometimes to bring new learning to the Irish environment and in the process learning that we had much to share.

In this context, BeLonG To developed strong international links on a number of fronts. Much of the alliances that were formed resulted from trips I made to South Africa and the United States as part of the 2009 Captain Cathal Ryan Scholarship Award. This extraordinary opportunity, provided by Declan and Danielle Ryan and the One Foundation, led to the development of a powerful global peer network. The relationships developed led to involvement in the production of the United Nations Educational, Scientific and Cultural Organization's (UNESCO) 'Education sector responses to homophobic bullying' in 2012 and subsequent convenings by UNESCO and Gay, Lesbian & Straight Education Network (GLSEN, USA) of activists working to make schools equal for queer youth across the world. We met in Rio de Janeiro, Johannesburg, Buenos Aires and Paris – supporting each other's work, carrying out research (UNESCO, 2012, 2016; Kosciw and Pizmony-Levy, 2013) and training together, and opening ourselves to new and inspiring thinking. Additional work with the Organization for Security and Co-operation in Europe (OSCE), during Ireland's first chairmanship in 2012, led to greater connections with and visits to LGBTQ+ organisations in both Russia and Eastern Europe at a key moment during the implementation of Russia's anti-LGBT laws (Walker, *The Guardian*, 12 March 2012).

During Ireland's EU Presidency in 2013, BeLonG To was positioned well to invite many of these organisations from across the globe to participate in the LGBT Youth and Social Inclusion Conference (Dublin, 17 June 2013) which we ran, supported by the Department of Children and Youth Affairs (Ireland) in collaboration with ILGA-Europe, IGLYO, the NYCI and the European Youth Forum. In 2015 I was invited by the Council of Europe (CoE) to join their Sexual Orientation, Gender Identity and Expression, and Sex Characteristics (SOGIESC) panel, and I wrote their first analysis of the 'challenges, gaps and opportunities in the field of human rights of lesbian, gay, bisexual, transgender and intersex children and the children of LGBTI families' (Barron, 2016). This work supported the development of further research and the mainstreaming of the rights of LGBTI children within the CoE's children's rights work.

This global connectedness provided deep links and enduring friendships which is vitally sustaining for activists, particularly those of us from minority communities when there are relatively so few of us at home. A heart-warming demonstration of these friendships came when the Russian LGBT Network, whom I had met in St Petersburg and worked together with at the OSCE, made a video for BeLonG To's youth voter registration drive ahead of the Marriage Equality Referendum in 2015 – appealing to people to register and vote. This was made during a time when the organisation and its people were being subjected to an intense state crackdown on their work and on them personally. The video and the discussions it provoked in Ireland were a powerful reminder of how swiftly authoritarian forces can remove rights from minority communities.

Direct relationships with politicians

As a small country with limited local government, historically shaped by the structure of the local parish, Ireland offers an unusually close level of access to national politicians, including government cabinet members, compared to other states (Carty, 2006). When functioning effectively, this proximity creates valuable opportunities for equality-focused civil society to engage directly with senior politicians – a dynamic explored throughout this book. For LGBTQ+ civil society, this was furthered in 2011 with the election of three openly gay TDs (members of parliament) – Jerry Buttimer, John Lyons and Dominic Hannigan – for the first time. They joined long-time member of the Seanad, queer rights champion Senator David Norris, and newly appointed Senator Katherine Zappone. These five LGBTQ+ members of parliament played very significant roles in advancing the rights of the LGBTQ+ community in general and LGBTQ+ young people in particular.

For this book, I had in-depth conversations with three former government ministers who played pivotal roles in shaping policy between 2008 and 2016: Barry Andrews, Frances Fitzgerald and Ruairi Quinn. Andrews and Fitzgerald served as Ministers for Children and Youth Affairs and are now members of the European Parliament, while Quinn, a former leader of the Labour Party, held roles as Minister for Education and Minister for Finance. Their reflections provide critical insights into how LGBTQ+ civil society engaged with the political landscape during this period, the challenges they encountered and the lessons learned.

Their perspectives, alongside insights from former ministers Richard Bruton and James Reilly, who succeeded them in education and youth portfolios, offer a broader understanding of the evolving relationship between civil society and the state.

Quinn offered a personal perspective on the evolving understanding of LGBTQ+ identities *and* into the dynamics of government decision making and civil society's role in influencing policy. He highlighted the slow pace of systemic change in Ireland, using the example of the 'Baptism Barrier' in school admissions to illustrate how issues can take years to progress through the political and administrative systems.

'The slow part is often the configuration of the Dáil,' he noted, explaining how institutional inertia can delay reform but also emphasising the long-term stability of changes once they are enacted: 'When there are champions who are articulate and convinced, change becomes inevitable, especially as attitudes within departments shift to reflect the broader changes in society.'

The insights shared by these ministers demonstrate the intricate relationship between civil society advocacy and political systems. They highlight the value of strategic patience, and the ability to build coalitions within and outside government. These lessons serve as a reminder that structural change needs persistence, adaptability and a deep understanding of the structures activists seek to transform.

BeLonG To's contribution to the Marriage Equality Referendum

The work described in the previous section laid the groundwork for a critical moment in 2015 – the Marriage Equality Referendum, which was a defining period in Ireland's history. It created legal equality for same-sex couples, but it signified a much bigger cultural shift towards valuing LGBTQ+ people within Irish society. While much has been written about the referendum's success, the role of BeLonG To and LGBTQ+ youth organising in shaping the campaign and creating many of the conditions needed for its victory has often been misnamed and even attributed to other organisations (Healy, 2017b). Here I reflect on BeLonG To's contributions – its decade-long work with LGBTQ+ youth, its proactive reframing of narratives and its ability to mobilise critical demographics. This work helped secure the Yes vote but also changed how LGBTQ+ young people were seen in Ireland.

It wasn't always clear that BeLonG To would directly campaign in the referendum. LGBTQ+ civil society had limited resources and, understandably, marriage was not seen as a youth issue by many advocates. Partner organisations like Marriage Equality, GLEN, the Irish Council for Civil Liberties (who together would form the main campaign vehicle Yes Equality) as well as the

Union of Students of Ireland (who had huge reach) and LGBT Noise (who organised hugely impactful marches, platforms for activists and engaged in very creative community building) were already doing this work.

Within BeLonG To, we had many staff meetings about what we should do, and as with all of our advocacy work, the answer came directly from the young people themselves whom we engaged with around the country. Youth workers nationally spoke to their members. I vividly remember being at such a meetings, and the overwhelming response was that they felt deeply about the Marriage Equality Referendum and wanted their voices to be heard. For young people, the forthcoming referendum was *not* about marriage equality per say; it was about how the country saw them and treated them. They saw this as a vote on what it meant to be LGBTQ+, and it was about acceptance versus rejection. With this information, we developed our messaging, which was not being used by other campaign groups. We moved our messaging away from the 'Love is Love' international/US-style messaging to messages that were bigger, broader, community focused and about young people. At this stage, BeLonG To had been campaigning to change public attitudes at a large scale for 12 years, and the organisation was adept at developing crisp, emotive messaging. We had learned that when campaigning to 'win hearts and minds', Irish people responded to community messaging (such as 'support your LGBTQ+ family and friends') over individual messaging (like 'Love is Love'). The messaging for the BeLonG To Yes coalition grew from the simple question 'What kind of country do we want our children to grow up in? Do we want them to experience acceptance, kindness, openness, or do we want them to experience mean spiritedness, small mindedness and violence?'

Our messaging was also consciously taking over the space which the anti-LGBTQ+ side wanted to occupy, and other groups were shying away from – the child protection space. Welsh children's rights communications specialist Carys Mairs Thomas was central to the development of this messaging and to ensuring that it was taken up widely in the media, and eventually by other marriage equality campaigns. Carys moved from Wales to Dublin for three months to work with me and knew the right messaging pitch as she had worked for a number of years with Ireland's Children's Rights Alliance. Children's rights was the arena that BeLonG To worked every day, so while we knew it was a tough role to play, we knew that we were the right people to do it.

As one marriage equality campaigner put it:

> The marriage equality movement managed successfully on most of the issues around marriage being between a man and a woman, marriage not being a church thing, most arguments we won. But the children one, it was always difficult. So, without having the children's rights

organisations and the youth organisations out there, we would never have won that argument because you know pitting the gays against 'what about the children?' Having BeLonG To support the children's rights organisations to come out and say 'well yeah, what about the children? What about the gay children?'

Building a foundation for LGBTQ+ youth empowerment

From the moment BeLonG To began in 2003, its mission to create spaces where LGBTQ+ young people felt safe, supported and empowered was clear. By 2015, these spaces had grown into a national network of over 30 regional LGBTQ+ youth groups, reaching over 4,000 LGBTQ+ young people annually. What stands out about this work was its ripple effect. The 'One in every family' saying about LGBTQ+ people started to appear to be true as more and more young people were empowered to come out in their families and communities. Families, schools and neighbours began to see LGBTQ+ young people not as abstractions but as vital, loved members of their own communities.

Looking back, this work, particularly outside of Dublin, was about far more than support. It was about visibility and agency. It ensured that LGBTQ+ young people weren't just passive recipients of change – they were active drivers of it. They told their stories, stood up in their schools and challenged prejudice in ways that were deeply personal and profoundly impactful. I remember travelling to Kilkenny, where I am from, for a marriage equality rallying event during the campaign. I saw first-hand that it was the BeLonG To-supported LGBTQ+ youth project, while wearing different hats, who were the people behind the rally and the campaigning. This was the case in many parts of the country. Local LGBTQ+ youth workers became marriage equality campaign leaders right across the country. They were ideally positioned to run local marriage equality canvassing groups as they were well networked nationally and locally into their communities because of the years of community building they had done in the previous years (Carey, 2015).

Taking charge of the child protection narrative

One of the most strategic interventions BeLonG To made was its proactive ownership of the child protection narrative. We knew from the beginning that the No campaign would centre their arguments on 'protecting children'. This wasn't new – this argument had been used against us in the past, often successfully as outlined in Chapter 2. In addition, I had visited *Minnesotans United for All Families* in 2013, which had successful prevented a ban on same sex marriage, and learnt how the child protection argument could play out in a referendum campaign.

Our response was built around one simple, powerful question: 'what kind of country do we want our children to grow up in?' This question shifted the debate entirely. Suddenly, it wasn't about hypothetical dangers – it was about the very real futures of LGBTQ+ young people in Ireland.

The #BeLonGToYES coalition brought together nationally trusted organisations like Barnardo's, the Irish Society for the Prevention of Cruelty to Children, the Children's Rights Alliance, Foróige, Youth Work Ireland, the Migrant Rights Centre, Headstrong, Pavee Point, Empowering People in Care (EPIC), the Institute of Guidance Counsellors, the UNESCO Child and Family Research Centre and the NYCI – all organisations that BeLonG To had spent over a decade building relationships with (Barron, 2016). Their support added credibility and weight to the core message about the kind of Ireland we wanted for children and young people. Together, we reframed the conversation: voting Yes wasn't just about marriage – it was about creating a society where all children, including LGBTQ+ children and youth, felt safe, valued and included (Carey, 2015).

It is also noteworthy that the BeLonG To Yes campaign brought a conscious focus to the intersectionality of the LGBTQ+ community – by including migrant, Irish Traveller, organisations for very vulnerable children and young people. It worked particularly hard to speak to working-class young people and communities, which was reflective of the young people who attended BeLonG To groups. Team members Gillian Brien, Ger Rowe, Sean Frayne, Lisa McKenny, Trina Tsai, David Carroll and chairperson Anna Quigley all campaigned tirelessly, leading groups within their own working class, rural, minority communities with messages about why the referendum mattered to queer youth and their families.

The respectful approach to this coalition building – one which drew on longstanding relationships and aligned the coalition with individual organisations' missions – was highlighted by several interviewees. As Mary Cunningham, Director of the NYCI, reflected:

> It was the work behind the scenes about awareness raising and education of the youth and children's rights sector. Because of the years and years of working with people building trust because you go to their stuff so they go to yours, they know you, you're a trusted group, a trusted brand.

Anna Quigley captured this perfectly: 'The child protection argument had been used against us for so long, but BeLonG To turned it into one of the most compelling reasons to vote Yes. It put LGBTQ+ young people at the heart of the campaign, and that made all the difference.'

This was a strategic win, and it was a deeply personal one for so many of us who had seen this argument weaponised against us for decades, and indeed as I will discuss in Chapter 8, has re-emerged as a far-right narrative tool.

Mobilising young voters and the role of 'It's in your hands'

Young people were always going to be key to the Marriage Equality Referendum. Polls showed their overwhelming support for marriage equality, but we also knew their historically low turnout rates posed a risk. The Union of Students of Ireland and Yes Equality did extraordinary work across Irish colleges in registering students to vote, and this is why BeLonG To made voter registration and engagement a cornerstone of its campaign (Carey, 2015).

The BeLonG To short film 'It's in your hands' became a focal point of this effort. The message was simple but powerful: *You have the power to shape Ireland's future.* It resonated deeply.

By the end of 2014, over 40,000 new voters had registered, many of them young people. On the day of the referendum, their turnout proved decisive. This was a logistical and political success, which bucked received wisdom – showing that when young people feel seen and valued, they show up – including to vote.

Mary McAleese, Enda Kenny and political leadership

BeLonG To's work resonates within communities and with national leadership. Former President Mary McAleese's public endorsement of a 'Yes' vote, at a BeLonG To Yes campaign event, was a defining moment. As a devout Catholic and respected public figure, her support carried immense weight, particularly for voters who were undecided. Her statement that a Yes vote would 'chip away at the architecture of homophobia' reinforced BeLonG To's framing and gave the campaign a moral clarity that was hard to ignore. As US magazine *The Nation* put it:

> When Mary McAleese, former president, announced her support for the marriage-equality amendment, she did so not only as an activist barrister who for forty years had striven to dismantle 'the architecture of homophobia', but as a parent of twins – one gay and one straight – who would have vastly different legal protections. (Spillane, 2015)

Dr McAleese's message was emotionally resonant because it built on her own family's life and that of her son Justin, who is gay and who himself played a major role in the referendum campaign. Speaking of the vote which was due to happen within days, she said of her and her husband Martin:

> We believed it to be about Ireland's gay children. What we both feel very strongly is, particularly as we approach 2016 [the centenary of Ireland's 1916 Proclamation of Independence], is that it is a debate about children. People have been saying it is about children and we

believe it to be about Ireland's gay children and their future. And about the kind of future we want for Ireland. We want, in the words of the proclamation, the children of the nation to be cherished equally.

Her intervention in the days leading up to the vote was deeply significant. By choosing to speak alongside BeLonG To – and to focus her message on children and young people – she built on nearly a decade of connection with the organisation. This was not a new concern: she had first publicly centred the well-being of LGBTQ+ young people in 2007, when she addressed the International Association of Suicide Prevention in Killarney, as explored in Chapter 3.

One of the most significant moments of the campaign was when Taoiseach (Prime Minister) Enda Kenny visited BeLonG To. The Taoiseach sat with LGBTQ+ young people and listened as they shared their stories. I remember one young person, in particular, who spoke about what a Yes vote would mean for their future. It was raw, heartfelt and impossible to not be moved by.

The Irish Times reported on the Taoiseach's meeting with LGBTI+ young people at BeLonG To, including how Mr Kenny met with young LGBT people and 'told them all political parties in Leinster House supported the referendum and said they had 15 days left to ensure people were sufficiently motivated and interested enough to actually vote'. The newspaper also reported how '[o]ne young BeLonG To member, Alison Kershaw, broke down as she told Mr Kenny she had a girlfriend for more than two years and they had a happy, successful relationship' (Minihin, 2015).

At BeLonG To, Mr Kenny said:

> If this vote were to not approve the referendum change it means that Irish citizens are denying other Irish citizens the right to an equal society or equality in society in terms of the marriage contract and the civil law. So it's a really important date, a really important day, a really important opportunity for this country to move to a different space, to show real leadership in terms of what equality actually means. (Minihan, 2015)

In the final days of the campaign, Kenny repeated those words in public, framing the referendum as a choice about the kind of Ireland we wanted to build. Hearing those sentiments echoed at the highest level of government was a testament to how central LGBTQ+ youth civil society had become – not just to the campaign but to the national conversation.

Building momentum and getting the vote out

Having used social media to reach large numbers of people for many years ahead of the referendum, BeLonG To significantly increased its online presence further. It's widely acknowledged that social media played a key role in securing the Marriage Equality Referendum, and the BeLonG To Yes coalition reached 4.7 million people online (Barron in Healy, 2017a).

A standout moment was when our short film 'Bring your family with you', directed by Aoife Kelleher and Hugh Rogers, based on a concept developed with my husband Jaime Nanci and myself, garnered over 650,000 views online, at a time when Ireland's voting population was just 3.4 million people (International Foundation for Election Systems, Election Guide, 2015). It brought more star power to the campaign, with internationally known actors Brian Gleeson, Aaron Heffernan, Ruth McCabe and Steve Wall playing central characters. Set in a rural Irish village, the film showed young people persuading their parents, aunties and grannies to join them in voting Yes to marriage equality. It was an empowering message to young people, showing them their ability to influence their families and communities. The film even made it on to the Last Week Tonight with John Oliver TV show in the United States as a parody, reflecting its widespread impact.

BeLonG To's online strategy also included short films explaining how to vote, a WhatsApp campaign reminding young people to vote on 22 May and the use of the 'I Voted' application on Facebook. These efforts, driven by Oisín O'Reilly, brought a new level of engagement and accessibility, helping us reach nearly 5 million people.

Reflecting on long-term change

The Marriage Equality Referendum was such an important moment, but the campaign brought up painful memories for many LGBTQ+ people and exposed the persistence of homophobic and transphobic rhetoric. BeLonG To saw this first hand. Our helplines were flooded with young people seeking support during the campaign, many of them grappling with being made the centre of a public debate, with shocking vitriol from the anti-equality side.

Notwithstanding the success at the polls in 2015 where 'Yes' was carried by 62 per cent to 38 per cent, it is important for me to note how difficult and retraumatising the referendum campaign was for the LGBTQ+ community in Ireland. Across the country, huge numbers of queer people and allies went door to door asking people to vote for LGBTQ+ equality. The anti-equality campaign were free to use highly derogatory comments about us – on posters and in the media. It was a violent and brutal time for us. For queer parents and young people, it was a particularly aggressive time, with the specifics of their lives being debated by bad actors.

But it did plant the idea in people's minds that equality is an element of Irish identity – people were proud of the result and the attention that Ireland received as a modern progressive society. As we will question in Chapter 8: has this connection between equality and Irish national identity held? Is there learning in this for how we face new anti-equality and far-right forces?

Five analytical takeaways

1. Strategic reframing as a tool for advocacy success

BeLonG To's ownership of the child protection narrative demonstrated the power of reframing opposition arguments into compelling reasons to support a marginalised community. By asking, 'What kind of country do we want our children to grow up in?', BeLonG To neutralised the opposition's most potent argument and turned it into a powerful pro-equality message. This highlights a critical lesson for us activists: anticipating and owning contentious narratives before they can be weaponised. This approach requires deep familiarity with public sentiment, strong alliances with trusted voices and the ability to align our messaging with both community voice and the wider national sentiment. .

2. The role of youth empowerment in cultural change

BeLonG To's long-term work with LGBTQ+ youth created a network of advocates who were drivers of change in their spaces. By supporting young people to share their stories and lead in their communities, the organisation contributed to a cultural shift in advance of marriage equality. This demonstrates the importance of grassroots empowerment in advocacy, where those most affected by an issue are positioned as its most credible and compelling voices. For activists and movements, this underscores the value of us investing in long-term capacity building and visibility for marginalised communities.

3. Coalition-building as a cornerstone of progress

By aligning with children and youth rights organisations, minority community organisations and health-promoting organisations, the BeLonG To Yes coalition expanded the reach and credibility of the marriage equality message. The coalition's strength lay in its respectful, trust-based relationships, built over years of collaboration. This provides a critical insight for us activists: successful coalitions are not transactional but relational, requiring ongoing effort to build alignment without compromising our missions.

4. Engaging politicians as active partners

BeLonG To's direct engagement with political leaders, including former President Mary McAleese and Taoiseach Enda Kenny, highlights the importance of cultivating relationships with decision makers. McAleese's major referendum intervention being held at BeLonG To lent moral authority to its message about supporting LGBTQ children and young people, while Kenny's visit to BeLonG To shows how personal stories from LGBTQ+ young people could shape political discourse. The key takeaway here is that proximity to political power – when handled strategically – can amplify marginalised voices and translate grassroots advocacy into national change. It further demonstrates that time we spend building alliances with politicians who are willing to listen and learn is time well spent.

5. Resilience in the face of hostility and trauma

The referendum campaign, while ultimately successful, was a deeply challenging time for Ireland's LGBTQ+ community. BeLonG To's preparation for the emotional toll of the campaign, including helplines and ceremonies, demonstrates the importance of supporting communities through difficult advocacy moments. This is a reminder that the pursuit of equality often comes at a personal cost to those involved, and care structures must be built into advocacy efforts. As activists, we can recognise that moments of triumph are often preceded by significant emotional labour and trauma, and by periods of re-traumatisation afterwards, which we need to acknowledge and address to sustain movements over time.

Figure 6.1: Michael Barron and husband Jaime Nanci kissing at Marriage Equality Referendum count centre

Source: Getty Images

Figure 6.2: Activists Lisa Kenny and Karen McLoughlin in the BeLonG To campervan for Yes

Source: BeLonG To – LGBTQ+ Youth Ireland

Figure 6.3: Michael Barron with former President of Ireland Mary McAleese and Dr Martin McAleese

Source: Belong To – LGBTQ+ Youth Ireland

Figure 6.4: Michael Barron with Minister Richard Bruton, ending baptism barrier announcement

Source: Author's own

Figure 6.5: BeLonG To Yes children's rights organisations coalition T-shirt

Source: BeLonG To – LGBTQ+ Youth Ireland

Figure 6.6: International LGBTQ+ activist panel discussion at the LGBT Youth forum in Croke Park

Source: BeLonG To – LGBTQ+ Youth Ireland

7

Self-organised community model for policy change

In this chapter, I draw together the analysis from the previous chapters to iterate the often invisible work of civil society of turning values into action, of making beliefs operational. In making these processes explicit, my aim is to share learning and move our shared thinking along.

The model I have produced is built on the experience of being a queer person, advocating for queer young people in mainstream policy environments. It also builds on my immersion as a queer academic in the world of public policy theory for many years, and from a queer justice analysis seeing how non-inclusive that space is. The theory and frameworks simply did not relate to my own experiences or worldview, and so I was compelled to reimagine them and create a framework that takes into account what it means to advocate for policy change from a minority or marginalised position. I had to develop a model for advocates who are seeking policy changes to protect their communities, changes which receive extremist opposition and institutional fear and exclusion. This was what I experienced in all my advocacy for LGBTQ+ young people over this period, and I know it is akin to the opposition faced by people seeking positive public policy change towards the Traveller community, communities of colour, migrant communities, disabled communities and communities with experience of drug use and of prison.

I set out in this book to make contributions, including producing tools, insights and a specific model for advocates for social justice. The model I produce centres the role of minority community organisations in the creation and implementation of government policies, including laws and constitutional changes. It's a model based on the experience of being part of a movement which brought marginalised needs 'from the community hall to the constitution'.

In the following pages, we look at a public policy-making model that recognises that this can and does happen.

In addition to immersing myself in theory and thinking through how it could be applied to real-life policy-making, I also explored it the opposite way – how my experiences and those of the people I interviewed could be matched to public policy theory. Former Irish Taoiseach (Prime Minister) Garret FitzGerald, described as 'the most intellectual Irish politician of his generation', is credited with saying 'That's fine in practice, but will it work in theory?' I applied some of this reverse thinking to this model also (Irish Times, 20 May 2011).

My intention is 'to be useful', and I present this chapter with a view to it sparking ideas and empowering activists, communities and those interested in justice to see legislative and policy change as accessible, and for policy makers to see communities as allies.

The research for this book revealed that LGBTQ+ civil society engaged in organised strategic processes of turning vision, values and ideas into action for the express purpose of developing a society, including public policies, which would be inclusive of LGBTQ+ young people. This strategy is outlined in organisational documents I studied and was discussed by those I interviewed. The purposefulness of this long-term strategic approach is key to understanding how much policy change has happened. Discussion of these approaches of consciously translating vision, values and ideas into tangible actions for policy change forms the basis of this chapter.

The vision and values which formed the basis of the work of civil society were ones of equality for LGBTQ+ young people, for all marginalised groups and for all in society. The ideas which accompanied this were to present an image of a society where LGBTQ+ young people experienced equality and in so doing to promote optimism and 'narrative change' on how LGBTQ+ youth were seen in society. These ideas allowed for a new, unapologetic presentation of LGBTQ+ young people (who had long been stigmatised or invisible), which allowed for public discussion of issues that needed to be addressed through policy change and for the development of various coalitions to work towards these changes.

The actions developed to manifest the vision, values and ideas into realities focused on public awareness campaigns, critical engagement of LGBTQ+ young people through youth work and active strategic engagement with government (public service and politicians) to develop LGBTQ+ youth-inclusive policies.

To develop the model, I draw from a set of public policy theories, primarily:

- John Kingdon's agenda setting policy framework;
- Sabatier and Jenkins-Smith's 'policy advocacy coalition framework';
- narrative policy framework (McBeth et al, 2017);
- problematisation (Bacchi, 2009).

It departs in significant ways from these frameworks and theories, however – particularly as it:

- centralises the role played by minority and marginalised communities in civil society across key aspects of policy development, from framing the problem to policy implementation;

- focuses on the significant role played by community youth work in the development of public policy;
- highlights the importance of civil society-driven narrative change;
- problematises the development of policy, particularly on issues which are subject to 'public moral arguments' (Fisher, 1984), such as LGBTQ+ youth rights;
- acknowledges the direct relationship between civil society (community workers and advocates) and politicians through lobbying and campaigns to change public attitudes.

Figure 7.1 illustrates the framework for civil society-driven public policy development which I have developed and below is an outline of each component and why they are significant in this context.

Civil society

Here I bring my experience in frontline community youth work, public campaigning public policy development and directing funding to social justice movements, to a this framework. It is a framework for self-organised communities to draw on in developing public policy.

This activist perspective is in line with an approach to promoting equality in Ireland, which 'has traditionally lent towards a focus on activism to mobilise, politicise and organise people who experience inequality and discrimination' (Crowley, 2015, p 5).

This perspective, together with the literature and theory, and the voices of those I interviewed, has led me to place civil society at the centre of this framework. This allows for the role of civil society and community organisations to be considered in all aspects of policy development. They and we are not simply 'interest groups', as much public policy theory

Figure 7.1: Framework for civil society-driven public policy development

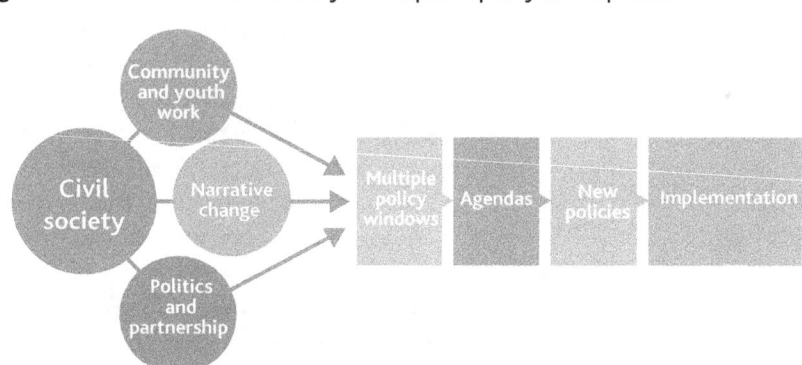

would say (Kingdon, 1984; Jenkinson-Smith and Sabatier, 1993), but are the people whose real lives are directly impacted by the policy or legislation in question.

In his work on public policy theory, Kingdon includes the character of the *policy entrepreneur*, a driven individual anywhere within the policy system who is willing to invest their energy promoting a particular issue and policy solution. I find this to be the case here, and I further suggest that LGBTQ+ civil society collectively demonstrated the qualities of the policy entrepreneur, including:

- having a claim to hearing due to their expertise on the topics;
- having a claim to hearing because they represented a community;
- they were or became politically connected over time;
- they were tenacious and persistent;
- they negotiated and brokered at key moments (such as during government formations) to exploit policy window opportunities.

It is significant to note that civil society activism by its nature is innovative and entrepreneurial – seeking out and attempting to find new opportunities for social change. Kingdon (1984, pp 131, 123) describes policy solutions whirling around in a 'policy primeval soup'. In this innovative and creative spirit, civil society is a core 'recipe-writer' for the 'soup' of policy ideas and hence gave birth to many of the policy processes relating to LGBTQ+ young people since the early 1990s.

Community youth work

Core to the inclusion of LGBTQ+ young people in Irish public policy was the role played by community youth work, including its work in politicising young people to advocate for justice. This central 'coal face' work involved building community, providing opportunities for young people to come together, when often there had been none. In terms of social memory, LGBTQ+ youth and community organisations enabled diverse young people, and those who cared for them, to share common experiences and histories and to understand that they were not alone. For so many, the feeling of 'I am the only one' was so demoralising, and indeed dangerous in terms of their mental health, so these opportunities in and of themselves were life changing. One of the great joys and privileges of being an LGBTQ+ youth worker in the early 2000s was witnessing young people transform from fear and anxiety to joy and fun, spending time with other young people with whom they shared an identity. For many when they walked into BeLonG To on their first day, it was the first time they had ever met another LGBTQ+ person in real life.

In addition to these transformative processes, LGBTQ+ civil society harnessed and directed the energies of queer youth into effecting social change. This work included:

- organising – creating LGBTQ+ organisations and infrastructure across the country, including over 20 LGBTQ+ youth groups by 2015;
- strategising – developing long-term measurable plans for social and policy change;
- community youth work – adopting social justice education and awareness-raising approaches, such as political education and activism programmes for young people;
- collective action and coalitions – working in partnerships and collaboratively with other communities for shared goals, for example working in partnership with migrant and Traveller organisations.

Narrative change

In order for LGBTQ+ civil society to engage in public policy, it was necessary for it to challenge some basic (prejudiced) assumptions and to alter the 'rules of the game'.

In Ireland, the LGBTQ+ community's use of cultural activism brought together creativity, technology and personal advocacy in powerful ways. Many queer people had long turned to the arts as a space for expression and refuge, often before fully understanding their identities. This deep connection to imagination and creativity became a strength in the equality movement, fuelling campaigns that blended artistic talent, marketing skill and authentic storytelling to capture hearts and drive narrative change. This community strength was drawn on by queer civil society when it:

- carried out a series of public campaigns aimed at changing public perceptions (including those of policy makers) on LGBTQ+ identity;
- carried out targeted work of 'narrative change', such as 'reclaiming' issues of child protection and bullying;
- 'problematised' policy-making processes, such as convincing public servants that requiring demographic statistics on the LGBTQ+ community was not possible or desirable;
- partnered with a wide variety of other minority communities to work on the development of equality legislation;
- undertook a long, slow, invisible process of 'equality mainstreaming' whereby LGBTQ+ young people would be included across a wide variety of mainstream policy – embedded so much in public policy in Ireland that it is now the 'new normal' for children and youth policy to include queer youth.

Politics and partnerships

A close and direct working relationship between LGBTQ+ civil society and elected politicians played a very significant role in the development of public policy to support LGBTQ young people. This relationship with parliament was spoken about in detail with the politicians who talked with me. They spoke of the significance of these direct relationships, the role played by civil society in generating policy solutions, lobbying them and in influencing public opinion through campaigns.

For politicians, the historical mistreatment of the LGBTQ+ community and a related commitment to the separation of church and state in public policy was a clear motivating factor for their engagement with LGBTQ+ youth issues (McAlinden, 2013).

The General Election in 2011 brought to power a Fine Gael–Labour coalition government, in which long-serving Labour TD (member of parliament), Ruairi Quinn, became the Minister for Education. Just two years earlier, the publication of the Report of the Commission to Inquire into Child Abuse (commonly known as the Ryan Report), detailed the shocking scale of physical, sexual and emotional abuse suffered by children in institutions run by a range of Catholic religious orders, but which were funded and inspected by the Department of Education. Responding as Labour Party opposition spokesperson on education in 2009, Mr Quinn said of the Department of Education and Science:

> There is a continuing culture of deferment and obedience to the Catholic Church and its religious orders in the Department of Education and Science that has continually frustrated getting answers to simple questions. Either officials in the department are members of secret societies such as the Knights of St Columbanus and Opus Dei and have taken it upon themselves to protect the interests of these clerical orders at this point in time in this year of 2009 or, alternatively the minister is politically incompetent. (The Irish Examiner 2009)

Remarking on how Quinn championed LGBTQ+ issues and challenged religious ethos issues, one civil servant I spoke to commented:

> You might not get every minister who would have wanted to do what Ruairi Quinn wanted to do, because he was quite happy to rattle people's cages on issues. So not every minister would have maybe taken it on. The minister was determined to try and drive change in the system, so maybe other ministers might not have pursued as many issues in that area as he did.

In 2011, the new government established the first dedicated department to focus on children and young people, which also provided an opportunity to further the development of LGBTQ+ youth policy. Former Minister for Children and Youth Affairs Frances Fitzgerald commented: 'It was the first full department for Children and Youth Affairs. It was a moment in time: a new department, a new minister, somebody with a background with families, children, background in social work, community development, equality particularly.'

The new department was to focus on delivering on a number of commitments in the Programme for Government, including:

- the holding of a referendum in relation to the rights of children under the constitution;
- the establishment of a Child and Family Support Agency on a statutory basis in order to fundamentally reform the delivery of child protection services;
- implementing the recommendations of the Ryan Report, including putting the 'Children first: national guidance' on a statutory footing.

These commitments were strongly focused on 'child protection' in the wake of the Ryan Report. This focus provided a significant link to work to combat homophobia and transphobia. In July 2013, in his sixth annual report to government, the Special Rapporteur on Child Protection (a position appointed by the Minister for Children and Youth Affairs) highlighted homophobic and transphobic bullying and its impact on children and young people, saying: 'It is recommended that homophobic and transphobic bullying in schools should be considered a child protection issue. As such, schools need to address homophobic and transphobic bullying through rigorous prevention and intervention measures' (Shannon, 2013, p 104).

It is of significance to note that the Special Rapporteur on Child Protection, Geoffrey Shannon, had developed an ongoing working relationship with myself and BeLonG To in the years preceding this 2013 report and addressed the launch of the BeLonG To Stand Up! campaign in 2012. This open and supportive relationship was a hallmark of much of our work during this time.

Former Minister for Children and Youth Affairs said 'People think that policy is something that's totally objective. Of course, it's driven by values. It's driven by experience. It's driven by things you want to see changed and by your experience' (politician).

Another politician spoke about issues they had with a particular senior civil servant whom they believed was blocking their agenda to develop anti-homophobia and transphobia policies, and that their political advisors told them that some civil servants were unhappy and that there was 'pushback – people saying there is no issue around bullying in schools and certainly no such thing as bullying as regards to homophobic bullying. There was a section of the civil service … that was very cautious.'

As with the civil service, the development of positive working relationships between politicians and LGBTQ+ civil society was vital. Politicians I spoke with mentioned feeling 'welcome and well received' at LGBTQ+ events and meetings and also spoke about receiving 'considered and sound' advice from LGBTQ+ groups. One politician stated that 'gay, transgender youth wasn't spoken about until BeLonG To made us listen' and spoke about the organisation being 'present in parliament and media'.

The significance of relationships between LGBTQ+ youth civil society and the political system was discussed by all the politicians I interviewed, as was the importance of relationships in the negotiation of policy change. This speaks well to notions of a 'policy community' in which actors from different locations can come together to develop coalitions. It also speaks to the specificities of policy development in an Irish context, in which this policy community is relatively small and civil society access to politicians is possible, and indeed welcomed at this time.

Former Minister for Children and Youth Affairs Barry Andrews spoke about finding a balance between challenging various positions and forming respectful relationships. They said:

> There's a good balance. You have to be robust, but you'll get very little done if there isn't respect. Respect doesn't mean you have to bend the knee, it just means acknowledging that individuals have their own constituencies and their own stakeholders and they have to be respected.

Frances Fitzgerald former Minister for Children and Youth Affairs spoke about the significance of how department officials discussed LGBTQ+ civil society, saying 'I remember people within the Department speaking very highly of BeLonG To's ability to negotiate and bring people with [them].'

Relationships with key public service champions

When it came to LGBTQ+ civil society, the important role played by a number of key public servants in the changing status of LGBTQ+ young people in public policy was vital. As one civil servant said of his colleague:

> Politicians are often guided by supportive civil servants who play a crucial role behind the scenes. People like Mary, for example, who write the speeches, frame the message and push the agenda forward, are essential to driving progress. Yet, their contributions are rarely visible or acknowledged. These advancements don't happen by chance – you need dedicated individuals committed to making them a reality.

I would describe the members of the Irish civil service (including 'Mary', referred to in the excerpt), as 'champions' – people who worked within their systems to advance the rights of LGBTQ+ people. Indeed, people from both civil society and politics referred to them by name and spoke of the significance of their actions. These individuals described how they were motivated by a variety of factors – including knowing LGBTQ+ family, friends and colleagues, as well as their own social justice analysis and their own 'work ethic'.

They were also motivated to act through the development of positive and trusting relationships with LGBTQ+ civil society groups. People I interviewed described LGBTQ+ civil society advocates as 'sound' and 'thinkers and doers', with BeLonG To being referred to as 'a solid group … so any proposals coming in from the group would have gotten due attention'. Another spoke of LGBTQ+ civil society groups being open and transparent – 'anytime we went to BeLonG To to look for information or support or anything [they] came back with the stuff, without any angle on it'.

Multiple windows and agendas

I have considered policy development over decades and as such have examined multiple and varying policy windows. These have included sexual abuse scandals in the Catholic Church, which allowed for a greater movement towards secularism and work on homophobic and transphobic bullying in schools and general elections and programmes for government negotiations.

The model also recognises that the processes in which civil society engages in policy development with government is not linear, nor are they impermeable, with the development of a new policy as a discrete endpoint. These processes are cyclical, and civil society is positioned throughout (both by itself and by the state) as a driver from initial concept development through to policy implementation, evaluation, review and policy redevelopment. This process is represented in Figure 7.2.

Partnerships between civil society and the state were crucial during this time. As civil society space currently narrows and multi-agency governance declines, key examples of state–LGBTQ+ community collaboration highlight opportunities to strengthen and build on this work in the future. Vision and values formed the basis by which civil society and the state worked in collaboration for the inclusion of LGBTQ+ young people.

The overarching framing of LGBTQ+ young people in terms of equality allowed for various focuses on tangible inequalities and various times. This required multi-level strategies by LGBTQ+ civil society to translate the ideal of equality into a reality of policy change and community building. The strategic use of optimism and imagination and campaigns of narrative change claimed a space in public life for LGBTQ+ young people – a group that has long been invisible and stigmatised.

Figure 7.2: Cyclical framework for civil society role in public policy development

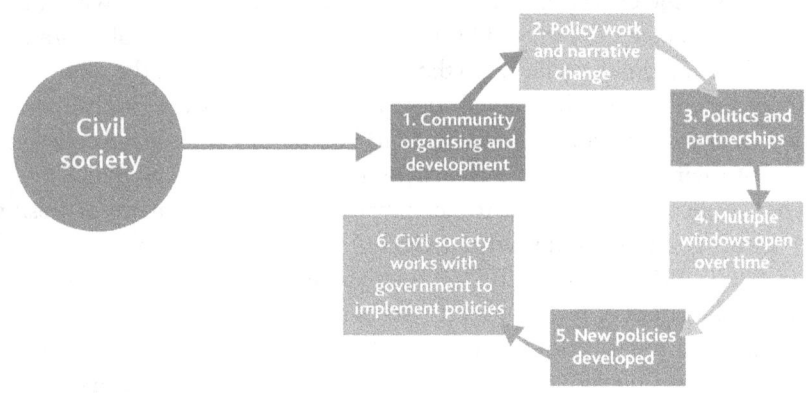

The significance of youth work as a vehicle for building community infrastructure, as a methodology for consciousness raising and as a platform for advocacy for policy change, is central to the story of how LGBTQ+ civil society worked to translate ideals into actions. The 'quiet inclusion of LGBTQ+ across mainstream public policy' was organised through long-term strategic focus on policy change.

When approached from an active, engaged and solution-focused civil society, civil servants and politicians demonstrated 'core relational and transformational capacities' (McInerney, 2014) in their engagement. In this era of shrinking civil society freedom and space, it is very important to reflect on this real-life work and the potential for partnership between civil society and the state to bring about genuine transformation in a once 'unmentionable' area.

Five takeaways

This chapter introduced a new model for understanding the role of civil society in driving public policy reform, based on the experiences of LGBTQ+ youth advocacy in Ireland. It emphasises the importance of self-organised community leadership, long-term strategic narrative work and collaborative partnerships in shaping and sustaining policy change.

1. Minority-led civil society

The chapter highlights the central role of minority-led civil society organisations in shaping public policy. LGBTQ+ youth organisations in Ireland were responding to injustices but were also consciously constructing solutions and bringing them to the public policy system. By centring the lives of marginalised communities, civil society was fulfilling its role of challenging inequality and centring social justice in public policy development. Minority-led civil society can position itself as a key architect of policy change, using its unique perspective to identify structural barriers and design effective, inclusive solutions. Mainstream civil society can support this, and government needs to elevate minority communities' role in developing policy about their lives. Communities are not 'special interest group' but are a cornerstone in developing public policy which effects them.

2. Community youth work

A cornerstone of the model is the role of community youth work in nurturing community leadership and advocacy. By creating safe and empowering spaces, LGBTQ+ organisations enabled young people to transition from isolation to collective action. This approach amplified LGBTQ+ young people's voices in policy making and public discourse. Community youth work is both support mechanism and a platform for systemic change – more resources, trust and imagination can be invested in young people to lead and shape social justice changes.

3. Narrative change

Strategic narrative change is central to the model, illustrating how advocacy efforts reframed social justice for the LGBTQ+ community as a universal issue tied to safety, dignity and fairness. LGBTQ+ organisations put a lot of time and energy into dismantling harmful stereotypes by reclaiming public narratives and aligning their messaging with shared socialvalues. This narrative work shifted public opinion and created a foundation for policy change.

4. Politics and partnerships

The model emphasises the importance of building trust-based partnerships with politicians, public servants and other stakeholders. Collaborative relationships allowed LGBTQ+ advocates to influence the policy-making process at critical junctures, ensuring that reforms were practical, informed and supported. These partnerships demonstrated how civil society and government could work together to implement meaningful change.

5. Multiple windows: the cycle of policy making and implementation

This chapter reinforces the importance of understanding and engaging with the cyclical nature of policy making and implementation. LGBTQ+

advocates leveraged multiple policy windows, from legislative reforms to public consultations, to embed LGBTQ+ equality into national frameworks. By maintaining a presence at every stage – from identifying issues to monitoring implementation – they ensured that progress was sustained over time. As activists, we can remain engaged throughout the policy cycle, using opportunities to influence, implement and sustain systemic change.

8

Defending our civil society platforms

Minority and marginalised communities have always faced institutional barriers to organising, along with violence from extremists and the state. The structural challenges in pursuing legal and policy change for equality and justice are nothing new. These challenges may take on new forms and faces, but they remain ever present and deeply entrenched. Achieving meaningful progress and embedding our rights so firmly in society that they cannot be dismissed is an uphill battle.

When we speak about the structural forces marginalised communities must fight, this is what we mean. These are not abstract concepts – they are tangible examples of how systems, policies and even civil society can be weaponised by powerful, bigoted people and groups to harm and silence us.

We are confronting real threats: the rise of far-right extremism, political shifts away from equality and the troubling notion that our hard-won rights are increasingly seen as negotiable or dispensable. Issues like government regulations and funding insecurities may seem bureaucratic, but their impact on marginalised communities and our advocates is profoundly destructive. Combined with the escalating threat of far-right ideologies worldwide, the need to defend and uplift civil society has never been greater. Civil society must remain a democratic space where marginalised communities can safely advocate for our rights.

With this backdrop, in this chapter I reflect on the critical role of civil society in a healthy democracy and the growing threats it faces from restrictive regulations, targeted attacks and entrenched institutional power. Drawing from personal experience, I explore how the mechanisms of governance, often intended to protect transparency and fairness, can be weaponised to suppress advocacy and silence dissent.

The fight for equality and justice is collectively and personally fraught with dangers for members of marginalised communities. This chapter examines the structural barriers we face when organising – how powerful institutions and systems, often presented as neutral, can be weaponised against us. Whether it's state funding tying civil society's hands, or policies being manipulated to harm rather than protect, I've experienced first hand how regulation, meant to promote transparency, can be used to do the opposite when it is allowed to be manipulated by bad actors.

Democracy relies on an independent civil society to amplify marginalised voices, challenge unjust policies and hold those in power accountable. Yet, in recent years, we've seen increasing constraints on this work – through overregulation, funding tied to compliance rather than advocacy and deliberate campaigns designed to undermine legitimacy. These pressures represent a fundamental challenge to the ability of civil society to contribute to public debate and push for social justice.

In this chapter, I look at what happens when these forces converge, how they impact those working for equality and justice and why defending the space for civil society is essential. I also highlight how important it is that we understand that it is primarily certain types of civil society – civil society led by and for minority communities which are targeted by conservative forces and the far right – that are most under attack and most in need of defending. These are organisations from communities of colour, Muslim communities, LGBTQ+ communities, Traveller and Roma communities, women, communities of people seeking international protection and those advocating with people with experience of drug use and prison.

Memory: The weaponisation of regulation – the real-life cost

As I sat in the window in Donegal reading the documents on a cold and wet September morning in 2018, the injustice of what had transpired over the previous years flooded over me. I had a pain in my chest, and I couldn't breathe properly. I was frozen in place, the extent and gravity of vitriol laid out in front of me in documents I had received through a Freedom of Information and a General Data Protection Regulation request to the Standards in Public Office Commission (SIPO) was frightening. I knew the complaints against our work at EQUATE to remove the Baptism Barrier from Irish schools were driven by bad actors, but I didn't know the full extent of it until that morning when I examined the almost 100 documents from a Freedom of Information request I had lodged with the regulator.

There was correspondence between myself, my colleague and Chairperson and an officer of SIPO, correspondence between that SIPO officer and our funders, correspondence between the same officer and those making unfounded complaints and seeking information. This did not surprise me, nor did the internal SIPO communications which in May and July indicated that there was no breach of regulation by EQUATE. What did surprise me was who the main complainant was. It was a member of the Church of Ireland who was hired at this time as a professional lobbyist to work for the Church of Ireland to pressure the government against our proposals to remove the Baptism Barrier (which allowed children to be discriminated against because of their religion) from state-funded schools. The sheer volume and doggedness of correspondence from this lobbyist was overwhelming. My colleagues and I had been battling this complaint since early in 2017, and it was now the end of 2018. The completely erroneous complaint (which if found to be true could have resulted in a criminal prosecution as the SIPO officer reiterated to me often) was found to have no basis in July 2017, but this lobbyist continued. The relentlessness and pressure on our funders meant that we couldn't do our work, and we couldn't raise the needed funds. While I was unemployed and staying in a cottage in Donegal, I read that even after EQUATE closed in October 2017 – leaving three of us without jobs – this lobbyist kept targeting us well into 2018.

After EQUATE closed, I had spent almost a year working as an individual to try to complete the work needed – a friend had told me that she was worried that I was losing my mind in the mountains! I was almost there and couldn't let it go, but I was consumed by anger, upset and crippling self-doubt by what had happened – and not knowing who was really behind this weaponising of a government regulatory body. It was a terrible time. But here, finally, was all the evidence needed to show the truth as my colleagues and I had always known it to be.

Other civil society organisations stopped returning my calls when news of a regulator query reached their boardrooms – it stung, and they were wrong. A Catholic newspaper ran front-page stories that led to 'What did you do wrong this time?' phone calls from my parents.

It was all a dirty tricks campaign aimed at blocking the passage of equality legislation. I had been on the receiving end of the wrath of a 1,500 years old institutional church with enormous wealth and influence. What I was feeling was what being in the target of such a powerful body feels like. I wasn't losing my mind. I sat there with my head spinning. I curled up on the sofa in front of the stove, rain pelting on the roof and cried.

The Business Post journalist Barry Whyte investigated the issue and confirmed that in July 2017 'the Standards in Public Office Commission (Sipo), Ireland's electoral spending watchdog, gave EQUATE a clean bill of health. The education equality group was not, Sipo documents from the time demonstrate, in contravention of campaign funding laws' (Whyte, 2018). He spoke with lobbyist Tony Goodwin, who confirmed that he was issuing complaints against EQUATE to SIPO, and to the Secretary of the Church of Ireland's General Synod Board of Education, Dr Ken Fennelly, who confirmed they had hired Goodwin 'as a consultant and adviser on the area of school admissions' (our work was part of school admissions reform) during this time. Both claimed that Goodwin's pursuit of EQUATE via SIPO was done in a private capacity, while he worked with them on the same issues (Whyte, 2018).

Speaking to *The Irish Times*, Liam Herrick, Director of the Irish Council for Civil Liberties, said: 'The experiences of Equate and other NGOs demonstrate how easy it is for individuals to target the work of an organisation they don't like.' He said it was 'unquestionably the case' that were the Electoral

Act (which governs SIPO) to properly function as it reads, civil society participation in public debate would effectively come to an end (O'Brien, *Irish Times*, 15 October 2018).

In parliament on 18 October 2018, Senator Fintan Warfield (2018) spoke about the misuse of the SIPO complaints system against EQUATE and said that 'there have been other instances where the Electoral Acts have forbidden people from speaking out for social change and it ultimately places a muzzle on activists and hurts democracy', pointing to concerns raised by the European Union Agency for Fundamental Rights.

I tell you this story to help build a picture of the stakes which were at play in the work to pursue social justice, particularly when such justice was at odds with Christian churches' interests during this time. I also tell it to expose the real human damage that the misuse of government regulatory bodies can do to people. At the time of writing this book, I know that far-right groups are using the complaints mechanisms of government regulators to try to derail the work of LGBTQ+ and equality organisations – just as Goodwin from the Church of Ireland had done to EQUATE. It further demonstrates:

- The embeddedness of the Christian churches within the delivery of basic state services – in this case, the state's education system, but also the state's health system and youth and community work systems. These churches are enormously wealthy and influential, in part due to the state subcontracting services to them.
- Establishing a civil society advocacy platform which directly challenged the Christian churches' hegemony and morality within the education system, health system and youth and community work system was radical.
- That getting a seat at the policy-making table for LGBTQ+ civil society organisations and activists was hugely challenging.
- How important it was to have independent and effective civil society organisations who could drive an equality agenda in these circumstances, as there was such opposition to progress and how important it is to defend civil society as a core pillar of democracy.
- How the state (in this case, SIPO) and the churches – in this case, a consultant working for the Church of Ireland – could still, after the introduction of marriage equality and abortion rights, conjoin to prevent progressive policy change.
- How the pushback against equality and human rights would increasingly be played out through the weaponisation of government regulatory bodies. This is a strategy which was to become adopted by far-right actors to attack organisations who worked with the communities they targeted with hate, including the trans community, the overall LGBTQ+ community, women and migrant communities.

- The vulnerability of equality advocates to highly personalised attacks and the use of disinformation which in this case led to three people losing their work in a precarious work market.

Limiting civil society – how governments control and contain

The use of government regulators to limit the work of an equality-focused civil society organisation highlights the broader issue of constraints being imposed on legitimate advocacy for a more equal society. The growth of anti-NGOism, as a core tenant of far-right and reactionary groups in recent years, both builds on pre-existing undermining of civil society and has now grown into a politically mainstream position. On 8 March 2024, two referendums were held to decide if changes should be made to the Irish constitution. The proposed changes were called: the Family Amendment and the Care Amendment. Both referendums failed to pass. This was seen by some as a victory for mainstream conservative and far-right groups, who framed the amendments as an attack on the Chistian traditional family unit. They also campaigned using considerable anti-NGOism (anti-civil society) sentiment. This sentiment continued into the local and European election campaigning in June of 2024.

The confluence of such significant forces creates conditions where for some time now, the basic work of civil society in advocating for a better, more just society for all is undermined (TASC [Think-tank for Action on Social Change], 2024), in part by the state. It is important to remember that this is not new. In 2002, then Minister for Justice and Equality Michael McDowell announced the closure of the Citizen Traveller Campaign, claiming it had 'failed to bridge the divide between Traveller and settled communities' (Burns, 2002). Earlier that year, the Citizen Traveller Campaign sharply criticised the government for legislation giving Gardai the power to confiscate illegally parked caravans without the knowledge of their owners – a clearly valid position for a Traveller campaign to take (The Irish Examiner, 4 November 2002).

This situation is, I believe, moving us to a position where the vital work of equality-focused civil society is becoming ever more precarious. Should this continue, I fear we are travelling to a place where minority communities will become even further isolated, and the progress that we have made will be greatly damaged. With this in mind, it is important that we consider the importance of an independent civil society, its role in a functioning democracy and how this role is curtailed by the state and by bad faith actors.

Civil society has played a central role in governance in Ireland. This has been included in the social partnership model and across a number of interagency oversight committees such as the National Drugs Task Force and the National Youth Work Advisory Committee. It influences public policy through lobbying and advocacy on their issues – work which LGBTQ+ advocates have proven to be very effective at.

The irony is that an independent civil society, with a focus on marginalised communities, is a concept which has been repeatedly iterated by the Irish government.

In 2000, the 'White Paper on a framework for supporting voluntary activity and developing the relationship between the state and the community and voluntary sector' described advocacy as a key function of the sector, contributing to policy development, planning and the creation of opportunities for participation in decision making. It states that '[a]dvocacy and provision of information are essential roles of the Community and Voluntary sector to support individuals facing disadvantage or discrimination to access and realise their rights'.

McInerney (2014) points to the dissonance between Irish government recognition of civil society groups internationally (as expressed in the 2006 'White Paper on Irish aid') and the lack of recognition for such groups' role domestically.

In practice, there is little evident valuing by government of the ideal of an independent civil society as a component of a healthy democracy. This contrasts with the clear recognition by the Irish government of the role of civil society organisations in countries many thousands of miles away. For civic engagement to take place and for democracy to deepen, there is a need for citizens and civil society organisations alike to express their voices without fear of control, domination or recrimination (McInerney, 2014, p 89).

Funding constraints

Brian Harvey's 2012 report for the Irish Congress of Trade Unions highlights the disproportionate impact of austerity on civil society. While overall government expenditure decreased by 4.3 per cent between 2008 and 2012, funding to civil society was slashed by 15 per cent. Harvey warned that by the end of the International Monetary Fund programme, the voluntary and community sector could shrink to just two thirds of its pre-crisis size. Similarly, a 2018 Community Foundation of Ireland report found that the non-profit sector experienced funding cuts of 35 to 40 per cent and a 31 per cent reduction in staffing following the recession in Ireland.

Austerity wasn't the only challenge. Concerns have also been raised about an anti-advocacy stance from state funders towards civil society. O'Connor and Ketola (2018) note that while the Irish constitution upholds the right to criticise government policy, some public agencies explicitly discourage publicly funded organisations from participating in policy debates, even when these organisations rely on independent funding to subsidise public services. Crowley (2015) echoes this, observing that funding dependencies have made civil society more cautious: dissent is muted, advocacy is confined to safe boundaries and survival has become the priority.

In 2024, the Irish Council for Civil Liberties' report, '"That's Not Your Role": State Funding and Advocacy in the Irish Community, Voluntary and Non-Profit Sector', shed light on the complex relationship between state funding and advocacy. While state funding is vital for supporting essential services, it often comes with explicit and implicit restrictions that stifle advocacy. Over 37 per cent of surveyed organisations admitted to scaling back their advocacy efforts due to fears of jeopardising their funding (Irish Council of Civil Liberties, 2024).

For LGBTQ+ organisations, these challenges are especially acute. Often operating with limited resources and precarious funding, these groups already work within a marginalised framework. The constraints imposed by funding relationships make it even harder for them to challenge entrenched societal norms and government policies. These restrictions undermine their freedom of expression and ability to represent marginalised voices, limiting their capacity to address systemic inequalities and push for transformative change.

Competitive tendering processes have further strained community organisations. As O'Connor and Ketola (2018) point out, larger organisations are better equipped to manage the scale and complexity of service commissioning contracts, effectively sidelining smaller, community-based groups. This shift risks undermining the diversity and grassroots focus of civil society, limiting its capacity to address the needs of marginalised communities.

Philanthropy

Philanthropy, while often well intentioned, can cause harm through its actions and approaches. A significant issue is the lack of transparency from donors and boards, with decision-making processes and funding priorities frequently shrouded in secrecy. This exclusion of key voices – particularly those from the communities being served – reinforces power imbalances and leaves those most affected without a say in interventions that shape their lives. When communities are sidelined, philanthropy risks becoming an exercise in power rather than partnership.

Too often, philanthropic efforts prioritise the needs and preferences of donors, geopolitics or pressure from investors over those of recipients. Donor recognition or personal agendas can take precedence, with funding directed towards causes that align with the markets rather than addressing the most urgent or systemic issues. This approach diverts resources away from marginalised groups and critical challenges, further entrenching inequality. Programmes shaped by donor priorities, geopolitics or market trends miss the mark and reinvolve injustice (Alden, 2024).

Moreover, philanthropy can fall into the trap of short-term fixes, dependency-inducing strategies and cultural insensitivity. These practices, rather than fostering empowerment or lasting change, can reinforce the very inequities they aim to address. When philanthropy centres its efforts on the desires of donors and operates without accountability, it undermines its potential to contribute to transformative progress. True change requires transparency, humility and a commitment to prioritising the voices and needs of those it seeks to serve.

Anti-LGBTI organisations are becoming increasingly well funded and coordinated, with resources that dwarf those available to LGBTI advocacy. In 2021–22, just three anti-LGBTI groups – the Alliance Defending Freedom, Focus on the Family and the Christian Broadcasting Network – reported a combined income of over $1 billion. To put this in perspective, that's more than the total funding received by over 8,000 global LGBTI grantees during the same period (Global Philanthropy Project, 2024).

These groups are using their substantial resources to push back hard against progress in LGBTI rights. They lobby for regressive legislation, spread disinformation and mobilise opposition in ways that directly threaten equality movements. For LGBTQ+ advocates, particularly in underfunded and hostile regions, this growing financial power of anti-LGBTQ+ campaigns represents an enormous and urgent challenge.

The '2021–2022 global resources report: government and philanthropic support for lesbian, gay, bisexual, transgender, and intersex communities' from Global Philanthropy Project (2024) highlights that without significant increases in funding for LGBTQ+ advocacy, especially in regions where these opposition movements are most active, we risk losing hard-won gains. The report makes it clear: to counter this threat, we need more than incremental funding changes. We need bold, sustained support to protect the future of LGBTQ+ rights.

Trans organisations are chronically underfunded and operating in an increasingly hostile environment. A key report from the Global Philanthropy Project highlights that most trans organisations worldwide work with budgets under $20,000 annually, and many in the Global South and East receive only a fraction of the resources available to groups in the Global North (Lukomnik et al, 2024). Meanwhile, these regions face some of the greatest challenges, leaving vital advocacy and community-building efforts struggling to survive. This funding inequity threatens the ability of trans movements to support their communities and push back against mounting threats.

What makes this even more alarming is the growing power and resources of the anti-trans movement. Well-funded opposition groups are intensifying attacks, from harassment campaigns to regulatory scrutiny, all designed to drain resources and delegitimise trans advocacy. Yet many human rights funders remain cautious, reluctant to provide the kind of bold, unrestricted and multi-year support these organisations urgently need. Without this, trans groups are left vulnerable, unable to effectively plan, respond to crises or resist these coordinated attacks.

Supporting trans work is about more than addressing funding gaps – it's about defending human rights and democracy against well-resourced opposition. This means funders being brave, trusting trans activists to lead so that the progress made in trans rights could be rolled back, leaving communities even more exposed to harm (Lukomnik et al, 2024).

Regulatory burden

Concurrent with cuts in state funding to civil society over many years, the government also introduced a series of significant compliance-related duties for civil society organisations. In 2009, the Charities Regulator (and the Charities Act) and the Revenue Commissioners introduced accounting and governance procedures requiring non-charities to register as companies. This was followed by the Companies Registration Office (and the Companies Act); the General Data Protection Regulations; the Register of Lobbying (and other requirements of SIPOC, such as the Electoral Acts); Garda Vetting; the Health and Safety Authority; and the Health Information and Quality Authority). Regarding programme staffing and employment, if (co-)funded by statutory agencies, government departments and agencies such as Child and Family Agency, Tusla, the Health Service Executive and Pobal also set specific compliance requirements (Carroll and Barron, 2019).

Far right attacks and shrinking civic space

In 2024, the Think-tank for Action on Social Change (TASC), in a report 'Civil society under duress' highlighted the multifaceted challenges LGBTQ+ organisations face in Ireland, particularly from far-right harassment, restrictive funding structures and diminishing civic space. Far-right groups have increasingly targeted LGBTQ+ organisations with coordinated attacks, including online abuse, protests at events and filing complaints with regulatory bodies to exhaust resources and undermine legitimacy. Public events, particularly those aimed at LGBTQ+ youth, have been disproportionately disrupted, forcing organisations to reduce visibility to protect staff and participants. This climate of hostility creates a precarious environment for advocacy and service delivery. As the report states, 'Far-right protests, particularly against LGBTQ+ youth events, have escalated, with organisations withdrawing public advertising to avoid repeated harassment and intimidation.' These actions make it harder for organisations to provide safe spaces for their communities and contribute to growing concerns about the safety and well-being of their staff and service users.

The report notes, 'Restrictions on advocacy funding have left many LGBTQ+ groups unable to respond to pressing issues, forcing them to prioritise compliance over community needs.' Far-right actors further exploit governance frameworks by filing vexatious complaints, diverting resources and focus from core organisational missions. Overregulation compounds these issues, forcing LGBTQ+ organisations to focus on administrative burdens rather than addressing systemic inequalities or developing transformative solutions.

The shrinking civic space has particularly severe implications for LGBTQ+ organisations, as their work is often framed as contentious or non-essential. Far-right narratives, amplified by social media, normalise discriminatory rhetoric, creating additional barriers to advocacy and fostering mistrust in LGBTQ+ communities. This narrowing space for dissent and public engagement disproportionately affects organisations representing marginalised groups, reducing their ability to advocate for equality and inclusion. As the report highlights: 'Previously stable democracies are seeing a decline in civic space, and LGBTQ+ organisations are among the first to experience the impact of these restrictions.' Furthermore, the intersectionality of harassment is evident, as anti-LGBTQ+ and anti-migrant campaigns are often intertwined, demonstrating how far-right groups exploit multiple forms of discrimination to weaken collective resistance. The report underscores the toll this environment takes on staff and volunteers, with one executive noting: 'Monitoring online platforms for threats has become an everyday part of the job to ensure staff safety.' This emotional and operational strain has led to burnout and, in some cases, scaling back public-facing activities, further diminishing the impact of LGBTQ+ advocacy.

The report further concludes that '[w]ithout systemic reforms, LGBTQ+ and other civil society organisations will remain vulnerable to escalating far-right attacks and restrictive regulatory environments' and 'the survival and effectiveness of these organisations are essential not only for the LGBTQ+ community but for the broader fight for equality, democracy, and human rights in Ireland' (TASC, 2024).

Takeaways

1. Weaponisation of regulations against advocacy

Regulations intended to promote transparency and fairness can be manipulated to suppress dissent and advocacy. Complaints filed through regulatory mechanisms are used to stifle progress and drain resources from equality-focused civil society groups. The experience of equality-focused civil society reveals how these tactics, often led by well-resourced and connected bad-faith actors, derail advocacy efforts and cause immense personal and community harm. Activists and organisations can come together in solidarity with one another now, providing genuine support to those being targeted and advocating for changes in regulation which allow for this to happen. There is a particular responsibility on mainstream civil society to step up and support minority people and organisations.

2. The growing threat of far-right tactics

Far-right groups, which are growing in influence, increasingly use coordinated harassment, disinformation and vexatious complaints to undermine LGBTQ+ and other equality-focused organisations. Public events, particularly those supporting marginalised communities, have become flashpoints for disruption. These tactics are violent and terrorising of minority communities, further eroding the capacity of civil society to engage in public discourse. Recognising and addressing far-right interference is critical to safeguarding civil society. This requires proactive measures, including coalition building, public education and robust government interventions to interrupt the spread of disinformation and hatred. Globally, the new reality that the anti-LGBTQ+ movement is funded at a significantly higher rate than the LGBTQ+ movement creates an urgency in the work with like-minded governments and funders to address this imbalance.

3. The fragility of advocacy-driven civil society under state control and shifting philanthropic priorities

Advocacy organisations often rely on state funding, which can come with restrictions that stifle their ability to challenge policies or systems of oppression. At the same time, private philanthropy is shifting its focus due to concerns about geopolitics, rising demands for transparency of family foundations and evolving priorities which shift depending on the political and investment climate, which can cause philanthropists to abandon communities. This dual challenge – state dependency and the unpredictability of philanthropic support – forces civil society into a precarious position, balancing survival with the need for dissent. Today, this is happening in a frightening global environment where human rights-focused civil society is out funded by anti-human rights organisations. Competitive tendering processes further marginalise smaller, community-driven organisations, limiting their capacity to address systemic inequalities and pitting groups against each other when we need unity. Advocacy groups and partners across government and other sectors can work to diversify funding models and advocate for systemic reforms that decouple financial dependency from political and market-driven controls.

4. The impact of coordinated opposition on marginalised communities

LGBTQ+ organisations, alongside groups representing migrants, women and racialised communities, are often the first targets of coordinated pushback against equality movements. The chapter underscores how intertwined forms of oppression, amplified by far-right narratives, disproportionately affect those already on the margins. This is violent and creates a chilling effect, reducing visibility and limiting opportunities for systemic reform. Advocacy can recognise the interconnected nature of discrimination and work collaboratively across movements to counter the structural and ideological forces that perpetuate inequality.

5. The central role of civil society in democracy

The essential function of civil society in holding power to account, advocating for marginalised voices and advancing equality needs to be better understood. Yet, as the chapter reveals, this role is increasingly under threat from restrictive regulations, anti-NGO rhetoric and resource constraints. Without systemic reform to protect and support civil society, the progress made in equality and human rights is at risk of being undone. Defending civil society is about safeguarding democracy.

Figure 8.1: Dublin far-right riots 2023, on Dublin's main street – O'Connell Street

Source: Sam Boal/RollingNews.ie

9

Conclusion

Writing this book has been a profound privilege. It is the culmination of decades of activism, decades also spent exploring this world as a queer man with a love of adventure and a deeply embodied desire for justice.

While writing this, I thought of so many people. My friend Kieran who brought a diverse and joyful world to me as a teenager, and my friend Eoin who was the first queer activist I ever met – who taught me to be both fast thinking and generous with my work. Both passed away in recent years, and both pushed me on to write this book.

I was wary of doing so. My doctorate thesis forms the spine of this writing – in fact, I set out to write a 'PhD conversion', but what emerged is quite different. I had a tough time completing the doctorate during the 2020–22 COVID-19 pandemic, a time I didn't want to revisit, and as I write in 2024/25 the world is a painful place for so many experiencing a genocide, wars, the climate crisis, White supremacy and rising Islamophobia and the very real life or death removal of care from women and trans people.

But writing this book was a totally different experience than I expected. I focused my mind on the countless young people I have met through my work and reconnected with so many of them. Some were 18 years old the last time I saw them in person. Now they are 20 years older, but we spoke like time had created no distance at all. I also reconnected with many of them 'lifers' – life-long activists – some of the incredible mentors and elders whom I learned so much from and continue to do so. Writing this book was a journey in reconnecting with what is important to me – communities of people who care for each other. With my husband Jaime, who put so much work into this book, we wrapped ourselves up in the generosity of friends who are activists, artists, writers, academics, and I feel that has been my greatest learning – that this warmth and generosity is alive and well.

So to you who are reading this, I encourage you to seek this out in your work and life as I share some final thoughts with you and as you reflect on this writing and your own journey.

What have we uncovered so far?

The power of self-organised civil society

I've learned that self-organised civil society has the power to transform lives and systems, particularly when rooted in the lives of marginalised communities. In

Ireland, LGBTQ+ youth organisations moved from the sidelines to the centre of public policy while being authentic. From changing education policy to contributing to the Marriage Equality Referendum, I've seen how centring the lives of our community contributed to cultural and legislative breakthroughs.

Historical context and structural challenges

Understanding the systemic barriers we face as a community is essential. Ireland's deeply Catholic past, institutional homophobia and the systemic silencing of LGBTQ+ voices created a wall we were not meant to break through. This institutionalised homophobia and transphobia was added to by funding dependencies shaped by neoliberalism and Catholic subsidiarity, which undermines our civil society's ability to pursue social justice. Today, far-right groups exploit societal fears through disinformation and moral panics. Progress is always hard won and can and will require us to address barriers head on, knowing that there will be personal cost.

Advocacy models and strategies

The most effective advocacy combines bold imagination with tangible, strategic actions. By reframing public narratives around equality, safety and shared values, LGBTQ+ organisations influenced public opinion and in turn public policy. Some of this work took decades – the quiet inclusion of queer youth national strategies across education, healthcare and youth policies. These strategies moved beyond responding to crises and media coverage and proactively imagined and articulated the kind of world we wanted LGBTQ+ young people to grow up in.

Where are we now?

Progress and precarity

We've achieved so much, from decriminalisation to marriage equality and gender recognition. Beyond that, we have embedded the rights of LGBTQ+ young people across mainstream policies and legislation. But these successes remain fragile. Far-right activism and the mainstreaming of its ideas and the re-emergence of 'child protection' narratives as a weapon against us shows how quickly progress can face backlash. We are navigating a landscape where progress is no longer guaranteed, and defending rights is essential.

The role of philanthropy and state dependency

I see how funding challenges have intensified. Philanthropic priorities shift due to geopolitics, market trends and individual interests, often leaving

LGBTQ+ organisations underfunded. State funding, while critical, frequently comes with constraints that can stifle our ability to address systemic injustices. This dual dependency leaves us in a precarious position, especially as public trust in institutions erodes and authoritarianism surrounds us.

Global trends and local impacts

Ireland's LGBTQ+ movement is deeply connected to global trends. Far-right tactics imported from abroad now target schools, libraries and public events. Yet, our ability to build international alliances and share strategies remains a key strength. This interconnectedness reinforces the importance of balancing local advocacy with global solidarity.

Looking ahead – where can we go next?

Reclaiming and protecting civil society

Civil society must remain a democratic space where marginalised communities can advocate for justice. To do this, we need to resist disinformation, restrictive regulations and funding conditions that threaten our independence. We must defend self-organised civil society as an essential tool for advancing a collective social justice agenda.

Healing and renewal

Advocacy is hard work, and I've seen how burnout and trauma can impact activists and movements. Healing is not a luxury; it's essential. We need to create space for renewal while building stronger coalitions across communities and movements. As we continue to battle against extremism and a precarious political landscape, we must also take time to heal. The weight of this work can be immense, and I've seen how it takes its toll on our people and movements alike. Healing isn't just about resting; it's about renewing our capacity to fight, to imagine and to create.

Embracing queer joy and imagination

At the heart of this work is queer optimism and queer joy – forces that have carried me through the hardest moments and reminded me why this work matters. Our communities have an incredible ability to build each other up, to create spaces where joy flourishes even in the face of hostility. I've experienced this joy of finding my own voice and providing space and tools that queer young people have used to find their voices. We have celebrated our identities, our campaign wins, our existence – our joy is political and reminds the world that we deserve happiness, dignity and celebration. Joy is not a distraction from the struggle — it is a vital part of it. As we move forward, we must find ways to nurture that joy, to hold each other through the battles and to ensure that our communities remain a space of creativity, care and hope.

Final thought

My advocacy has always been shaped by the margins — the places where exclusion is felt most deeply. Early in my work, I spent time alongside homeless young people and young people seeking asylum. I learned to seek out the margins within our own LGBTQ+ community, recognising that true justice means amplifying the voices of those who are most silenced. This understanding has framed my worldview and shaped my approach to advocacy, where our communities are communities of colour, Muslim communities, disabled communities, queer communities, Traveller and Roma communities, communities of migrants and people seeking asylum. I wrote this book with a queer justice lens, which means I wrote it with all these communities and friends in mind.

The most profound change comes from the power of marginalised communities working together — not just to resist harm but to reimagine what is possible. When we align our struggles, we amplify our strength. I've seen this first hand in coalitions that brought LGBTQ+ youth together with others fighting for dignity and equality.

This understanding has framed my worldview and shaped my approach to advocacy. We shared the same determination to create a world where we are all liberated, and in doing so, we became each other's allies, strategists and protectors.

Love, Organise, Resist.

Conclusion

Figure 9.1: Love, Organise, Resist! Artist and cultural activist Holly Pereira stands in front of her design created with queer elder and lifer Rita Wild and ResiStickers Ireland, which was used in an anti-hate campaign following the Dublin riots

Source: Author's own

References

Alden, W. (2024) 'Defunding dissent: philanthropists have quietly withdrawn funding from grassroots groups that spoke out for Gaza, imperiling a broad range of social justice movements', *Jewish Currents*, 19 December. Available at: https://jewishcurrents.org/defunding-dissent (Accessed: 9 April 2025).

Alinsky, S.D. (1971) *Rules for Radicals: A Practical Primer for Realistic Radicals*, New York: Vintage Books.

Aston, J. (2001) 'Research as relationship', in A.L. Cole and J.G. Knowles (eds) *Lives in Context: The Art of Life History Research*, Walnut Creek, CA: AltaMira Press.

Auerbach, D. (2014) 'When AOL was GayOL: how LGBTQ nerds helped create online life as we know it', Slate.

Ayoub, P. and Paternotte, D. (2019) 'Europe and LGBT rights: a conflicted relationship', in M.J. Bosia, S.M. McEvoy and M. Rahman (eds) *The Oxford Handbook of Global LGBT and Sexual Diversity Politics* [online], Oxford: Oxford University Press. Available at: https://www.oxfordhandbooks.com (Accessed: 8 April 2025).

Bacchi, C. (2009) *Analysing Policy: What's the Problem Represented to Be?*, Frenchs Forest, NSW: Pearson Education.

Bacchi, C. (2012) 'Why study problematizations? Making politics visible', *Open Journal of Political Science*, 2(1): 1–8.

Bailey, S. (2016) 'From invisibility to visibility: a policy archaeology of the introduction of anti-transphobic and anti-homophobic bullying guidelines into the Irish primary education system', *Irish Educational Studies*, 36(1): 25–42.

Barron, M (2013) 'Advocating for LGBT youth: seeking social justice in a culture of individual rights', in A. Mullhall (ed) 'Queering the issue', *Irish University Review*, 43(1): 151–57.

Barron, M. (2016) *Equal Opportunities for All Children: Non-discrimination of Lesbian, Gay, Bisexual, Transgender and Intersex (LGBTI) Children and Young People*. Strasbourg: Council of Europe. Available at: https://edoc.coe.int/en/children-s-rights/7051-equal-opportunities-for-all-children-non-discrimination-of-lesbian-gay-bisexual-transgender-and-intersex-lgbti-children-and-young-people.html (Accessed: 7 April 2025).

Barron, M. (2017) 'BeLonG To and marriage equality', in G. Healy (ed) *Crossing the Threshold: The Story of the Marriage Equality Movement*, Dublin: Merrion Press, pp 292–305.

Barron, M. (2018) 'An overview of the issues relating to the removal of the baptism barrier: removing the baptism barrier is no small thing', *The Irish Times*, 10 May, Available at: https://www.irishtimes.com/opinion/removing-the-baptism-barrier-is-no-small-thing-1.3489449 (Accessed: 22 August 2019).

References

Barron, M. and Bradford, S. (2007) 'Corporeal controls: violence, bodies and young gay men's identities', *Youth and Society*, 39(2): 232–61.

Barron, M. and O'Hagan, L. (2016) 'LGBTI safe and supportive schools', Dublin: Health Services Executive and BeLonG To.

BeLonG To and Equality Authority (2006) 'Making schools safe for LGBTI+ students booklet'

BeLonG To (2007) 'Delivering youth work in lesbian, gay, bisexual and transgender youth groups: a resource for setting up an LGBT youth group with quality guidelines and BeLonG To accreditation scheme', Dublin: Author.

BeLonG To (2008) 'BeLonG To youth services: strategic plan 2008–2011', Dublin: Author.

BeLonG To (2011) 'BeLonG To youth services: strategic plan 2011–2015', Dublin: Author.

BeLonG To (2012) *Annual Review 2012*. Dublin: BeLonG To Youth Services. Available at: https://www.belongto.org/app/uploads/2023/07/Belong-To-Annual-Review-2012-1.pdf (Accessed: 6 April 2025).

Boardman, M. (2024) 'New York club kids, then and now, remember Nelson Sullivan', *Paper Magazine*, Available at: https://www.papermag.com/nelson-sullivan-world-of-wonder#rebelltitem3

Bryan, A. and Mayock, P. (2012) 'Speaking back to dominant constructions of LGBT lives: complexifying "at riskness" for self-harm and suicidality among lesbian, gay, bisexual and transgender youth', *Irish Journal of Anthropology*, 15(2): 8–15.

Bryan, A. and Mayock, P. (2017) 'Supporting LGBT lives? Complicating the suicide consensus in LGBT mental health research', *Sexualities*, 20(1–2): 65–85. Available at: https://doi.org/10.1177/1363460716648099 (Accessed: 6 April 2025).

Bryant, L. and Bryant, K. (2019) 'Memory work', in P. Liamputtong (ed) *Handbook of Research Methods in Health Social Sciences*, Springer Nature, pp 527–40. https://doi.org/10.1007/978-981-10-5251-4_88

Byrne, R. and Devine, D. (2017) '"Catholic schooling with a twist?: a study of faith schooling in the Republic of Ireland during a period of detraditionalisation', *Cambridge Journal of Education*, 48: 461–77.

Burns, J. (2002) 'Campaign by travellers "is a failure"', *The Sunday Times*, 3 November. Available at: https://www.thetimes.com/uk/politics/article/campaign-by-travellers-is-a-failure-mjvm6zmst9x (Accessed: 8 April 2025).

Canning, D. and Reinsborough, P. (2010) *Re:Imagining Change: How to Use Story-Based Strategy to Win Campaigns, Build Movements, and Change the World*. Oakland, CA: PM Press.

Careaga Pérez, G. (2014) 'The protection of LGBTI rights: an uncertain outlook', *SUR: International Journal on Human Rights*, 11(20): 143–9.

Carey, A. (2015) *BeLonG To Yes: Voices from the Marriage Equality Campaign*. Dublin: BeLonG To.

Carroll, A. and Barron, M. (2019) 'Equality Fund report', Dublin: Social Innovation Fund Ireland.

Carty, R.K. (2006) *Party and Parish Pump: Electoral Politics in Ireland*. Vancouver: University of British Columbia Press.

CIVICUS, World Alliance for Citizen Participation (2010) 'Turning principles into practice: a guide to legitimacy, transparency and accountability', Johannesburg, South Africa.

Coolahan, J. (1981) *Irish Education: Its History and Structure*, Dublin: Institute of Public Administration.

Council of Europe (2018) 'Safe at school: education sector responses to violence based on sexual orientation, gender identity/expression or sex characteristics in Europe', Strasburg: Council of Europe Publishing.

Cover, R. (2012) *Queer Youth Suicide, Culture and Identity: Unliveable Lives?*, London: Routledge.

Creswell, J.W. (2009) *Research Design: Qualitative, Quantitative and Mixed Methods Approaches*, Thousand Oaks, CA: Sage Publications.

Crickley, A. and McArdle, O. (2010) 'Community work, community development: reflections 2009', *Working for Change: The Irish Journal of Community Work*, 1: 15–27.

Crotty, W. (1998) 'Democratisation and political development in Ireland', in W.J. Crotty and D.A. Schmitt (eds) *Ireland and the Politics of Change*, London: Routledge, pp 1–26.

Crowley, N. (2011) *A Roadmap for a Strengthened Equality and Human Rights Infrastructure in Ireland*, Equality and Rights Alliance.

Crowley, N. (2015) 'Equality and human rights: an integrated approach', Dublin: Equality and Rights Alliance.

Dalton, E. (2024) 'Parties in Northern Ireland executive agree to extend Britain's ban on puberty blockers', *The Journal*, 11 December. Available at: https://www.thejournal.ie/puberty-blockers-northern-ireland-6568777-Dec2024/ (Accessed: 10 April 2025).

Department of Children and Youth Affairs (2014) *Better Outcomes, Brighter Futures: The National Policy Framework for Children & Young People 2014–2020*. Dublin: Stationery Office.

Department of Children and Youth Affairs (2015) *National Youth Strategy 2015–2020*. Dublin: Government Publications. Available at: https://www.gov.ie/en/policy-information/91394c-youth-affairs/ (Accessed: 6 April 2025).

Department of Children and Youth Affairs (DCYA) (2017) 'LGBTI+ national youth strategy: report of the consultation with young people in Ireland', Dublin: Government Publications.

Department of Community, Rural and Gaeltacht Affairs (2009) *National Drugs Strategy (interim) 2009–2016*. Dublin: Department of Community, Rural and Gaeltacht Affairs. Available at: https://www.citywide.ie/resources/2009-2016-national-drugs-strategy/ (Accessed: 6 April 2025).

Department of Education and Skills (1995) 'Report of the expert advisory group on relationships and sexuality education', Dublin: Government Publications.

Department of Education and Skills (2013a) 'Action plan on bullying', Dublin: Government Publications.

Department of Education and Skills (2013b) 'Anti-bullying procedures for primary and post-primary schools', Dublin: Government Publications.

Department of Education and Skills, Health Service Executive, Gay and Lesbian Equality Network, and BeLonG To Youth Services (2012) *Growing Up LGBT: A Resource for SPHE and RSE*. Dublin: Department of Education and Skill.

Devlin, M. (2003) 'A bit of the "other": media representations of young people's sexuality', *Irish Journal of Sociology*, 12(2): 86–106.

Devlin, M. (2008) 'Youth work and youth policy in the Republic of Ireland 1983–2008: "still haven't found what we're looking for?"', *Youth and Policy*, 100: 41–54.

Dukelow, F. and Considine, M. (2017) *Irish Social Policy: A Critical Introduction* (2nd edn), Bristol: Policy Press.

Dunphy, R. (1997) 'Sexual identities, national identities: the politics of gay law reform in the Republic of Ireland', *Contemporary Politics*, 3(3): 247–65. https://doi.org/10.1080/13569779708449929

Equality Authority (2002) 'Implementing equality for lesbians, gays and bisexuals', Dublin: Equality Authority.

Equality Employment Act (1998) 'No 21/1998', Dublin: Stationery Office.

Equate (2017) Dialogue on Education Reform, Dublin: EQUATE.

Fartukh, A. (2023) 'Fascinating GAZE documentary showcases the history of Dublin's beloved LGBTQ+ bar The George', Dublin: Gay Community News, Available at: https://gcn.ie/gaze-documentary-the-george/

Finnegan, B. (2018) 'Baptismal barrier removal will have particular significance for LGBTs: gay community news', [newsletter], Available at: https://gcn.ie/baptismal-barrier-removal-will-particular-significance-lgbts/ (Accessed: 22 August 2019).

Fisher, W.R. (1984) 'Narration as a human communications paradigm: the case for public moral argument', *Communication Monographs*, 51(March): 1–22.

Foody, M., Murphy, H., Downes, P. and O'Higgins Norman, J. (2018) 'Teachers' self-efficacy and intervention in bullying: the role of empathy', *Irish Educational Studies*, 37(4): 523–37. Available at: https://doi.org/10.1080/03323315.2018.1484290 (Accessed: 6 April 2025).

Foucault, M. (1984) 'Polemics, politics and problematizations, based on an interview conducted by Paul Rabinow', in L. Davis (trans) *Essential works of Foucault*, vol 1, *Ethics*, New York: New Press.

French, Scot A. (1995) '"What is social memory?"' *Southern Cultures*, 2(1): 9–18. Project MUSE, https://dx.doi.org/10.1353/scu.1995.0049

Gay and Lesbian Equality Network (GLEN)/Nexus (1995) 'Poverty: lesbians and gay men; the economic and social effects of discrimination', Dublin: Combat Poverty Agency.

Gender Recognition Act 2015 (Act No. 25/2015) (Ir.). Available at: https://www.irishstatutebook.ie/eli/2015/act/25/enacted/en/html (Accessed: 6 April 2025).

Global Philanthropy Project (2024) *2021–2022 Global Resources Report: Government & Philanthropic Support for LGBTI Communities*. Available at: https://globalresourcesreport.org/ (Accessed: 8 April 2025).

Goffman, E. (1963) *Stigma: Notes on the Management of Spoiled Identity*, New York: Simon & Schuster.

Gordon, A., Hite, K. and Jara, D. (2020) 'Haunting and thinking from the Utopian margins: conversation with Avery Gordon', *Memory Studies*, 13: 337–46. 10.1177/1750698020914017.

Haiven, M. and Khasnabish, A. (2014) *The Radical Imagination: Social Movement Research in the Age of Austerity*. London: Zed Books.

Harvey, B. (2012) 'Downsizing the community sector: changes in employment and services in the voluntary and community sector in Ireland, 2008–2012', Dublin: Irish Congress of Trade Unions, Available at: https://www.drugsandalcohol.ie/17025/

Healy, G. (ed) (2017a) *Crossing the Threshold: The Story of Marriage Equality in Ireland*, Dublin: Merrion Press.

Healy, G. (2017b) 'Good Practice Guide on Values Based Campaigning for Legal Recognition of Same-Sex Partnerships'. Council of Europe.

Health Service Executive (HSE) (2005) 'Reach out: national strategy for action on suicide prevention 2005–2014', Dublin: HSE.

Higgins, A., Doyle, L., Downes, C., Murphy, R., Sharek, D., DeVries, J. et al (2016) 'The LGBTIreland report: national study of the mental health and wellbeing of lesbian, gay, bisexual, transgender and intersex people in Ireland', Dublin: BeLonG To and GLEN.

Higgins, A., Downes, C., O'Sullivan, K., DeVries, J., Molloy, R., Monahan, M., Keogh, B., Doyle, L., Begley, T. and Corcoran, P. (2024) *Being LGBTQI+ in Ireland 2024: The National Study on the Mental Health and Wellbeing of the LGBTQI+ Communities in Ireland*. Dublin: Belong To – LGBTQ+ Youth: Ireland. Available at: https://www.drugsandalcohol.ie/40915/ (Accessed: 6 April 2025).

Hurley, L. (1992) *The Historical Development of Irish Youth Work (1850–1985)*, Dublin: Irish YouthWork Centre.

Hurley, L. and Treacy, D. (1993) *Models of Youth Work: A Sociological Framework*, Dublin: YouthWork Press.

Hyland, Á. and Bocking, B. (2016) 'Religion, education and religious education in Irish schools', in Berglund, J., Shanneik, Y. and Bocking, B. (eds) *Religious Education in a Global-Local World. Boundaries of Religious Freedom: Regulating Religion in Diverse Societies*, vol 4. Springer, Cham. https://doi.org/10.1007/978-3-319-32289-6_8

Inglis, T. (1998) *Moral Monopoly: The Rise and Fall of the Catholic Church in Modern Ireland* (2nd edn), Dublin: University College Dublin Press.

International Foundation for Electoral Systems (IFES) (2015) 'Country Profile: Ireland'. Available at: https://www.electionguide.org/countries/id/105/ (Accessed: 7 April 2025).

Irish Council for Civil Liberties (ICCL) (1990) 'Equality now for lesbians and gay men', Dublin: ICCL. Available at: https://www.iccl.ie/wp-content/uploads/2017/11/Equality-Now-for-Lesbians-and-Gay-Men1990pdf.pdf (Accessed: 8 April 2025).

Irish Council for Civil Liberties (2024) *"That's Not Your Role": State Funding and Advocacy in the Irish Community, Voluntary and Non-Profit Sector*. Dublin: ICCL. Available at: https://www.iccl.ie/wp-content/uploads/2024/04/Thats-Not-Your-Role-WEB.pdf (Accessed: 8 April 2025).

Irish Examiner (2006) 'Schools could be liable for bullying', Irish Examiner, 25 October. Available at: https://www.irishexaminer.com/news/arid-30282564.html (Accessed: 9 April 2025).

Irish Examiner (2009, May 12) 'Taoiseach makes "long overdue" state apology', Retrieved 8 April 2025, from https://www.irishexaminer.com/news/arid-20093898.html

Irish Times (2008a) 'President links sectarianism and homophobia', *The Irish Times*, 31 October. Available at: [URL] (Accessed: 9 April 2025).

Irish Times (2008b) 'You shall go to the ball', 11 October, Available at: https://www.irishtimes.com/life-and-style/you-shall-go-to-the-ball-1.894652?mode=print&ot=example.AjaxPageLayout.ot

Irish Times (2009) 'LGBT youth at risk of self-harm and suicide', *The Irish Times*, 11 June.

Irish Times (2011) 'Taoiseach's speech on Cloyne motion', 20 July, Available at: https://www.irishtimes.com/news/taoiseach-s-speech-on-cloyne-motion-1.880466

Jenkins-Smith, H. and Sabatier, P. (1993a) 'The study of public policy processes', in P. Sabatier and H. Jenkins-Smith (eds) *Policy Change and Learning: An Advocacy Coalition Approach*, Boulder, CO: Westview Press, pp 1–9.

Jenkins-Smith, H. and Sabatier, P. (1993b) 'The dynamics of policy-oriented learning', in P. Sabatier and H. Jenkins-Smith (eds) *Policy Change and Learning: An Advocacy Coalition Approach*, Boulder, CO: Westview Press, pp 41–56.

Jessop, B. (2004) 'Multi-level governance and multi-level metagovernance: changes in the European Union as integral moments in the transformation and reorientation of contemporary statehood', in I. Bache and M. Flinders (eds) *Multi-Level Governance*, Oxford: Oxford University Press, pp 49–74.

Kemmis, S. and Wilkinson, M. (1998) 'Participatory action research and the study of practice', in B. Atweh, S. Kemmis and P. Weeks (eds) *Action Research in Practice: Partnerships for Social Justice in Education*, London: Routledge, pp 21–36.

Kerrigan, P. (2024) *Reeling in the Queers: Tales of Ireland's LGBTQ Past*, Dublin: New Island Books.

Kingdon, J.W. (1984) *Agendas, Alternatives and Public Policies*, New York: Longman.

Kosciw, J.G. and Pizmony-Levy, O. (2013) *Fostering a Global Dialogue about LGBT Youth and Schools: Proceedings from a Meeting of the Global Network Combating Homophobic and Transphobic Prejudice and Violence in Schools*, New York: GLSEN.

Lukomnik, J., Frazer, S., Cabral Grinspan, M. and Nepon, E. (2024) 'The state of trans organizing (3rd edition)', Global Philanthropy Project.

Langley, E. (2024) 'I research how people creatively express queer joy online – here are three tips for trying it yourself', *The Conversation*, 28 March. Available at: https://theconversation.com/i-research-how-people-creatively-express-queer-joy-online-here-are-three-tips-for-trying-it-yourself-224306 (Accessed: 7 April 2025).

Lynch, K. and Lodge, A. (2002) *Equality and Power in Schools: Redistribution, Recognition and Representation*, London: RoutledgeFalmer.

Lyons, T. (2013) 'Investment in BeLonG To youth services for lesbian, gay, bisexual and transgender young people: a One Foundation case study', Dublin: One Foundation.

Manor, J. (1999) 19991803781, English, Miscellaneous, USA, 0-8213-4470-6, Washington, DC, The political economy of democratic decentralization (x + 133 pp.), World Bank, The political economy of democratic decentralization.

Mayock, P., Kitching, K. and Morgan, M. (2007) 'RSE in the context of SPHE: an assessment of the challenges to full implementation of the programme in post-primary schools', Dublin: Crisis Pregnancy Agency.

Mayock, P., Bryan, A., Carr, N. and Kitching, K. (2009) 'Supporting LGBT lives: a study of the mental health and well-being of lesbian, gay, bisexual and transgender people', Dublin: BeLonG To Youth Services and Gay and Lesbian Equality Network.

McAleer, M.C. (2018) *An Oral History of the National Youth Council of Ireland 1967–2017: 50 Voices from the Last 50 Years*, Dublin: National Youth Council of Ireland.

References

McAlinden, A.-M. (2013) 'An inconvenient truth: barriers to truth recovery in the aftermath of institutional child abuse in Ireland', *Legal Studies*, 33(2): 189–214.

McArdle, O. (2020) 'Rocking the boat while staying in it: connecting ends and means in radical community work', *Community Development Journal*, 56. 10.1093/cdj/bsaa021 (Accessed: 6 April 2025).

McBeth, M.K., Jones, M.D. and Shanahan, E.A. (2017) 'The narrative policy framework', in P.A. Sabatier and C.M. Weible (eds) *Theories of the Policy Process*, New York: Routledge, pp 173–213.

McCormack, O. and Gleeson, J. (2010) 'Attitudes of parents of young men towards the inclusion of sexual orientation and homophobia on the Irish post-primary curriculum', *Gender and Education*, 22(4): 385–400.

McDonagh, P. (2020) 'Abortion, gay rights, and the National Gay Federation in Ireland 1982–1983', *Journal of the History of Sexuality*, 29(1): 1–27. Available at: https://muse.jhu.edu/article/744872 (Accessed: 9 April 2025).

McDonagh, P. (2021) *Gay and Lesbian Activism in the Republic of Ireland, 1973–93*. London: Bloomsbury Academic.

McDonagh, P.J. and Kerrigan, P. (2021) '"Cherishing all the children of the nation equally": gay youth organisation and activism in Ireland', in D. Marshall (ed) *Queer Youth Histories, Genders and Sexualities in History*, London: Palgrave Macmillan, pp 169–85.

McDonald, D. (2004) 'Church anger as gay campaign targets schools', *The Sunday Times*, 22 February, Available at: https://www.thetimes.co.uk/article/church-anger-as-gay-campaign-targets-schools-cfw5snvsm02

McInerney, C. (2014) *Challenging Times, Challenging Administration: The Role of Public Administration in Producing Social Justice in Ireland*, Manchester: Manchester University Press.

Minihan, M. (2015) 'Referendum No vote would deny citizens equal rights, Kenny says', *The Irish Times*, 7 May. Available at: https://www.irishtimes.com/news/politics/referendum-no-vote-would-deny-citizens-equal-rights-kenny-says-1.2203591 (Accessed: 7 April 2025).

Minton, S.J., Dahl, T., O'Moore, A.M. and Tuck, D. (2008) 'An exploratory survey of the experiences of homophobic bullying among lesbian, gay, bisexual and transgendered young people in Ireland', *Irish Educational Studies*, 27(2): 177–91.

Murphy, S. (2018) 'From 1983 to the Fairview March Memorial 2018', *Gay Community News*, [newsletter] 31 March 2018, Available at: https://gcn.ie/1983-fairview-march-memorial-2018/

National Youth Policy Committee (1984) *Final Report*, Dublin: Stationery Office. Available at: https://www.lenus.ie/handle/10147/45430 (Accessed: 6 April 2025).

Nolan, A. and Larkan, F. (2015) 'Vectors of transnationality in the adoption of a liberal public health response to HIV and AIDS', *Global Social Policy*, 16(3): 253–67.

Norman, J. and Galvin, M. (2006) 'Straight talk: an investigation of attitudes and experiences of homophobic bullying in second-level schools', Dublin: Dublin City University, Centre for Educational Evaluation.

O'Brien, C. (2018, October 15) Group against Baptism bar derailed after complaints. *The Irish Times*. Retrieved 8 April 2025, from https://www.irishtimes.com/news/education/group-against-baptism-bar-derailed-after-complaints-1.3660330

O'Connor, N. and Ketola, M. (2018) 'Enabling citizens, powering civil society: active citizenship supported by a thriving, independent community, voluntary and charity sector', Dublin: The Wheel.

O'Kelly, C. (2004) 'Being Irish', *Government and Opposition*, 39(3): 504–20. https://doi.org/10.1111/j.1477-7053.2004.00130.x

O'Higgins Norman, J. and Galvin, M. (2006) Straight Talk: An Investigation of Attitudes and Experiences of Homophobic Bullying in Second-Level Schools.

Office of the Minister for Children and Youth Affairs and BeLonG To (2010) 'Addressing homophobia: guidelines for the youth sector in Ireland', Dublin: Government Publications.

Pal, L.A. (2014) *Beyond Policy Analysis: Public Issue Management in Turbulent Times* (5th edn), Toronto: Nelson Education.

Pross, A.P. (1995) 'Pressure groups: talking chameleons', in M.S. Whittington and G. Williams (eds) *Canadian Politics in the 1990s*, Toronto: Nelson Canada, pp 252–75.

Reygan, F. and Moane, G. (2014) 'Religious homophobia: the experiences of a sample of lesbian, gay, bisexual and transgender (LGBT) people in Ireland', *Culture and Religion*, 15(3): 298–312.

RTÉ (2017) 'Remembering Ireland's early AIDS history', [TV programme] 29 November, Available at: https://www.rte.ie/eile/brainstorm/2017/1129/923640-remembering-irelands-early-aids-history/

Rubin, H.J. and Rubin, I.S. (2012) *Qualitative Interviewing: The Art of Hearing Data* (2nd edn), Thousand Oaks, CA: SAGE Publications.

Ryan, G.W. and Bernard, H.R. (2003) 'Techniques to identify themes', *Field Methods*, 15(1): 85–109.

Sabatier, P. (1988) 'An advocacy coalition framework of policy change and the role of policy-oriented learning therein', *Policy Sciences*, 21(2–3): 129–68.

Sabatier, P. (1993) 'Policy change over a decade or more', in P. Sabatier and H. Jenkins-Smith (eds) *Policy Change and Learning: An Advocacy Coalition Approach*, Boulder, CO: Westview Press, pp 13–39.

Sarma, K. (2007) 'Drug use amongst lesbian, gay, bisexual and transgender young adults in Ireland', Dublin: BeLonG To.

Shannon, G. (2013) 'Eighth report of the Special Rapporteur on Child Protection', Dublin: Stationery Office/Department of Children and Youth Affairs.

Snediker, M.D. (2008) *Queer Optimism: Lyric Personhood and Other Felicitous Persuasions*, University of Minnesota Press.

Spillane, M. (2015) 'How the Irish became the world's leading gay activists', *The Nation*, 15 June.

Stielau, A. (2015) 'Towards a queer futurity: the utopian impulse in the work of Athi-Patra Ruga and Milumbe Haimbe', *Agenda*, 29(1): 127–39.

TASC (2024) *Civil society under duress: Assessing the impact of political, financial, and governance pressures on CSOs*, Dublin: Think-tank for Action on Social Change. Available at: https://www.tasc.ie/publications/civil-society-under-duress-assessing-the-impact-of-political/ (Accessed: 8 April 2025).

The Irish Examiner (2002) 'Citizen Traveller Campaign criticises government over caravan confiscation powers', 4 November. Available at: [URL] (Accessed: 8 April 2025).

Towards Standards Ad Hoc Group (2008) *Towards Standards for Quality Community Work: An All-Ireland Statement of Values, Principles and Work Standards*. Galway: Community Workers' Co-operative. Available at: https://www.cwi.ie/wp-content/uploads/2016/03/All-Ireland-Standards-for-Community-Work.pdf (Accessed: 6 April 2025).

Thompson, N. (2003) *Promoting Equality: Challenging Discrimination and Oppression* (2nd edn), Basingstoke: Palgrave Macmillan.

Tiernan, H. (2021) 'Remembering Ireland's iconic drag spectacular Alternative Miss Ireland', Dublin: Gay Community News, Available at: https://gcn.ie/remembering-alternative-miss-ireland-part-1/

Tiernan, H. (2024) 'The history of H.A.M.: the iconic club that permanently altered Dublin's queer nightlife', Dublin: GCN, Available at: https://gcn.ie/the-history-of-h-a-m-dublins-iconic-club/

United Nations Educational, Scientific and Cultural Organization (UNESCO) (2012) 'Education sector responses to homophobic bullying', Paris: UNESCO.

United Nations Educational, Scientific and Cultural Organization (UNESCO) (2016) 'Out in the open: education sector responses to violence based on sexual orientation and gender identity/expression', Paris: UNESCO.

Vaid, U. (1995) *Virtual Equality: The Mainstreaming of Gay and Lesbian Liberation*. New York: Anchor Books.

Walker, S. (2012) 'St Petersburg bans "homosexual propaganda"', *The Guardian*, 12 March. Available at: https://www.theguardian.com/world/2012/mar/12/st-petersburg-bans-homosexual-propaganda (Accessed: 7 April 2025).

Warfield, F. (2018, October 18) Seanad Éireann Debate.

Weeks, J. (1977) *Coming Out: Homosexual Politics in Britain from the Nineteenth Century to the Present*, Quartet Books.

Weible, C.M., Sabatier, P.A. and McQueen, K. (2009) 'Themes and variations: taking stock of the advocacy coalition framework', *Policy Studies Journal*, 37(1): 121–40.

Wilson, A.E. (2024) 'I research how people creatively express queer joy online – here are three tips for trying it yourself', *The Conversation*. Available at: https://theconversation.com/i-research-how-people-creatively-express-queer-joy-online-here-are-three-tips-for-trying-it-yourself-224306 (Accessed: 9 April 2025).

Whyte, B.J. (2018, October 14) 'Fix "ambiguous" electoral act, says baptism barrier campaigner', *The Sunday Business Post*. Retrieved 8 April 2025, from https://www.businesspost.ie/news-focus/fix-ambiguous-electoral-act-says-baptism-barrier-campaigner/

Young, I.M. (1990) *Justice and the Politics of Difference*, Princeton: Princeton University Press.

Youth Work Act (2001) 'No 42/2001', Dublin: Stationery Office. Available at: http://www.irishstatutebook.ie/eli/2001/act/42/enacted/en/html

Index

A

academic counter narratives 90–5, 99
advocacy 53–4, 64, 76, 119–20
  documenting LGBTQ+ histories 54
  healing and renewal 167
  importance of 158
  intersectionality 98
  long-term strategies 89–90
  models and strategies 166
  responding to crises 99
  rigorous evidence 77
  state funding 159
  strategic reframing 135
  weaponisation of regulation against 154–7, 162–3
  youth voices 98
advocacy coalition framework 19
agenda setting framework 19
Alliance Defending Freedom 160
alliances 123–36
  in the education sector 125–6
  international 126–7
  minority community youth organisations 124
  relationships with politicians 127–35, 135–6
  in the youth sector 123–5
Alternative Miss Ireland (AMI) 6
Andrews, Barry 117, 124–5, 127, 148
angel shift 116, 119
anti-LGBTI organisations 160
anti-NGOism 94, 157
anti-trans movement 160
Aston, Jacquie 13
austerity 158
autoethnography 15–16

B

baptism barrier 128, 138, 154–6
Barnardo's 131
Barron, Michael 80, 81, 99, 101, 136, 137, 138
BeLonG Teeny Bop 107
BeLonG To 7, 8, 30, 48, 72, 74
  'Addressing homophobia: guidelines for the youth sector' 124
  alternative future 119
  campaigns 112–13, 119
  child protection narrative 130–1, 135
  community support 69
  contribution to Marriage Equality Referendum 128–30, 132, 133–4
  credibility 76
  cultural activism 109–11
  drug use report 75
  early manifesto 106
  experiences of members 79–83, 97
  founding of 29
  framing issues 99
  gay poster 110–11
  International Day Against Homophobia and Transphobia 33–4
  leadership 63–4
  messaging 129
  online strategy 134
  poster campaign 113
  sense of belonging 105–6
  social change 84, 112–13
  'Start-Up Pack' 65–6
  strategic plans 90, 112–13
  strategy 65–6
  youth empowerment training 84
BeLonG To Yes
  Campaign for Marriage Equality 109
  coalition 131, 134, 135
#BeLonGToYES coalition 131
'Better outcomes, brighter future' 34–5, 87
body dysphoria 80
Braun, V. and Clarke, V. 15
BreakOut 86, 98
Brien, Gillian 7, 131
Bruton, Richard 128, 138
Bryan, A. and Mayock, P. 92
bullying 69, 70, 110
  anti-bullying procedures 88–9
  see also homophobic bullying; transphobic bullying
Buttimer, Jerry 127
Byrne, Suzy 47, 48, 126

C

Canning, D. and Reinsborough, P 111
Captain Cathal Ryan Scholarship Award (2009) 126
Care Amendment referendum 157
Carey, Anna 76
Carroll, Dr David 7, 71, 80, 89–90, 131
Casement, Roger 41
Catholic Church 37–8
  clerical sex abuse scandal 117, 118
  deferment and obedience to 146
  dominance and influence of 41–2
  end of deference to 117
  influence in schools 42, 49–50
Charities Regulator 161
child abuse 31
Child and Family Agency 161

Child and Family Research Centre (UNESCO) 131
Child and Family Support Agency 147
child protection 129, 130–1, 135, 147
child sexual abuse 62
Children's Research Centre 74
children's rights 31, 129, 147
Children's Rights Alliance 129, 131
Christian Broadcasting Network 160
Christian churches 156
Church of Ireland 154, 155, 156
Citizen Traveller Campaign 157
CIVICUS World Alliance for Citizen Participation 63
Civil Partnership Act (2010) 33
civil service 147–9
civil society 10–12
  advocacy innovation 77
  central role of 164
  defence of 153–64
  definitions 10
  funding constraints 158–9
  government controls and limitations on 157–62
  independence 157–8
  minority-led 150–1
  partnerships 12
  partnerships with the state 149
  philanthropy 159–61, 163
  policy development 143–4
  power of 165–6
  public policy development 150
  reclaiming and protecting 167
  regulatory burden 161
  state investment 89
  strategic and planned approach 89
  weaponisation of regulation 154–7, 162–3
  see also LGBTQ+ civil society; self-organised civil society
civil society organisations 63
'Civil society under duress' report (TASC, 2024) 161–2
class 7
class analysis 124
clerical sexual abuse 33
Cloyne Report (2011) 33, 117–18
coalition building 77, 87, 98, 123, 131, 135
Collins, Eoin 66, 67, 68, 73
Combat Poverty Agency 67
community development 67–8
Community Foundation of Ireland report (2018) 158
community work 84–5
Community Workers' Co-operative 85
community youth work 83–6, 144–5, 151
Companies Registration Office 161

'Connecting for life' strategy 35–6
control mythologies 111
Coolahan, Professor John 49
Cork Traveller Visibility Group 2
Council of Europe (CoE) 10, 44, 127
creative activism 110
Criminal Law Amendment Act (1885) 41, 44
critical social education model 84, 86
Crotty, W. 10
Crowley, Niall 66–7, 69, 70, 74, 114, 158–9
cultural activism 109–11, 119, 145
Cunningham, Mary 63, 131

D

Day, Geoff 60
decolonisation 18
decriminalisation 28, 38, 41, 47, 66, 68, 87
democracy 153–4, 164
Department of Children and Youth Affairs (Ireland) 126
Department of Education and Science 146
Department of Education and Skills 38, 88
  Action Plan on Bullying 34, 70, 74, 87–8, 90, 94, 99
  Growing Up LGBT: A Resource for SPHE and RSE 96
devil shift 116
Devlin, Maurice 45, 52
dirty tricks campaign 154–6
documentary analysis 15
drugs 74–5
Dublin Lesbian and Gay Youth Group 47
Dublin North Inner City Drugs Task Force Strategy 75
Dublin Pride Festival 107, 108
Dublin Statement 34
Dunne, Kieran 5

E

Education and Welfare (2000) 70
education system *see* schools
Electoral Act 155–6
Employment Equality Act (1998) 68
Empowering People in Care (EPIC) 131
Equal Status Act (2000) 68–9, 87
equality 19
Equality Authority 73
Equality Employment Act (1998) 28, 49
equality, Irish tradition of 114
equality mainstreaming 115, 145
Equality (Miscellaneous Provisions) Act (2015) 36
Equality Status Act (2000) 29
EQUATE 154–6
EU Presidency LGBT Youth and Social Inclusion Conference (2013) 34

European Court of Human Rights 44
European Union Agency for Fundamental Rights 156
European Youth Forum 127
evidence base 72–6, 77
    drug policy 74–5
    early stage 73
    evidence gathering 73
    mental health 75–6
    policy change 74
    'Poverty, lesbians and gay men: the economic and social effects of discrimination' report (1995) 73
    research 74
    research ethics code 73
    seminar 74

F

Fairview Park 43
Family Amendment referendum 157
Family Solidarity 39, 116
far-right groups 4, 12, 156, 161–2, 163, 166
far-right ideologies 3, 153
Farrell, Colin 110
Fennelly, Dr Ken 155
Fine Gael-Labour coalition 146–7
    Programme for Government 147
Finnegan, Brian 64–5, 65, 69
Fiona (case study) 97
Fisher, W.R. 111
Fitzgerald, Frances 117, 127, 147, 148
Fitzgerald, Garret 141–2
Flynn, Bishop Thomas 39
Flynn, Declan 43
Focus Ireland 6
Focus on the Family 160
Foróige 131
Forum on Patronage and Pluralism 49
Frayne, Sean 131

G

Gaffney, Caoimhe 108–9
Garda Vetting 161
Gay and Lesbian Equality Network (GLEN) see GLEN
Gay and Lesbian Visions of Ireland: Towards the Twenty-First Century (Collins & O'Carroll) 112
Gay Health Action 43
gay identity 66
Gay, Lesbian & Straight Education Network (GLSEN) 126
Gay Men's Health Project 7
Gay Prom 107–8, 119
Gay Switchboard 47
Gaydar 62
gender dysphoria 80

gender ideology 4
Gender Recognition Act (2015) 35, 83
General Data Protection Regulations (GDPR) 161
Gleeson, Brian 134
GLEN 31, 67, 128
Global Philanthropy Project 160
global trends 167
Goffman, E. 111
Goodwin, Tony 155
Gordon, A. 11–12
governance 19
Gowran, Sandra 88, 126
Growing up Gay 32, 104–6, 109

H

Haiven, M. and Khasnabish, A. 112
Hannigan, Dominic 127
Harvey, Brian 158
haunting 11, 18, 40–1, 51
Headstrong 131
healing 167
Health and Safety Authority 161
Health Information and Quality Authority 161
Health Promotion 125
Health Service Executive see HSE
Heffernan, Aaron 134
Herrick, Liam 155–6
Hirschfeld Centre 45
HIV/AIDS 43
homophobia 11, 22, 28, 32
    mental health 72, 75–6
    in schools 49
homophobic bullying 29, 30, 69–70, 89, 118
    government programme 33
    religion 37–8
    in schools 36–7, 50, 70, 74, 147
    seminar (2006) 30
    Stop Homophobic Bullying campaign 30
homosexuality 44
    Catholic teaching 42
    criminalisation of 41
    decriminalisation of 44
    moral panic 39
hormone blockers 81
HSE 71, 161
    investments and funding 71
    National Office for Suicide Prevention 60, 65, 72, 75–6, 89, 96
human rights 19
Hurley, L. and Treacy, D. 84

I

IGLYO 46, 47, 126
ILGA-Europe 126
illegality 2

independence 117
IndividualiTy 80–3, 97, 98
Ingles, Roisin 107–8
Inglis, Tom 41
Institute of Guidance Counsellors 131
International Association of Suicide Prevention Conference (2007) 60–1
International Day against Homophobia and Transphobia 33–4
International Lesbian, Gay, Bisexual, Transgender, Queer and Intersex Youth and Student Organisation *see* IGLYO
intersectionality 18, 98
Irish constitution 41–2, 43, 44
Irish Council for Civil Liberties (ICCL) 46, 128
  'Equality now for lesbians and gay men' report (1990) 50–1
  'That's Not Your Role' report (2024) 159
Irish Refugee Council 6
Irish Society for the Prevention of Cruelty to Children 131
The Irish Times 72, 133, 155–6

K

Kavanagh, James 121
Kelleher, Aoife 104, 134
Kenny, Enda 118, 133, 135
Kenny, Lisa 137
Keogh, Bernard 45
Keoghan, Barry 110
Kershaw, Alison 133
Kingdon, John 93, 142, 144
Kirby, Simone 110
Knights of St Columbanus 146

L

Larkin, Junior 47
Lavigne, Danielle (case study) 79–83, 97
legitimacy 63–6, 76
LGBT Asylum Seeker and Refugee Project 32
LGBT Noise 129
LGBT Youth and Social Inclusion Conference (2013) 126
LGBTQ+ civil society 4, 22, 73
  activist tradition 93
  advocacy 72
  authenticity 63
  community youth work 83–4
  engagement in education system 93–5
  engaging with politicians 127–8
  evidence gathering 74
  hostility and risk 94
  mental health policy 90
  narrative change 145
  politicians 147–8
  social change 145
  state investment in 89
LGBTQ+ community
  advocacy for social justice 92
  building the evidence base *see* evidence base
  civil society groups 63–4, 73
  global recognition 62
  HIV/AIDS crisis 43
  identity 42–3
  internet and technology 62
  investment 72
  mainstreaming 115–16
  mobility 96
  'at-risk' group 71
  social media 62
  solidarity 98
  tackling harms 92
  targets of extremists 53
LGBTQ+ rights 3–4, 10
  ICCL report (1990) 50–1
  inherited British laws 41
  legislation 44
  opponents of 39, 44, 116
  opportunities 64
  policy implementation 96–8
  strategies for change 90
LGBTQ+ Safe and Supportive Schools model 35, 96, 125
LGBTQ+ youth
  academic counter narratives 90–5, 99
  activism 45–7
  advocacy campaigns 109
  advocacy discourses 92
  advocacy for social justice 92
  building a foundation for empowerment 130
  building the infrastructure 65–6
  civil society organisations 11
  country-wide network 85–6
  discrimination and stereotyping 52
  as drivers of change 130
  engagement in education system 94–5
  framing of issues 66–72
  government policy 8
  growth of 66
  historical context 40–5
  identity 106
  intersectional nature of 87
  legacy of criminalisation and stigmatisation 51
  life experiences 34–5
  Marriage Equality Referendum 129
  movement 9
  negative images of 92
  network of groups 130
  as an oppressed group 111
  optimism *see* queer optimism

policy framing 93
policy integration 86–9
presence in society 10
ramifications of Catholic teachings 42
risk and violence 8
stigma and stereotyping 39–40
strategic framing 76–7
strategic persistence 77
systemic barriers 166
visibility of 61–2, 64–5
weaponisation of morality against 54
youth empowerment project 96
Lil Nas X 110–11, 120
Logan, Emily 40, 81
Lovett, Ann 43
Lyons, John 127

M

Madonna 5
Madrigal-Borloz, Victor 4
mainstreaming 115–16
Making Schools Safe for LGBT Young People 109
marginalised communities 153, 158, 164, 168
marriage equality 38–9
Marriage Equality Act (2015) 35, 87
Marriage Equality group 30–1, 128
Marriage Equality Referendum (2015) 35, 72, 86, 111, 113, 123
  anti-equality campaign 134
  BeLonG To's contribution 128–30, 132, 133–4
  'Bring your family with you' film 134
  influence of young people 132
  'It's in your hand's' film 132
  McAleese's influence 132–3
  social media 134
  voter turnout 132, 133–4
Marrinan, Jack 43–4
McAleese, Justin 132
McAleese, Martin 132, 137
McAleese, President Mary 61, 69–70, 132–3, 135–6, 137
McAlinden, Anne-Marie 118
McArdle, Dr Oonagh 67–8, 85
McBeth et al 114
McCabe, Ruth 134
McDowell, Michael 157
McGrattan, Enda 107
McInerney, C. 158
McKenny, Lisa 131
McKinney, Ciaran 60
McLoughlin, Karen 137
McVeigh, Fran 7
medication 37
memory work 2
mental health 71–2, 75–6
Mhaol, Gráinne 41

Migrant Rights Centre 124, 131
Minnesotans United for All Families 130
minority communities 153, 157
Moloney, Sinéad 37
Moore, Phil 47
Murphy Commission Report 117

N

Nanci, Jaime 47, 99, 104, 136
narrative change 145
narrative policy framework 19–20
The Nation 132
National Action Plan on Bullying 34, 70, 74, 87–8, 90, 94, 99
National Association of Principals and Deputy Principals 126
National Drugs Strategy (2009) 75, 87
National Drugs Task Force 157
National Gay Federation (NGF) Youth Group 45–7, 46
National Network of LGBTQ+ Youth Services 31
National Office for Suicide Prevention 60, 65, 72, 75–6, 89, 96
National Parents Council 38
National Policy Framework for Children and Young People 2014–20 34–5
National Strategy for Action on Suicide Prevention (2005) 87
National Youth Council of Ireland (NYCI) 38, 45, 46, 124, 126, 131
National Youth Policy Committee 83
National Youth Strategy 2015–20 35, 87
National Youth Work Advisory Committee 124, 157
National Youth Work Development Plan (2003) 29
Nolan, A. and Larkan, F. 43
Norris, David 44, 46, 121, 127
nuclear family 41

O

O'Brien, Dr Carol-Anne 7, 48, 88, 126
O'Brien, Jamie 78
O'Connell, Joan 48
O'Connor, N. and Ketola, M, 158, 159
O'Connor, Sinéad 5, 26
Offences against the Person Act (1861) 41, 44
O'Higgins, Chief Justice 44
One Foundation 89, 126
oppression 18
optimism 107
  see also queer optimism
Opus Dei 146
O'Reilly, Oisín 126
Organization for Security and Co-operation in Europe (OSCE) 126

OutYouth 6, 48
'OutYouth report' (1998) 48–9

P

Parents Enquiry 47
partnerships
  civil society and state 149
  politics and 146–9, 151
Pavee Point 67, 124, 131
Pereira, Holly 169
Pérez, Gloria Careaga 41
philanthropy 159–61, 163, 166–7
Pobal 161
policy change 141–52
policy communities 14, 20, 148
policy development 87–8
policy entrepreneur 144
politicians 127–35, 135–6
politics, partnerships and 146–9, 151
poverty 67
Prendiville, Patricia 16, 126
problematising 20
puberty blockers 2, 4
public moral arguments 111, 116
public policy theory 144
public service champions 148–9

Q

qualitative interviewing 13–15
queer futurity 18
queer joy 18, 107, 167–8
queer optimism 104–22, 167–8
  cultural activism 109–11
  effecting policy change 114–16
  envisioning and imagination 112–14
  independence 117
  movement building 108
  narrative chain 108
  policy solutions 108
queer scene 6
queer youth *see* LGBTQ+ youth
Quigley, Anna 7, 63, 64, 106, 131
  youth work 84
Quinn, Ruairí 49, 88, 126, 127, 128
  on the Department of Education and Science 146

R

radical community work 85, 86
radical imagination 112
radical pragmatism 85, 86, 98
Rafter, Jean 7
Ratzinger, Cardinal 50
Reachout National Strategy for Action on Suicide Prevention 30, 71
Register of Lobbying 161
regulation 154–7
regulation, weaponisation of 154–7, 162–3

Reilly, James 128
Report of the Commission to Inquire into Child Abuse *see* Ryan Report
resilience 136
resistance 77
ResiStickers Ireland 169
Revenue Commissioners 161
Rodgers, Anna 104
Rodgers, Hugh 104, 134
Roe, Ger 7, 131
Roma community 2
Rubin, H.J. and Rubin, I.S. 13
Russell, Roweena 126
Russian LGBT Network 127
Ryan, Danielle 126
Ryan, Declan 89, 126
Ryan Report 117, 118, 146, 147

S

Sabatier, P. and Jenkins-Smith, H. 142
schools
  baptism barrier 49, 51
  Catholic ethos 49–50
  Catholic primary school 49–50
  homophobic and transphobic attitudes 52
  homophobic and transphobic bullying 36–7, 49, 50, 70, 74, 147
  influence of Catholic Church 42, 49–50
  secularising 118
  violence in 36–7, 38–9, 42, 68–9
self-harm 30, 60, 71, 72
self-organised civil society 10–12
self-organised communities 59
self-organised community model 141–52
  civil society 143–4
  community youth work 144–5, 151
  limiting civil society 157–62
  minority-led civil society 150–1
  multiple windows and agendas 149–50, 151–2
  narrative change 145, 151
  politics and partnerships 146–9, 151
Sexual Orientation, Gender Identity and Expression, and Sex Characteristics (SOGIESC) 127
Shannon, Geoffrey 147
Sheehan, Brian 88, 126
shoehorning 67
ShoutOut 34
Snediker, Michael 106
So Gay! Campaign 29, 38
social change 83–4, 117, 119, 145, 161–2
  campaigns 112–13
social justice 107, 156
  pursuit of 52–4
social memory 18

Special Rapporteur on Child
  Protection 147
SPHE programme 29, 74
  'Growing up LGBT in Ireland'
    curriculum 34
Spillane, M. 132
Stand Up!
  Don't Stand for Homophobic
    Bullying 109, 110
  LGBTQ+ Awareness Week 32, 109, 122
  Support Your LGBT Friends 109
  video 33
Standards in Public Office Commission
  (SIPO) 154–6
state, the
  church-state relations 118
  investment in LGBTQ+ civil society 89
  neglect 53–4
  partnerships with civil society 149
stigma 18
Stop Homophobic Bullying in Schools
  Campaign (2008) 70
subsidiarity 124
suicide 60–1, 71–2
Supporting LGBT Lives study (2009) 32

T

Teacher Training Programme Development
  for Social and Personal Health
  Education *see* SPHE programme
That's So Gay! 109
thematic analysis 16–17
theoretical framework 17–20
Think-tank for Action on Social Change
  (TASC) 161–2
Thomas, Carys Mairs 129
trans organisations 160–1
Transgender Equality Network Ireland
  (TENI) 30, 80, 83

transphobia 11, 28, 32
  mental health 72, 75–6
  in schools 49
transphobic bullying 29, 34, 69–70, 89
  in schools 36–7, 50, 70, 74, 147
Traveller community 2
Trinity College 30, 74
Tsai, Trina 131
Tusla 161
Twieg, Esther 121

U

UNESCO 126
Union of Students in Ireland 38, 129, 132

V

violence
  against queer individuals 94
  in schools 36, 38–9, 42, 68–9

W

Wall, Steve 134
Walsh, Tonie 45–6
Ward, Neil 88
Warfield, Senator Fintan 156
Weeks, J. 41
well-being 71–2
Whyte, Barry 155
Wild, Rita 169

Y

Yes Equality 132
youth empowerment 84, 96, 130, 135
youth work 84–5
  see also community youth work
Youth Work Ireland 131

Z

Zappone, Katherine 127

www.ingramcontent.com/pod-product-compliance
Lightning Source LLC
Chambersburg PA
CBHW051547020426
42333CB00016B/2132